THE CHOSEN
WHEN JESUS BECAME GOD ON EARTH

THE 'UNVARNISHED' HISTORY

BY

DEAN R. EYERLY

Contents

PREFACE

*B*ecause Judaism, Christianity, and Islam all base their teaching on a history of the Promised Land, this book follows the Christian Bible timeline from Creation through Revelation, with historical discovery added where it might be of interest to you, the reader. The book is an unvarnished history with emphasis placed on a new sect of Judaism who were followers of Christos – the Anointed One. Many divinely inspired stories you are about to read were either ignored or discarded by the early church fathers on their way to building a new religion that Jesus came to inaugurate. Dates given are best case estimates, give or take a year.

Historicity of the Bible is the question of its acceptability as a history. In the study of the Bible, scholars incorporate fields which range from archaeology and cultural anthropology to historical linguistics and comparative literature. They examine biblical passages, comparing them to non-biblical evidence. They have discovered that a tremendous amount of credible information is stored in a collection of writings called Pseudepigrapha which are non-canonical texts written for purposes other than the teaching of scripture.

Discoveries made in the 21st century lend little support to Old Testament stories as being history while offering challenging New Testament stories as well. Discovery of the *Dead Sea Scrolls* and *Nag Hammadi Codex* have placed a new light into first century Palestine. Translation of Josephus's *Jewish War* and *Antiquity of the Jews* from ancient Greek into English highlights a diversity of Jewish belief as well as shared expectations and teachings. These discoveries have had the effect of centering Christianity much more within its Jewish roots than was previously thought.

The Christian belief system began with Jews living in exile who spoke the Greek language and had been exposed to the Greek god Zeus and the coming of a King David figure. What separated the first followers of Jesus from non-believers was their belief that he was the resurrected Messiah with that belief having its roots in literature of the second century BCE which promised a future anointed leader who would re-establish the "Kingdom of God" in place of the foreign rulers of that time.

For scholars, Apostle Paul is the originator of Christianity as it is his vision of Jesus that accounts for over one half of the New Testament.

Because of the differences that exist between the picture of Jesus painted by his first followers and the picture painted by Apostle Paul, scholars question the accuracy of his description.

One of the main elements in the study of the Bible is to recognize the difference that exists between the *pre-Easter* and *post-Easter* Jesus with the former referring to the "earthly view" people had of him before the crucifixion as compared to the "divine view" after the resurrection when Jesus became a bright light and a voice from on high with the earthly story of Jesus the Nazarene being removed from the Christian story by the fourth century so that, Paul's version of Jesus could more easily compete with the many gods of the pagan world.

By connecting the dotted lines of research done by biblical scholars, history surrounding an "earthly" man named Jesus of Nazareth can be given with fairly good accuracy.

INTRODUCTION

The modern study of history has led to greater interest in Jesus, as we have come to realize that those who read the gospel account of Jesus are prone to make many wrong assumptions about the meaning of the texts since our modern culture differs greatly from that of two thousand years ago. Times have changed, literary styles have changed, and words and catchphrases have changed. As modern people we think historically, asking the question, "What really happened in the past?" Pre-modern people did not ask that question, they remembered the past through myths. From *Jesus and the Lost Gospels*, scholars Timothy Freke and Peter Gandy give an explanation for Christian myth stories as compared to the more factual history you are about to read:

> The Christian myth cycle is a mythological explanation of where we came from and where we are going. It begins with the myth of origination and ends with the myth of return. The myth seeks to explain the greatest mysteries of all – the arising of something from nothing, the nature of God, and the creation of the cosmos and its purpose. Pagan and Christian myths of origination imagine God as a Big Mind that thinks the cosmos into existence. According to Plato, the ultimate aim of the Mysteries was to instruct the initiate in the "way to return." The myth of origination is an explanation of how we got into our present predicament and a map to guide us on the return journey home to our essence and source. This is because "the way down and the way up are the same."

For most Christians, the New Testament is considered a charter document that came into existence like the Constitution of the United States whereby all the authors of the New Testament were present at the beginning of this new religion writing their gospels and letters for the purpose of founding the church that Jesus came to inaugurate. Unfortunately this is not the way it happened as Christianity was not established until four hundred years after Jesus death by the followers of Apostle Paul.

Christianity began as a movement within Judaism first led by Apostle Paul when he received both a revelation and a commission while traveling on the Damascus road to persecute the followers of Jesus. Based upon revelation, he believed that Jesus was the heavenly exalted son of God; based upon commission, he viewed himself as being a prophet sent by God to serve the Gentiles, preaching the good news of salvation through faith in Jesus. After the crucifixion, Paul began to preach a new version of his Christ belief that entailed the abolishment of Torah revelation and redefining Israel as "all those with faith in Christ." The more distinct Paul's view of Jesus separated from the Jerusalem church of James, brother of Jesus, the more Paul suggested that only he understood who Jesus was. While maintaining several major assumptions from Judaism, he was changing the meaning of the Hebrew Bible and replacing it with his own theology. The Jewish distress over Paul's new interpretation of the Hebrew Bible was caused by their belief that if they turned away from God's commandments, their community would suffer as the commandments were the only language God had given them to express their love for him, which meant that they would lose their share of the world to come.

To understand the teaching of Jesus, one must be versed in the philosophy of the major Jewish sects of his time as their thinking was extremely diverse as each group attempted to establish their ideal sacred community. Jesus would have discussed the law with the Pharisees – He would have debated the concept of bodily resurrection with the Sadducees – He would have submitted to the practice of immersion by the Essene – with several of his followers belonging to the Zealot movement.

Writing in elegant Greek, Flavius Josephus's (36 – 100 CE) most important works were *Jewish War* and *Antiquities of the Jews* with Jewish War recounting details of the first Jewish revolt against Rome while Antiquities of the Jews provides a detailed history of the world giving insight into first century Judaism and the roots of early Christianity. In Antiquities, Josephus describes the Jewish sects at the time of Jesus:

Pharisees were distinguished scholars of the law and traditions of Israel. They were against war with Rome. They believed everything was predetermined by God except for human obedience to the Torah which was up to individual choice with God giving reward or punish accordingly.

Sadducees were the aristocratic class which cooperated with the Romans in ruling the country. They did not believe in bodily resurrection, afterlife or divine intervention – death is final.

Essene believed that the Roman invasion had come as a punishment for their failure to keep the law. They viewed themselves as being the true temple priesthood in exile; they awaited the coming of a messiah figure such as Judas Maccabeus.

Zealots were Essene activists who sought the downfall of the Roman Empire through open rebellion; they were looking for a messiah figure who would overthrow Roman rule.

NAG HAMMADI CODEX

*I*n 1945, at the foot of an exceptionally impressive cliff called Jabal-al-Tarif that graced the Nile River as it flowed around the great river bend near Aswan in Upper Egypt, a collection of ancient manuscript called the Nag Hammadi Codex was discovered. Until this discovery, most of the information scholars had about the first followers of Jesus were derived from writings of the later-day church Fathers, who viewed the early followers of Jesus with distain due to their beliefs. What differentiated the "lost" gospel from orthodoxy was the emphasis placed on the earthly life of Jesus. What differentiated the early teaching of Jesus from orthodoxy was the idea that knowledge of God and self alone, will save as opposed to faith which means that the individual has it within himself to obtain salvation. The first followers took focus on Jesus as being their esteemed teacher of knowledge. They believed that he was born to Joseph and Mary in normal fashion; he had brothers and sisters who were involved with his movement; he was the founder of their "kingdom of God" school of thought; he led a perfect and pure life; his consort was Mary Magdalene who knew ALL; the crucifixion was public notice of Jesus incorruptibility; that his 'spirit' raised-up prior to the crucifixion. These followers considered the principle element of salvation to be direct 'knowledge' of God as compared to belief in God. Jesus was seen as a divine being which had taken human form in order to lead humanity back to the light through his teaching and knowledge of God with this belief being widespread until it was deemed unacceptable by the Church of England. Modern response to this new found scripture goes something like this:

"Isn't Nag Hammadi Codex considered *gnostic*? Isn't *Gnosticism* an ancient Christian heresy?"

Clement, bishop of Alexandria (150 -217 CE), first used the word *gnostic* to describe a Christian sect whose spiritual development surpassed all others. The word *Gnosticism* was first coined by Henry More (1614 - 1687)

, an English Puritan author, to describe an early Christian movement not approved by the Church of England. He did so, not because he was interested in ancient Christianity, but because he needed something he felt was heretical to compare with his seventeenth-century Catholic rivals.

DEAD SEA SCROLLS

*I*n 1947, ancient scrolls were discovered in caves located high up in the cliffs overlooking Khirbet Qumran which is located at the north end of the Dead Sea. Excavation of Khirbet Qumran has revealed a large complex of buildings that were once occupied by a strict Jewish sect known as the Essene with this discovery changing modern thinking about religion in Palestine at the time of Jesus. It is believed that Judas Iscariot, as head of the East Manasseh Magians, was in charge of the scribes at Khirnet Qumran.

The writings found are of two different kinds: biblical and non-biblical. Biblical texts are the oldest known copies of the Hebrew Bible with this cache including all books of the Old Testament, except, for the Book of Esther which was missing. Non-biblical writings are of particular interest to scholars because they shed new light on the inner workings of a group of believers known as "The Way." These works include legal dicta about marriage with the laws being extremely revealing for anyone interested in the late Second Temple period at the time of Jesus, for the documents are a window revealing how people of early first century Palestine lived their lives. Of the non-biblical scrolls, the following are of most interest to scholars as they pertain to the Christian religion. *Damascus Scroll* is a group of sermons describing how God has always judged the wicked and rewarded the faithful. At the end of the manuscript is a document titled *Foundation of Righteousness: An Excommunication Text* which indicates to some scholars that Apostle Paul was excommunicated from the Jerusalem church because he had expanded his understanding of Jesus beyond that which the Jerusalem church could tolerate. *Community Rule Scroll* governed the community living of Essene scattered throughout Palestine with believers referred to as "Children of the Light" with their association being called "The Way." *Thanksgiving Hymn Scroll* recounts the history of persecution at the hands of those who were opposed to the writer's ministry with *Temple Scroll* giving insight into Jewish life in the first century which is not found in the Bible. Robert Eisenman, professor emeritus of Middle East Religions at California

State University, Long Beach, and author of *The Dead Sea Scrolls and the First Christians* explains why the biblical presentation of Jesus does not go nearly far enough:

"All the New Testament documents about Jesus, except for Paul's letters, have been rewritten and overwritten. If you want the real picture of what happened in Palestine in the first century, the place to go is the Scrolls. The Scrolls offer an unadulterated picture of Palestine, and these texts don't accommodate anyone. If you read the historian Josephus or the Dead Sea Scrolls, this is not the atmosphere of the times. – they depict Palestine seething with political revolution."

WHO WAS JESUS?

*U*pon the study of writings of those who were exposed to Jesus in the first century, his uniqueness begs the question—Who was he really?

Was he a Philosopher? There were some similarities between Jewish religious leaders and contemporary Greek philosophers in that they achieved freedom in a world of tyranny by desiring and possessing nothing that could be taken away from them. They believed that virtue is the only good and that its essence lies in self-control and independence.

Was he a Rabbi? Jewish teachers were interpreters of scripture and repositories of legal traditions and master of logical analysis of scripture. In those instances where Jesus is presented as debating scriptural in a rabbinic way, there is good reason to believe that these texts were not original to Jesus but were attributed to him by the later church.

Was he a Zealot? While Jesus stood-up for the poor and the outcast, he was not a 21st century style protester. He was a gadfly who infuriated those sinners who were asleep spiritually.

Was he a Prophet? A prophet is one who receives a message from God and speaks that message to the people with those words becoming scripture. Informally, the word prophet is used to describe one who is wise, predicts the future and sets a direction for the nation.

Was he the Messiah? The followers of Jesus gave him the title "Christos" which, in Greek, means "anointed one" similar to King David with Apostle Paul's messiah differing dramatically from Jewish expectations. Paul's messiah figure dies rather than winning military victory – Paul's messiah rules over a spiritual realm without affecting political change – Paul's messiah represents salvation from sin whereas salvation is achieved through repentance – and Paul's messiah saves mankind from sin instead of earthly oppression.

Was he Son of Man? The earliest title given to Jesus was "son of Man" with the term referring to an angelic being mentioned in the book of Daniel (7:9-14).

Was he a charismatic Preacher and Healer? Stories about Jesus demonstrate the belief that he had the unique capacity to draw God's saving grace into the world. Parallels between Jesus and 'charismatic' miracle-worker of Talmudic legend are: Jesus was perfect and sinless; Jesus had an intimate father-son relationship with God; Jesus performed healings; Jesus was looked upon by authority figures with distain; Jesus was held in great standing with the common folk; and He was an example of virtue and wisdom.

A RABBI AND THE STRANGER

*T*he opening scene – Jews of Judah are struggling to break free from the cruel dominion of Rome. They despise the Romans for their brutality and deeply held pagan beliefs. They reject paganism and steadfastly hold to the law of Moses.

A teacher emerges from the gloom. Only about thirty-two years old, he is blessed with extraordinary charisma. With remarkable courage, he rises up and publically decries the Romans, the corrupt temple priests, and uncaring wealthy. In speeches from the hilltops and market square all over Galilee, he proclaims that the Jews must earn their redemption. He exhorts his people to mindfully practice God's law once again. He inspires the wary Jews to overcome their fears of Rome. The teacher's rhetorical style is electric, complementing home-spun parables with fierce fighting words to inspire in his listeners a craving to make things right. If the Jews reassert their true fidelity to God, he says, they will be victorious. At the heart of the teacher's message is a single commandment: his followers must commit themselves to the Torah's laws and values. If they love each other and embrace true unity, their enemies can never break them. He amasses a huge following as his message of spiritual renaissance and contempt for Rome takes root. The time of redemption is fast approaching. The teacher's reputation is growing. His eloquence has captured a spirit of populism and an enthusiasm for Jewish self-rule. He has become certain of what he only suspected before: it is his destiny to lead God's children from oppressive Roman rule. His many followers believe he is the long-promised Jewish redeemer. The teacher travels with his disciples from Galilee to Jerusalem, the cradle of ancient Jewish civilization, currently contaminated by pagan Roman culture. Crowds greet him and hail him as their leader. The teacher exudes a sublime light. He swells with courage, and rhetorical brilliance. He uses parables to communicate his deeply spiritual teachings. He inspires both the learned and the ignorant. Many in the crowd recognized him for what he is. He must be the one. On the night before the final confrontation with Rome, the teacher gathers his disciples together. He orders them to collect swords. They must prepare to seize the temple by force if necessary. They will demonstrate to the people of Jerusalem their teacher's courage in the face of Roman oppression. When the people see their actions, they will follow them, sparking a massive rebellion. The Romans will have no choice but to retreat. The next morning, the teacher and his followers enter the courtyard of the temple in Jerusalem. His message of revolt against Rome has attracted a following. Those who listen to him are inspired, but their fear is palpable. His sermons escalate. The teacher intends to win over the Jewish leaders and especially the Pharisaic priests. He knows that without the support of his priestly colleagues he cannot hope to win the complete allegiance of the people. They offer him moral support, but the ultimate test of his messiahship is his success. If the Romans are defeated and the prophecies fulfilled, he must indeed be their long awaited messiah. Then calamity strikes. Just as the teacher's preaching in Jerusalem reaches its crescendo, reports of the rabble-rouser reach the ears of the Jewish high priest who is the chief enforcer of Rome among the Jews. He serves as the emperor's muscle and can scarcely afford a rebellion in Jerusalem for which he would be held accountable. Before the teacher can mount his revolt, Roman centurions seize him at the behest of the high priest. Without so much as a trial or hearing, the Romans lead the teacher to the same death that awaits all political rebels: crucifixion. When the tragedy of the mourning comes to an end, his followers debate the meaning of the teacher's mission and their own future. They remain devoutly Jewish. They believe in the Torah. They believe in the prophets. And most of all, they believe in their teacher. They debated among themselves, they grieve, but they live on in hope, studying their teacher's words devoting themselves to the Torah.

Without warning, a mysterious stranger arrives. He presents himself to the teacher's followers. He admits he has only met the teacher once in Damascus, but has nonetheless become enamored with the teacher's story. With a strong mystical bent, the mysterious stranger begins to reinterpret the mission of the teacher. He shocks the devoted disciples by suggesting the teacher was more than a man, more even than the messiah. He suggests the teacher was outright divine—literally, the 'son of God.' The stranger ascribes a meaning to the teacher's death that the original followers never could. The teacher did not die in vain as his demise constituted part of his mission from God, the fulfillment of an ancient, divine plan. The teacher had been sent to die for the sins of mankind. The teacher came to earth on a spiritual mission rather than a political one. His purpose involved not freedom from Rome but rebellion against the corrupt Jewish establishment and Torah observance that had become into an obstacle to salvation. The teacher lived to end the tyranny of Satan, not to destroy Rome. He came to inaugurate a new religion, not to reinforce old spiritual truths. His death served as atonement for the iniquity of humankind. Salvation is available to all, if they only believe. And finally, the stranger tells the stunned disciples that Jesus' death brought all the laws of the Torah to completion. His execution abrogated all obligations - no teaching could have given greater shock to a Jewish system.

New adherents flocked to the stranger's attractive message. People delighted in the idea of an invisible, all-powerful, personal god willing to heed individual prayers. The stranger offered up to the teacher's followers a Jewish God that has been stripped of Jewish ritual with salvation resulting from good faith rather than good acts. Moreover, the stranger combined the Greek belief in many gods with the Jewish belief in one invisible god, arguing there is a father-god, transcendent and invisible, a son-god, earthly and human with the stranger advocating the divine nature of the rabbi. Little by little, as time passed and the influence of the stranger percolated through the teacher's followers, their belief system changed as Greek speaking followers of the stranger overtook the original Jewish disciples of Jesus. The character of the teacher's entire movement transformed dramatically, no longer resembling what had begun as a pious movement within Judaism designed to throw off Roman rule.

LAND OF MILK AND HONEY

*T*he Middle East is the only place in the world where three continents come together. It is a crossroads that links Asia, Africa, and Europe. In ancient times, the Middle East was often in turmoil, much as it is today. The armies of the Assyrians, Babylonians, Persians, Romans, Greeks, Seleucids, and Ptolemaic conquered all or part of the region and then imposed their own way of life on the people conquered. In the centuries before Jesus, it was not unusual for Jews to move from one country to another. Some felt they had no choice as they were fleeing from an invading army or being forced into exile after their homeland had been conquered. Most, however, packed up their belongings in order to escape poverty at home or to seek opportunities abroad, just as people do today.

In the ancient world, Jews were not easily distinguished from their neighbors. They did the same kinds of work, built similar homes, and in many ways lived similar lives. Yet there was one important difference: they worshipped one invisible God at a time when most of their neighbors prayed to a wide variety of gods who looked like animals or humans. In such a world, the Jewish devotion to one God was seen as being odd as monotheism was still a new idea. When one group defeated another, the newly conquered people were expected to accept the gods of the victor. After all, the new gods had triumphed over the old and were therefor entitled to praise and honor. But most Jews, who committed themselves to the one God, refused to pay their respects to the gods of the conquerors with this stubborn refusal raising the question: Why do Jews refuse to worship the same gods as everyone else? Why do they choose to stand apart?

The land in which the Old Testament was born was located along the east coast of the Mediterranean Sea, a meeting point of Africa, Asia, and Europe. In the northeast was a fresh water lake named the Sea of Galilee. It flowed into the Jordan River to the south. The river flowed in a straight line south and emptied into the Dead Sea, which was thick with salt and was surrounded by hot wilderness. The northern part of the country was fertile, the center of the country had beaches and lowlands along the Mediterranean coast to the west, and the southern part of the country was desert. It was hot and humid along the coast; it was drier in the hills, still drier in the desert. As striking as the variety of the land was, the variety of its people was even greater, with native Jews becoming the dominant people within the border from the twelfth century BCE on. The population was both urban and rural. The dominant belief across the Near East was the pagan belief. The God of Israel was Yahweh, who the people of Israel spoke of in terms of his acts in history.

Jewish political life was organized around twelve tribes which had distinct geographical territories. There were individuals within the community who acquired authority by virtue of their position in society. Judges did not hear legal cases but were in charge of the military. Priests, who wore white gowns were often referred to as being 'angels' who came from the tribe of Levi. Prophets were called by the deity to perform a special task, be it to encourage or criticize in the realm of politics, ethics, or ritual.

Information contained in this historical timeline covers all writings found in both the Old and New Testament with "other" gospel stories added that were omitted for various reasons. Sources used, are both biblical and non-biblical with modern scholarship added.

4004 BCE

CREATION OF THE UNIVERSE

In 1650, Archbishop Ussher of Armagh, in *Annales Veteris et Novi Testamenti,* determined that Creation took place based upon his life-long study of the Hebrew Bible.

Based on a major DNA study, the first humans left the Garden of Eden about 100,000 years ago with exact location of the garden being traced to the African nation of Botswana south of the Zambezi River in the country's north. For 70,000 years, our ancestors thrived in that area until climate change turned Africa's largest fresh water lake into what is now the Katahari Desert forcing the population to migrate.

3630 BCE

The notion of chance – good luck and bad luck depended on the belief that nothing in the world was accidental but only happens due to intention. Good actions beget good rewards; bad actions beget bad rewards. Life was expected while death came from the outside, from the invisible spirits – enter the God of the Old Testament!

3600 BCE

In Greek mythology, the Trojan War was waged against the city of Troy by the Greeks after Paris, a Trojan prince, took Helen from her husband Menelaus, king of Sparta.

Scholars believe there is a core of truth to the story with the conflict dating between the 12th or 11th century with the stories *Iliad* and *Odyssey* being composed three hundred years after the event. In 1871, the city of Troy, which dates between 3600 and 3000 BCE was discovered. Troy was a wealthy and sophisticated Anatolian city located at the mouth of the Dardanelle Straight which connects the Black and Aegean Seas with Troy controlling all trade in that part of the world. The city covered seventy-five acres, was surrounded by stone walls measuring thirty-three feet high and ten feet thick. Population approximated 7,500 residents.

2675 BCE

Based on ancient Egyptian sources, scholars have determined that a large mass of nomads led to the collapse of the Canaanite city state system of government with this happening during the Early Bronze Age (3300 – 1200 BCE).

2204 BCE

In the ancient Hebrew language, the word "Adam" refers to humanity. In Christianity, Adam and Eve represent the dignity and shame of the human race which committed sin causing a need for redemption.

According to the Hebrew Bible, Noah, who was a hero due to his blameless piety was chosen by God to perpetuate the human race after his wicked contemporaries had perished in the great flood. When the floodwaters receded, the world was repopulated. As mankind multiplied upon the face of the earth, some found favor with God, because of their faithfulness while others committed sin. For scholars, the Noah flood narrative is reminiscent of much older Babylonian epics that describe a huge flood. One is the *Epic of Gilgamesh* which describes a flood on the Euphrates River and the other *Epic of Atrahasis* which describes a huge flood on the Tigris River. Based on archaeological digs, the authors of these two epics were flood survivors who lived in villages on the lower part of either river where the flood waters covered their villages to a depth of several feet for a great distance so great that no land could be seen giving the appearance that the whole world was under water.

1996 BCE

God said to Abram: "Go from your country and your kindred and your father's house to the land that I will show you. I will make of you a great nation and I will bless you, and make your name great" (Genesis 12:1-2). Abram then traveled from Ur to the city of Haran in Canaan together with his family. After he had built an altar to god in the northern highlands, famine forced them to continue south to Egypt. In fulfillment of his father's wishes, Abram then led his clan southwest to Canaan because Terah had received word from kinsmen that the southern part of the unoccupied pastureland of Canaan would be given to them their arrival.

Readers of the Bible will assume that Abram's monolithic faith had already taken root before he came to Canaan. However, the Bible makes no distinction between the god of Terah and god of Abram. The break with the old deities happened when Abram was in Canaan because the cities of Ur and Haran were followers of the moon-god Sin with Abram being high priest and leader of the Habiru tribes. The famous Covenant made between Abram and the Lord was not concluded until he reached Elonei Mamre where Abram exchanged his Mesopotamian moon-god Sin for the Canaanite high god Elyon as is indirectly confirmed by the words spoken by Joshua (24:14-15):

> "Throw away the gods your forefathers worshipped beyond the (Euphrates) River and in Egypt, and serve the Lord. But if serving the Lord seems undesirable to you, then choose for yourselves this

day who you will serve, whether the gods of your forefathers served beyond the River, or the gods of the Amorites, in whose land you are living. But as for me and my household, we will serve the Lord"

For scholars, the change of name from Abram to Abraham and rite of circumcision are not signs of religious reform but of the adoption of a new faith and new union with a new god – Elyon, the lord of heaven and earth with this new religion containing elements of monotheism which became the foundation on which Moses would build his monotheistic faith. Scholars believe that Abraham's family history is actually the family history of the Habiru and Sutu tribes with events, such as the patriarch's 99 year old wife giving birth added to show the omnipotence of God. Scholars view the patriarchal age and period of Judges as a literary construct that does not relate to any historical era and that after a century of archaeological investigation, no evidence has ever been found for a historical person named Abraham.

1938 BCE

Northern Hebrew tribes from Canaan first arrive Egypt.

1927 BCE

Abraham's 99 year old wife Sarah bore him a son named Isaac. Upon reaching manhood, Isaac married Rebecca who bore him twin sons. Jacob, who was given the name Israel who fathered twelve tribes while his brother Esau fathered the Arab nations.

1881 BCE

Joseph, who received a coat of many colors from his father as a sign of his birthright, was sold into slavery by his jealous brothers to a passing caravan of traders who took him to Egypt where he became a servant in the house of Potiphar and his wife Zuleika. Scholars linking this story about Joseph's ascent to grand vizier to the turmoil of the Second Intermediate Period (1780-1550 BCE) with this era marked by a divided Egypt with the Hyksos tribes holding power in the north, Egyptian rule in the center of the country, and Nubians ruling in the south.

1800 BCE

The period following the conquest of Canaan but before the creation of the United Monarchy, is called the period of the 'Judges' who were leaders of the individual tribes. The Hebrew tribes that settled in Canaan acted independently of each other with each tackling problems in their own way. Contrary to what the Deuteronomists wrote in the Bible, there was no conflict between monotheism and paganism because worship of Yahweh was not a monotheistic religion of the kind that it became centuries later. Confrontation between the cult of Yahweh and Canaanite cult of Elyon was not a fight over belief, but a contest for political influence and material resources. Levites and Aaronites were not competing for the triumph of one god over another, they were fighting to preserve their own positions in the face of competition from other cults.

1750 BCE

The Bible tells us hardly anything about the 430 year stay that the Hebrew tribes spent in Egypt. This silence by the Deuteronomists was an attempt to hide the fact that the Hebrews initially comprised two ethnically close, but distinct tribal groups – the northern tribes of Israel-Joseph and the southern tribes of Jacob-Judah; and that these two peoples arrived in and left Egypt in different centuries; the 15th and 12th.

The biblical account of the Hebrews' arrival in the Nile Delta, the peaceful life they lived there, and their enslavement by the pharaohs and dramatic exodus under the leadership of Moses related only to the southern tribes with the northern tribes having a completely different experience because they were an integral part of the people that conquered Egypt sharing in its rise and fall.

The Hyksos were two distinct Amorite tribes. The main difference between the two was the political role each played and the tribes arrival date in Egypt. Because of the northern tribes alliance with the pharaohs and their defeat, a mass exodus of the northern tribes out of Egypt to Canaan, Lebanon and Syria began reaching its climax in the 15th century. It is for this reason that the authors of Exodus thought it best to keep silent about the extensive time period that the Hebrews spent in Egypt.

1700 BCE

Babel is the setting for the story of the Tower of Babel with the city of Babylon raising to prominence under Amorite king Hammurabi (1792-1750 BCE). Scholars believe Tower of Babel, a structure built in the land of Shinar (Babylonia) after the great flood given in Genesis 11:1-9 is a biblical construct which relates to the arrogance of man's pride because he wanted to build a tower "with its top in the heavens" so as to contradict God's orders. God disrupted the work by so confusing the language of the workers so they could no longer understand each other with those people being dispersed over the face of the earth. It is thought that the myth may have been inspired by the Babylonian tower temple north of the Marduk temple which was called Bab-ilu (Gate of God) and need to explain the many different languages found in the world.

1450 BCE

The Northern tribes stay in Egypt ended when they were forced to leave for Canaan during the course of 300 years with this determining the formation of the tribal alliance. The fact that the Hebrews returned to Canaan in three stages makes scholars believe that initially they consisted of – a northern group (Israel), a southern group (Judah), and the Amorite tribes of Issahar, Zebulun, Gad and Asher at the time of the Exodus.

1402 BCE

While Yahweh's origins are mysterious, one theory is that the name is a shortened form of the Canaanite god *eldu yahwi saba ot,* "Elyon who creates the hosts," meaning the heavenly army that accompanied Elyon as he marched beside the earthly armies of Israel. Yahweh's first appearance in history is from the time of Amenhotep III (1386-1349 BCE) based upon inscriptions found on stone tablets. A widely accepted hypothesis among scholars is that traders brought Yahweh to Israel along the caravan routes from Egypt to Canaan.

1391 BCE

According to Book of Exodus, because the Jews in Egypt continued to multiply, Ramesses I (1184-1153 BCE) ordered every newborn Jewish male infant to be drowned in the river. Upon hearing this news, a young couple from the tribe of Levi decided that in order to save their baby, they would set him afloat on the river in a basket made of sticks and waterproof pitch. Eventually, Pharaoh's daughter Bithia discovered the basket and took the baby in and thusly the Hebrew male child was raised at the court of the Egyptian king Seti I (1290-1279 BCE) and named Moses. During the reign of Ramesses II (1279-1213 BCE), Moses was forced to flee to Midian after killing an Egyptian overseer. In Midian, God charged Moses to lead the Jews out of bondage and bring them to the Promised Land. To punish Pharaoh, God sent a series of plagues to Ramses but only the 10th plague finally broke his resistance. The plague called for all of Egypt's firstborn males to be slain. To ensure that God's angels would bypass the Hebrew families, each family had to slaughter a lamb, roast it, and brush blood on "the two door posts and the lintel of the houses with this moment being celebrated in Jewish history as the "Lord's Passover".

For scholars, the term 'firstborn' in the Bible means the heads of clans and their families. What most likely happened during the night known as 'Passover' was that the adversaries of pharaoh attempted a coup, trying to eliminate both he and his supporters. Conspirators, led by Setnakht, sent a messenger to the enslaved Semites promising them freedom if they helped him storm the capital as he regarded the Hebrew tribes allies and so it was that the 'angel of death' passed over their homes. When Irsu and Setnakht (1189-1186 BCE) were contesting for the throne, the Hebrew tribes became the deciding factor shaping the balance of power in the region. Book of Exodus emphasizes the fact that the Hebrews did not simply leave Egypt, they left in great haste having been payed handsomely as a reward for their services. When Pharaoh said "Let my people go," his staff did not lead them by a short route but by a much longer route toward the Sea of Reeds. Realizing that the Egyptians were catching up to reclaim their payment, Moses decided to use the extreme ebb of the tide to cross to the Sea of Reeds opposite shore at Nuweiba through shallow water. The idea was that the muddy sea bottom would prove no obstacle to cattle and people on foot, but would be impassable for the wheels of the Egyptian war chariots. Stranded and broken, the chariots held up the progress of the Egyptian army. "At daybreak the sea went back in place the water flowed back and covered the chariots and horsemen…not one of them survived" thus ending the 430-year stay of the 'house of Jacob' in Egypt.

Scholars believe that Moses is a legendary figure with no references to him appearing in any Egyptian sources prior to the fourth century BCE. Non-biblical writings with references to the role of Moses, first appeared at the beginning of the Hellenistic period in the 3rd century BCE. For biblical scholars, the Bibles first attempt at telling a story about the formation of Israel is given in Book of Genesis featuring Abraham and his family travels with a second attempt being Book of Exodus in which the account of Moses is given.

1390 BCE

Israel emerged as part of the Canaanite city-state system which believed that Elyon, "the kind, the compassionate, the creator of creatures," was the chief of all gods with the goddess Asherah as his consort. This pair made up the top tier of the Canaanite pantheon acting as administrators of the cosmos. The second tier was made up of their seventy children. Prominent among this group was *Baal* of the northern kingdom, and his brother *Yahweh*, of the southern kingdom, whose sphere of influence was the thunder-storm and its life giving rains.

In ancient literature, Yahweh is pictured as being a warrior for his people, a storm-god marching out from the region of the south or southeast of Israel with a heavenly host of stars and planets making up his army. By 600 BCE, the temple priests in Jerusalem gave Yahweh all the powers previously possessed by his brother Baal.

1361 BCE

Prior to unification, each tribal group had its own leader. The northern tribes of Israel were led by Moses while the southern tribes of Judah were led by Joshua with both leaders wanting an alliance convinced that without it conquest of Canaan would be impossible.

The first unification of the tribes occurred in central Transjordan thus a majority of the Hebrew tribes (10 out of 12) were together again after two and a half centuries of divided history from the middle of the 15th to the beginning of the 12th centuries BCE. In recognition of his advanced age, experience, and record of achievements, Moses was recognized as head of the tribal union. During the exodus from Egypt, Moses received the commandments of God at Mount Sinai. There the tribes built the Ark of the Covenant to house the stone tablets upon which the Commandments were written. To the followers of Moses, the Ark represented the embodiment of Yahweh and the sign of his presence on earth. Because Moses was too old to rule, the real power over the tribes was placed in the hands of Joshua, leader of the 'house of Joseph-Israel', and Eleazar, head of the priestly southern clan of the 'house of Jacob-Judah.' In order to lead religious services of the alliance, there needed to be a common religious cult. The southern tribes worshipped Yahweh, while the norther tribes worshipped Elyon. So the leaders of the Northern tribes adopted Yahweh the God of the southern tribes as their main God with Eleazar being high priest of the entire alliance.

1325 BCE

Battle of Jericho was the first battle fought by the Israelites in the course of the conquest of Canaan. Led by Joshua (1355-1245 BCE), the Jews entered the Promised Land organizing their political life around twelve tribes. The tribes had distinct geographical territory, with ten tribes (Dan, Naphtali, Gad, Asher, Issachar, Zebulon, Ephraim, Manasseh, Benjamin, and Reuben) being located in the northern kingdom of Israel and two tribes (Simon and Judah) being located in the southern kingdom with archaeological facts partially confirm the biblical version and partially contradict it.

- The Tribes conquest of Canaan was not a simultaneous military campaign taking place over a short period of time but stretched out over several centuries.

- The Israelites were not aliens in Canaan but an integral part of it.

- The sacking of Canaanite cities cannot be attributed to only Hebrew tribes but can be attributed to Egyptian pharaohs Seti I, Ramesses II and Thutmose III who conducted regular marches into Palestine.

In 1868, Charles Warren identified Tell es-Sultan as the site of biblical Jericho with the first major excavation being done in 1930 and again in

1952. It was determined that the five acre city, with a population of 600, met its fiery demise between 1400-1550 BCE due to a major earthquake.

1246 BCE

Scholars cannot find a written record of the Exodus in the annals of Egyptian history. In *The Journal of American Research Center in Egypt*, Alan Schulam made the following observation about Egyptian history:

> The recording of historical facts was only incidental to the purpose of royal documents … we should understand that the royal historical document was a piece of controlled government propaganda, intended mainly, if not solely, to propagate a royal myth.

It may come as a surprise to many students of the Bible that in the original text the body of water the Israelites crossed when leaving Egypt is called "Sea of Reeds" not the Red Sea. The "Red Sea" phrase came into the account with the incorrect third century BCE translation of the Hebrew Bible into Greek.

1190 BCE

Philistines first appeared in the southwest of Canaan shortly before the second wave of Hebrew tribes arrived from Egypt. The Philistines came as raiders and enemies of Egypt and then as mercenaries and colonists, having been given the region of Gaza by Egypt as a place in which to settle. Philistines were of Indo-European origin who came from over the sea, from the northwest. They were numerically inferior to the Hebrews but were superior in terms of military organization and quality of weaponry. It was the Philistines who brought the Iron Age to Canaan. They knew how to produce iron and used this metal to make weaponry. They seized Canaanite cities and created communities under the command of their own leaders, called 'Seranim' - meaning 'Tyrant'. Philistine country was known as the Pentapolis, the union of the five cities of Gaza, Ashkelon, Ashdod, Ekron, and Gath.

1117 BCE

Michmash Campaign and exploits of Jonathan, eldest son of Saul, who single-handily routed the Philistines, is the backstory for the biblical narrative of the famous battle between David, representing the small rural country of Israel, and Goliath, representing the large urbanized Greek cities of the eastern coastal region.

In 1999, archaeologists found the biblical city of Timnah were book of Judges states (14:1) that Samson, from the tribe of Dan, met, fell in love and married Philistine Delilah. Today, the site is a flat-topped mound known as Tel Batash, with the site dating between 1150 and 1100 BCE. Samson in the Bible is best known for his supreme strength, but in reality, he serve as judge in Israel for twenty years and was one of the last divinely inspired following in the footsteps of Deborah, Joshua, and ultimately Moses.

1100 BCE

Shiloh became the first resting place for the Ark of the Covenant.

1050 BCE

The United Monarchy was established at the height of the Philistines' military aggression against the Hebrew tribes. The tribes, realizing that they needed to be unified, selected Samuel as leader, a man who was a judge, a priest, and a prophet. He, in turn, appointed Saul as first commander of the army or "king" of Israel who soon proved his military leadership. Saul mobilized the tribal militias and rushed north to defeat the invading forces of the king of Ammon. Flush with victory, he led his army to attack the Philistines in the highlands. When Saul led his army to meet the Philistines at Mount Gilboa, badly wounded, he fell on his sword. After his death, Samuel selected Saul's sons, Ishbaal and David, to rule the country. Shortly thereafter, David became sole ruler (1002 - 970 BCE) of both the north and south because Ishbaal had been assassinated.

Unification of all twelve tribes occurred during the late 11th century. The tribes consisted not of one, but three different West Semitic groups of Amorite origin, which made their alliance unstable. Worship of Yahweh was likewise not a unifying factor. Until their departure for Egypt, and in Egypt itself, these groups had different histories. The main thing that had united them had been their status as Habiru/Apiru tribes and their dramatic memories of their stay in Egypt. The people had become a nation. They had been redeemed from slavery in Egypt; they had been given the law. They were committed to a life of obedience to God, and a religion which constantly reminded them of their dependence on God's forgiveness and mercy.

1020 BCE

Saul, 1st King of Israel

1002 BCE

When David became king, he ruled the nation from the city of Jerusalem. With a standing army of 50,000 men, he quickly expanded his kingdom to include modern-day Lebanon, Jordan, and Syria. Surprisingly, he chose to ignore the Philistine threat on the coast instead marching on the city of the Jebusites, known as Jerusalem because he wanted to anchor his newly unified nation in a proper capital and establish a shrine for Yahweh. He built an elaborate palace in Jerusalem placing the Tabernacle which would house the Ark of the Covenant on top of the mount previously used by the Jebusites as a threshing floor. He expanded his territory until Israel had become the dominant state in the area absorbing the nations of Ammon, Moab, and Edom. His
greatest achievement was the fusion of the twelve quarrelsome tribes into one nation.

In 1913, archaeologists discovered King David's tomb located on a path off the Kidron Road. The tomb consists of a hewn tunnel fifty-two feet long, eight feet wide, and thirteen feet high, lowered to six feet where David's sarcophagus was placed. Upon his death, rule of the Kingdom was turned over to Solomon, son of his favorite wife Bathsheba.

970 BCE

The Bible depicts Solomon's reign as an era of unprecedented prosperity. As wealth poured into the country, he fulfilled his father's promise to God to build a temple to house the Ark of the Covenant in Jerusalem. Because he tolerated the growing popularity of pagan deities introduced by his foreign born wives, the prophet Ahijah convinced Solomon's ministers to overthrow him. When the conspiracy was discovered, Jeroboam, one of Solomon's ministers who was involved in the plot, fled to Egypt.

Marib, the 60 acre capital of the ancient kingdom of Saba, was home to the legendary Queen of Sheba. According to *Antiquities of the Jews*, queen of Sheba or Saba, was queen of Egypt and Ethiopia. In *Targum Sheni to Esther*, the queen's name was Makeda and she was a Sun worshipper. In the Hebrew Bible, Sheba brings valuable gifts to King Solomon. In Gospels of Matthew and Luke, because Solomon spoke with great wisdom, Makeda converted to Judaism with Ethiopian Jews tracing their ancestry to Menelik I, son of King Solomon, and Makeda. Archaeologists have not yet discovered inscriptions in the capital city of Marib bearing the legendary Queens name.

In 2010, archaeologists discovered a twenty-five acre copper smelting operation at Khirbat en Nahas, located thirty miles south of the Dead Sea in Jordan, with this location thought to be the famed site known as King Solomon's mines. Adjacent to the mines is a large fortress complex which includes the ruins of an old guardhouse suggesting slaves were used to work the mines. Located a few miles away from the mines is also a cemetery containing more than 3,500 tombs dating to the same period.

958 BCE

The national god of the northern kingdom of Israel and the southern kingdom of Judah was named Yahweh. For scholars, the earliest plausible mention of him are in Egyptian texts that place him among the nomads of the southern Transjordan (region that encompasses modern-day Israel, Lebanon, Syria). In the oldest biblical literature, Yahweh is an ancient near eastern "divine warrior" who leads a heavenly army against Israel's enemies. Over time, the royal court and temple priests promoted Yahweh to being god of the entire cosmos, possessing all the positive qualities previously attributed to other gods and goddesses. By the end of the Babylonian exile in 538 BCE, the very existence of foreign gods in Israel and Judah was denied as Yahweh was proclaimed the creator of the cosmos and true God of all gods.

957 BCE

Construction of Solomon's 1st temple in Jerusalem was completed with Ark of the Covenant moved from Shiloh to Jerusalem.

931 BCE

Upon Solomon's death, his son Rehoboam, became king of the tribal alliance alienating the Samaritan tribes of the north because he favored the south's policy and religious practices. He removed Abiathar as high priest of the northern tribes marginalizing the Levite class. He implemented taxes on the north to support a military that was designed to protect the south from invasion by Egypt. He oversaw the redistricting of tribal boundaries in the north which cut across family ties. Because of these displeasures, the United Kingdom of Israel began to fall apart when the northern tribes refused to accept Rehoboam as their new king. Upon separation, the elders of the north formed their own kingdom calling it "Israel" so as to rob the south of its legitimacy. With the elders anointed Jeroboam king (931 - 910 BCE) of the northern kingdom, he immediately reorganized it as a modern state in much the same way as Solomon, had done. He created rival shrines in the former cult centers of Bethel and Dan commissioning golden calves – the traditional symbol of Elyon. Deuteronomists depicting this idolatry as being "a sin" (I Kings12:30). With the priests of the north, who were badly treated, recording their history as they saw it and Judean priests in the south, who were treated favorably, recording history through their life experience which was good, two distinctly different views of history were being recorded from the time of Moses which would cause problems at a later date.

885 BCE

King Omri (885-874 BCE) was one of the most successful rulers of the northern kingdom. He ended the long-running state of war with the southern kingdom of Judah by signing a pact with King Asa ending a half century of enmity between the two Hebrew realms. He then signed a treaty with King Ithobaal of Sidon on the Phoenician coast. The alliance was sealed with the marriage of Omri's son, Ahab, to Jezebel, daughter of King Ethbaal. He then defeated his hostile neighbor to the east, Aram-Damascus, bringing peace to the kingdom. With the political situation secure, Omri directed his attention to building a new capital of the northern kingdom (I Kings 16:23-24) which he would call "Samaria".

King Ahab (874-853 BCE), of the north, honoring a peace treaty with Judah in the south, spurring growth of trade with neighbors like Phoenicia. When Jezebel, Phoenician wife of Ahab enters the scene, she is an idol worshipper who seems to be the power behind her husband's misdeeds. Book of Kings says that she was brought to the northern kingdom of Israel to wed the newly crowned Ahab (1Kings 16:31) by her father, Ethbaal of Tyre, king of the Phoenicians, who was ancestor of the Canaanites who worshipped Baal and Asherah. As king, not only was he high priest of the Canaanite religion, so to, was his daughter Jezebel a priestess. When she came to Israel, she brought with her pagan gods which had an immediate effect on Ahah who accepted them. For this reason Jezebel was vilified by Deuteronomists, whose goal was to stamp out paganism from the Promised Land. According to the Deuteronomists, as Jews settled into the Promised Land and separated into northern and southern kingdoms, God's chosen people in the north went astray by worshipping pagan deities.

Jezebel's arranged marriage to Ahab was a political alliance providing Phoenicians and Jews military protection from powerful enemies to the north as well as valuable trade routes. Israel gained access to the Phoenician ports on the Mediterranean while Phoenicia gained passage through Israel's central hill country on the King's Highway, the heavily traveled route connecting the Gulf of Aqaba in the south with Damascus in the north. Although the marriage made sense as sound foreign policy, it was intolerable to Jeremiah because of her pagan ways. For scholars, Jezebel was an outspoken woman in a time when females had little status and few rights; a foreigner in a xenophobic land; an idol worshiper in a place where the worship of Yahweh was a state religion; a meddler in the political affairs of a nation of strong patriarchs; a non-believer in the territory where the commandments originated. In a kinder analysis, she emerged as a fiery and determined person. She is true to her religious belief and native customs; she is loyal to her husband. Throughout her reign, she boldly exercises what power she has and in the end, having lived her life on her own terms, faced death with dignity.

850 BCE

Elijah and Elisha gave testimony to God in the northern kingdom of Israel while Joel gave testimony in the southern kingdom of Judah. The worship of Yahweh alone began when he gradually absorbed all the positive traits of all other gods and goddess of the cosmos.

A new study led by Tel Aviv University concluded by excavations made at the Judahite fortress at Arad in southern Israel, that the Hebrew Bible was written before the Babylonians destroyed Jerusalem and the temple built by Solomon. *Biblical Archaeology Review* (BAR) believes that in a kingdom of some 100,000 people, at least several hundred could read and write.

785 BCE

Hosea and Jonah prophesized in the northern kingdom of Israel.

781 BCE

King Uzziah (781-740 BCE), of the southern kingdom of Judah, observed the pagan developments in the north with alarm.

769 BCE

An alliance between King Jeroboam II (783 -743 BCE) of the northern kingdom of Israel and King Uzziah (769-740 BCE) of the southern kingdom of Judah was formed recreating the original kingdom of King Solomon which included most of Lebanon, Syria, and Jordan.

760 BCE

Amos prophesized in the northern kingdom of Israel.

755 BCE

Book of Amos denounces the crimes against humanity committed by the Gentile nations, telling Israel that even though they have sinned and are guilty of the same crimes that the restoration of the House of David will occur. The central theme of the book is that God puts his people on the same level as the surrounding nations. As it is with all nations that rise up against the kingdom of God, even Israel and Judah will not be exempt from the judgement of God because of their idolatry and unjust ways. The nation that represents Yahweh must be made pure of anything or anyone that profanes the name of God.

750 BCE

City of Rome was founded by Romulus.

745 BCE

After Tiglath-pilesar III ascended to the thrown of Assyria (745-727 BCE), he invaded Israel capturing "Kedesh, Hazor, Gilead, Galilee and all the land of Naphtali. He carried the captive people of Israel to Assyria with the purpose of this deportation to make room for his Assyrian settlers. Upon arrival in Assyria many of the captive Jews intermarried with the foreigners causing them to be considered a new sect of Judaism.
With one stroke, the Assyrian king had taken possession of all the important agricultural land of Israel as well as a substantial section of the Transjordan. The only area of the northern kingdom which remained intact was around the capital city Samaria.

740 BCE

Book of Hosea denounces the worship of gods other than Yahweh and states that there will be an eventual reconciliation between Yahweh and the northern kingdom of Israel.

736 BCE

King Ahaz of Judah (736-716 BCE) recognized that it was pointless to try to fight the Assyrians. Instead, he pursued a policy of accommodation with the Assyrian king refusing to join the anti-Assyrian coalition with this move incurring the wrath of both King Pekah of Israel and King Rezin of Syria. In response to their hostility, Ahaz sought Assyria's protection causing Judah to become an Assyrian vassal state by default. Ahaz welcomed the influx of Assyrian culture incorporating Assyrian rituals into temple worship.

Ahaz encouraged his subjects to worship the many gods of Israel alongside Yahweh in the temple in Jerusalem.

735 BCE

Micah prophesized in the southern kingdom of Judah.

727 BCE

King Shalmaneser of Assyria, had little interest in foreign adventure. Upon his death, King Sargon II, a far more aggressive personality, decided to storm the Samarian citadel with King Hoshea's forces crumbling under the Assyrian onslaught causing a second major deportation of 27,000 Jews.

718 BCE

King Hezekiah (718-687 BCE) of the southern kingdom earned praise because he had decided to destroy the idolatrous shrines that had been allowed to flourish under his father, King Ahaz. Like his father, he could not resist engaging in political brink-man-ship when he began to solicit Egypt's help in a possible revolt against Assyria with the initiative being of deep concern for the prophet Isaiah because he was firmly committed to preserving the Davidic dynasty and the temple in Jerusalem as God's throne on earth. Knowing of the futility of confronting Assyria's might, Isaiah denounced Hezekiah's move without first asking for his council. Isaiah was proven correct when around 701 BCE, Assyrian king Sennacherib (704-681 BCE) led a powerful invasion force to suppress Judah's revolt.

714 BCE

The northern kingdom of Israel, with its capital in the city of Samaria, loved their pagan gods. When King Sargon II (714-711 BCE) of Assyria conquered the northern kingdom, the inhabitants of the southern kingdom, who worshipped Yahweh were not sympathetic.

The Assyrians took the Jews from the north and replaced them with their own people thereby forcing the ten northern tribes to assimilate into other cultures and disappear from history. Still, many of the Jews living in the capital city of Samaria and surrounding area remained in their homeland and continued to practice the faith of Moses while at the same time intermarrying with their new Assyrian visitors. Because of the destruction of the north, the priestly class of both the northern and southern kingdoms, who were treated much differently, wrote two different histories of the nation which was later inserted into the books of Genesis, Exodus, Leviticus, and Numbers.

702 BCE

Isaiah prophesied from Jerusalem through the reign of Uzziah, Jotham, Ahaz and Hezekiah, the kings of Judah. His mission was to urge the people to repent of their sins as salvation was given only by God and not by man. When the Assyrian army was hammering on the gates of Jerusalem during Hezekiah's reign, the king took Isaiah's advice and the city was saved.

In 1830, archaeologists found hexagonal clay prisms at the sight of the King Sargon II palace. The prisms make the following observations about the event Isaiah described:

> As for Hezekiak, the awful splendor of my lordship overwhelmed him, and the irregular and regular troops which he had brought in to strengthen Jerusalem, his royal city, and had obtained for his protection, together with 30 talents of gold, 300 talents of silver,precious stones, antimony, large blocks of red stone, ivory inlaid couches, ivory arm-chairs, elephant hide, elephant tusks, ebony-wood, box-wood, all kinds of valuable treasure, as well as his daughters, concubines, male and female musicians, he sent to me later to Nineveh my loyal city.

The vision of God in all his glory in the temple of Jerusalem colored Isaiah's whole mission. He had seen God as the 'Holy One of Israel' and he never forgot it. He had seen human sin for the appalling thing it was, and he never forgot that either. Spiritual and secular leaders had gone soft and failed in their jobs (56:9-12). The nation had gone running after pagan gods, joining in sexual rites and child-sacrifice (57:4-13; see 2 Chronicles 33:1-9). Religious observance was a hollow mockery: the people loved neither God nor their fellow man (58). Society was rotten to the core, riddled with lies, dishonesty, injustice, malice and violence (59:1-13) with no one having time for truth and justice (59:14-15) with all these things standing in stark contrast to all that God wants for his people (57:14-19; 58:6-14; 59:20-21).

God is sickened by their moral degradation, social injustice and religious hypocrisy yet he still offers forgiveness (18). For these reasons, God made use of the proud and cruel Assyrian nation to punish his people. Jerusalem will be saved from Assyria by God, but the city will fall to the Babylonians and the captive people will then be taken into exile if they don't mend their ways. In the unbridgeable gap between the shame of Israel and her glory stands God the Avenger and Redeemer (59:16-21) with his judgment being on the whole world and everyone in it.

687 BCE

During the reign of King Manasseh (687 - 642 BCE), the Ark of the Covenant was removed from the temple in Jerusalem by Levite priests and taken to Elephantine Island located in the Nile River near Aswan in Egypt. The Ark was removed because the king was planning to place a statue of the pagan goddess Asherah in the holy of Holies along-side Yahweh.

In 1893, Egyptologist Sir William Flinders Petrie discovered the remains of a temple located on Elephantine Island that had been manned by a militant colony of Jews that acted as mercenaries for Egypt guarding the southern border of the country. The soldiers established a township and built a temple fashioned after the Jerusalem Temple to house the Arc before the coming of the Persians in 526 BCE, when Cambyses, son of Cyrus II conquered Egypt. In 1910, archaeologists discovered 175 papyri written in the 5th century BCE on Elephantine Island stating that Yahwist priests from Jerusalem brought the Ark of the Covenant to the island and that the Ark was later moved to Ethiopia where it is house at Axum.

686 BCE

Nahum (686-612 BCE) prophesized in the northern kingdom of Israel.

640 BCE

King Josiah anxious to reverse the policies of his father Manasseh, initiated a purge of all pagan influences while at the same time presiding over a restoration of ritual and legal practices related to the worship of Yahweh. He destroyed the shrine of Bethel in Samaria and announced his realm cleansed of alien gods. He decreed that all Israel should live in full compliance with the laws. After extensive repairs and cleansing of the Jerusalem Temple, he asked the Levite priests to return the Ark of the Covenant to Jerusalem from Egypt. Since the relationship between the southern kingdom of Judah and Levite priests had dramatically deteriorated over the years, Josiah was in no position to force the return of the Ark from the Isle of Elephantine where priests had built a temple to house it.

Zephaniah prophesized in the southern kingdom of Judah.

625 BCE

Book of Deuteronomy, is thought to have been written by Jeremiah. Chapter 1-30 consists of three speeches delivered to the Israelites by Moses on the plains of Moab, shortly before they enter the Promised Land. The first speech recounts the forty years of wilderness wanderings which had led to that moment, and ends with an strong urge to observe the law of Moses. The second speech reminds the Israelites of the need to follow Yahweh and the laws he has given them, on which their possession of the land depends; and the third speech offers comfort that even though Israel should prove unfaithful and so lose the land, with repentance all can be restored. The final four chapters (31-34) contain the Song of Moses, the Blessing of Moses, and narratives recounting the passing of the mantle of leadership from Moses to Joshua and, finally, the death of Moses on Mount Nebo. In Deuteronomy, the belief that God can be human is the ultimate heresy as the chasm separating God and man is infinite and unbridgeable.

624 BCE

Assyrians fell to the Egyptians with the Egyptians then falling to the Babylonians with both the northern and southern kingdoms entering a period that Jews refer to as being the "Babylonian Exile".

622 BCE

Jeremiah made his last prophecy about the Ark of the Covenant.

614 BCE

Book of Nahum was written as a prophecy about the approaching final destruction of Nineveh, the capital city of the Assyrian empire. Nahum describes the siege and frenzied activity of Nineveh's troops as they try in vain to halt the invaders. Nahum's writing testifies to his belief in the righteousness of God and how God will deal with those Assyrians in punishment according to their cruelty. Nahum shows God slow to anger, but that God will by no means ignore the guilty; God will bring his vengeance and wrath to pass. God is presented as one who will punish evil, while protecting those who trust in Him.

According to Babylonian clay tablets discovered in the 19th century named the *Fall of Nineveh Chronicle*, there was a bitter 12-year struggle between Babylon and Assyria (628 – 616 BCE), as well as civil wars in Assyria itself. The Assyrians had, by the accounts of their own records, been brutal rulers even by the standards of the time. The fall of the city of Nineveh took three months.

612 BCE

Habakkuk prophesized in the southern kingdom of Judah.

609 BCE

King Jehoiakim , son of king Josiah, did not share his father's enthusiasm for religious reform. Before long, pagan practices were once again being performed which explains the reason Jeremiah stood in the temple courtyard and delivered his famous sermon urging his people to repent of their ways and observe the tenets of God's covenant. Jeremiah warned the king that his course of action would lead to catastrophe with his prophecy being fulfilled in 598 BCE when Nebuchadnezzar marched on Jerusalem. Thousands were either slaughtered or sent off into captivity with Jeremiah being spared. Thus began the period of the Babylonian captivity.

608 BCE

Book of Joel is a call to national repentance in the face of God's judgment; promise of future blessings and coming judgement on Judah's enemies: Philistines, Kingdom of Edon, and Kingdom of Egypt.

603 BCE

Daniel was a Judean exile in the court of Babylon. He was taken there as a young boy in the third year of the reign of Jehoiakim. He belonged to a noble family and was exceptionally able serving in the court as magistrate. In his later years, King Belshazzar held a great feast and in a drunken state, drank from a sacred vessel which had been taken from the temple of Solomon upon its destruction. Because of this blasphemous act, hand-writing mysteriously appeared on the wall of the palace. David, interpreting the handwriting, told the king that he would lose his kingdom to the Persians. That very night he was assassinated with his successor being Darius the Mede of Persia. After the Persian conquest of Babylonia, Daniel became one of three administrators of the empire. When the king decided that Daniel should administer over the entire kingdom, other jealous officials plotted his downfall with Daniel being saved by God due to his righteousness.

Scholars agree that stories told in Book of Daniel actually happened but not in the sequence given because the book was written in 166 BCE. They also agree that King Belshazzar was, in fact, Nabonidus crown-prince and governor while his father was in Arabia between 553 and 543 BCE who had returned to Babylon years before its fall. They also agree that Darius the Mede is literary fiction.

600 BCE

Book of Exodus describes the Israelites' deliverance from slavery in Egypt through the hand of Yahweh, the revelations at Mount Sinai, and the subsequent divine indwelling of God with Israel.

In 1984, archaeologists discovered the location of Mount Sinai as being at Jebel-al-Lawz in Saudi Arabia. Josephus describes Mount Sinai as being "the highest mountain in the city of Madian" whereas Philo of Alexandria described Mount Sinai as being located east of the Sinai Peninsula and south of Palestine.

In 1985, archaeologists discovered the crossing site for Exodus as being located at Nuweiba, Egypt where two giant inscribed columns erected by Solomon mark the spot. In addition to this, discovery of the buried columns, many four, six, and eight spoked golden wheels from the Pharaoh's chariots plus remains of humans and horses were found on the seabed floor on either side of the quarter mile wide crossing point between Ehypt and Saudi Arabia. On either side of the land bridge is located the Eilat Deep and Aragonese Deep, which reach depths of 3,000to 5,000 feet.

599 BCE

Book of Numbers is about Israel's exodus from oppression in Egypt and journey to take possession of the land God promised their fathers. It draws to a conclusion the themes introduced in Genesis and played out in Exodus and Leviticus. God has promised the Israelites that they shall become a great nation, that they will have a special relationship and that they shall take possession of the land of Canaan. Numbers demonstrates the importance of holiness, faithfulness and trust.

598 BCE

The Chaldeans, under the leadership of King Nebuchadnezzar, made their first assault on Jerusalem placing Zedekiah in the position of puppet king of Judah. Ten years later, Zedekiah rebelled against the rule of Babylonia causing Nebuchadnezzar to re-enter Jerusalem. This time, Nebuchadnezzar following standard Mesopotamian practice, deported the Jews after he had conquered the city. The deportations were large, but didn't involve the entire nation. Around 10,000 were forced to relocate to the city of Babylon, the capital of the Chaldean empire. There, the exiled Jews were exposed to Greek culture and language. This period, called the "Exile" in Jewish history, ended when Darius the Great of Persia overthrew the Chaldeans.
Ezekiel was among the upper-class Jews who were exiled to Babylon from Jerusalem. At that time, he was active as a prophet in the northern kingdom retaining this gift when he arrived in Babylon. He saw his people's sin in all its blackness; he saw the inevitability of God's judgment. As he declared God's message his most constant theme was the individual's responsibility

before God for their actions. For Ezekiel, there had been a total departure from the true religion of Israel as the Canaanite goddess Asherah had been set up in the temple of Yahweh in the days of King Manasseh.

In 1900, archaeologists discovered the ruins of king Nebuchadnezzar's palace complex, the famed Temple of Marduk and the remains of the Ishtar Gate.

597 BCE

Book of Genesis is the inspired word of God because no human observer was present during creation of the world. The flood story is based on ancient stories about an actual catastrophic regional flood events with the inspired author re-casting these older stories in order to teach about the seriousness of sin and the merciful love of God. The story focus is on conflict and resolution. God's purpose is to have his presence fill the earth bringing about order and fruitfulness in creation. Conflict enters the story until God brings judgement and mercy. Genesis is the founding story of humanity, ending in crisis. It is the founding story of the nation with whom the covenant is eventually made in Sinai.

In 1965, while working at Bab edh-Dhra on the Dead Sea's Lisan Peninsula, archaeologists discovered the biblical cities of Sodom and Gomorrah, with their flourishing population suddenly ceasing to exist around 2100 BCE due to fiery circumstances as noted in Genesis. Geologists discovered that the local inhabitants main occupation was the mining of bitumen, and that a major seismic event occurred igniting the heaps of bitumen causing an uncontrollable inferno, which for any onlooker would have looked like brimstone raining down from the sky.

586 BCE

Obadiah prophesized in the southern kingdom of Judah.

When the Babylonians conquered the southern kingdom of Judah, they destroyed the temple in Jerusalem built by Solomon forcing thousands of Jews into exile with these Jews not disappearing from history because Nebuchadnezzar allowed them to practice their own religion. Those who settled in Egypt, Lebanon, Syria and elsewhere outside of Judah were exposed not only to the Greek language but to the pantheon of Olympian gods. Zeus, like Yahweh, was the sky and thunder god with the fate of men and nations held in his hands.

Samaritans, who were exiled Jews of the northern kingdom, resisted paganism by developing their own version of worship, using only the Pentateuch while rejecting other books of the Hebrew Bible. They built their own temple on Mt. Gerizim stating that their mountain was the true dwelling place of the Lord because the temple in Jerusalem had been polluted. The major rift between Samarians and Judeans intensified when the Samaritans offered to help the south rebuild Solomon's temple but were 'rudely' dismissed because of their acceptance of pagan gods, inter-marriage between races, and the way in which their religious practice differed from the south:

- Both north and the south believed they came from the seed of Abraham.

- Both worshipped the same God of Abraham, Isaac, and Jacob.

- Both considered Moses to be the law-giver and prophet of God.

However:

- Samaritans accepted only the Pentateuch as Holy Scripture rejecting otherprophets sent by God as well as the Talmud.

- Samaritans made their sacrifices and celebrated their high holy days on Mt. Gerizim.

- Samaritans considered Levite priests to be the highest religious authority with the southern kingdom looked to the temple priests.

- Samaritans rejected the idea of resurrection after death because it was not written in the Pentateuch.

- Samaritans awaited a prophet who would establish a period of peace and justice on earth while the south was awaiting a messiah who would militarily overthrow the Romans and give them back their land.

Book of Obadiah is an oracle based on the fall of Edom, a mountain dwelling nation whose founding father was Esau. Obadiah describes his encounter with God, who addresses Edom's arrogance and charges them for their violent actions against their neighbor, the house of Jacob. When Nebuchadnezzar sacked Jerusalem, the Edomites helped the Babylonians loot the city with Obadiah, suggested that they should have helped their brothers saying God's judgement would wipe out the house of Esau forever.

581 BCE

Jeremiah (627-582 BCE) began to prophesize to the southern kingdom when the power of Babylon to the north and Egypt to the south was on the rise with Babylon finally emerging supreme thereby becoming the instrument by which God judged his godless people. In Jeremiah's opinion, the destruction would take place because the northern kingdom had been unfaithful by worshiping the pagan gods. He had witnessed the destruction of Jerusalem by Nebuchadnezzar's army, after which he continually warned the inhabitants of the south to mend their ways before it was too late. And when catastrophe finally came to Jerusalem, he was the one who bitterly lamented Israel's fate in *Book of Lamentations* which he authored. Because of the fall of the northern kingdom, Jeremiah decided that the history of the northern and southern kingdoms had to be combined into one because of the political and social realities of the day. This uniting of the two histories reflected the reuniting of the two communities after two hundred years of division explaining the reason for the fall of the north, as Jeremiah believed that if two visions of history were put side by side at a later date, the reader would be reminded of the dual history of the Jewish nation, diminishing the authority of both. Jeremiah arranged the two stories so that the law would stand as covenant and the foundation of history. He depicted the fate of the people as dependent on how faithfully they kept their covenants with God. The turning point in Jeremiah's ministry came when he had Baruch, his scribe, commit to writing all the prophecies he had given and read them in the Jerusalem temple with his warning to king Zedekiah being that he should surrender Jerusalem to Babylon as it was God's will, and that if he did not, the Babylonians would defeat Judah in war and destroy the city.

575 BCE

Book of Habakkyk is a discussion between God and Habakkuk about growing from a faith of uncertainty and doubt to the height of absolute trust in God. He addresses his concerns over the fact that God will use the Babylonian empire to execute judgment on Judah for their sins. God explains that He will also judge the Chaldeans, and much more harshly. Habakkuk expresses his ultimate faith in God, even if he doesn't fully understand what He is doing. The message "the just shall live in faith" (2:4) plays an important role in Christian thought.

574 BCE

Zoroaster (612 – 535 BCE) was born in eastern greater Iran. He was an Iranian religious reformer who challenged the tenets of contemporary Iranian religious belief having a significant impact on Judaism, Christianity, and Islam. He saw the human condition as a struggle between the forces of good and evil. He emphasized the freedom of the individual to choose between right and wrong and the individuals responsibility for one's deeds. The purpose of mankind is to sustain and align itself to creation – the ethical participation in life and exercise of constructive good thoughts, words, and deeds. Central to Zoroastrianism is the profound dichotomy between good and evil, and the idea the universe was created by the one God, Ahura Mazda ("Wise Lord"), in order that the two forces could engage with one another with the evil one, Ahriman, being incapacitated. Immortal souls that balance in favor of good over evil go to what Zoroaster simply referred to the "best existence" – or heaven – and those immortal souls that balance in favor of evil go to the "worst existence" – or hell, and remain there until the end of time. One of the most important differences between Jewish monotheism and Zoroastrian monotheism is that Jews recognize the one God as the source of both good and evil, while Zoroastrians think of God only as the source of Good. Because there is no creation story in Zoroastrianism, the origin of Ahriman's and the legions of demons he commands is unknown.

571 BCE

Book of Ezekiel records six visions of the prophet while exiled in Babylon between 593 to 571 BCE. The visions are structured in three themes: Judgment of Israel; Judgment of Nations; and future blessings of Israel. Its themes include the concepts of God, purity, Israel as a divine community, and individual responsibility to God.

560 BCE

Book of Kings 1 and 2 present a history of Israel and Judah between 960 – 560 BCE. In King David's old age, Adonijah proclaimed himself David's successor but supporters of Solomon arranged for him to be the successor. At the beginning of his reign, Solomon assumed God's promise to David by bringing splendor to Israel and peace and prosperity to his people with the centerpiece of his reign being the temple in Jerusalem. In the end, Solomon followed other gods and oppresses Israel. As a consequence of Solomon's failure to stamp out pagan worship, the kingdom of David was split in two during the reign of Rehoboam. In the final chapters, God brings Nebuchadnezzar against Jerusalem with Yahweh withholding aid from his people with the city being razed and the temple destroyed, with the priests, prophets and royal court being led into captivity.

553 BCE

Book of Lamentations is a collection of poetic laments for the destruction of Jerusalem by Babylon. The book mourns the desertion of the city by God, its destruction, and ultimate return of the divinity. The tone is bleak, the degree of suffering is undeserved, and expectations of future redemption minimal. In chapter 1, the city sits as a desolate weeping widow overcome with miseries. In chapter 2 these miseries are described in connection with national sins and acts of God. Chapter 3 speaks of hope for the people of God saying that the chastisement would only be for their good; a better day will dawn for them. Chapter 4 laments the ruin and desolation of the city and temple, but traces it to the people's sin. Chapter 5 is a prayer that Zion's rejection may be taken away by repentance and recovery of the people.

551 BCE

Book of Judges covers the time between the conquest in the Book of Joshua and the kingdom established in Book of Samuel. The stories follow a consistent pattern: the people are unfaithful to Yahweh and he therefore delivers them into the hands of their enemies; the people repent and beg Yahweh for mercy, which he sends in the form of a leader; the judge delivers the Israelites from oppression and they prosper, but soon fall again into unfaithfulness and the cycle is repeated. The text gives accounts of six major judges and their struggles against oppressive kings of surrounding nations and brief stories about six minor judges. Because the story was written 550 years after the time of the actual judges, chronological order of events and historical facts have been distorted by the huge gap in time. The main problem – none of the judges, not even Gideon, Jephthah, Ehud, and Samson ruled all the tribes at once but only some of them.

The Hebrew tribes who returned to Canaan made up a third of the entire population of the country. While the advance of the northern tribes was kept in check by Egyptian rule over Canaan, the second wave of returning Hebrew tribes settled the fate of Canaan. The land was not conquered by military means but by the assimilation of the Hebrew tribes with the local people.

In 1920, archaeologists discovered the biblical city of Hazor as being a twenty-five acre mound off the road running north from the Sea of Galilee. Hazor was a Canaanite city of temples which house a magnificent palace that suffered catastrophic destruction in 1275 BCE.

550 BCE

Cyrus the Great of Persia (590-530 BCE), conquered Babylon, Egypt, and everything in between including Judah.

Book of Ruth tells about her accepting the god of the Israelites and the people as her own. Ruth teaches that foreigners who convert to Judaism can become good Jews, foreign wives can become exemplary followers of Jewish law, and there is no reason to exclude them or their offspring from the community. Ruth's identity as a non-Israelite and emphasis on the need for an inclusive attitude towards foreigners suggests Book of Ruth was written when intermarriage with foreigners had become controversial.

549 BCE

Book of Samuel 1 and 2 begins with the prophet Samuel's birth and God's call to him as a boy. The story of the ark of the Covenant that follows tells of Israel's oppression at the hands of the Philistines, which brought about Samuel's anointing of Saul as Israel's first king. Because Samuel proved unworthy, God turned to David who defeated Israel's enemies. David purchased the threshing floor, where his son, Solomon built the first temple and brought the Ark to Jerusalem. God then promised David and his successors an everlasting dynasty. Second Book of Samuel concludes with four chapters (chapter 21 to 24) which lie outside the chronical narrative of Saul and David. The narrative is resumed with the first Book of Kings which relates how, as David lies dying, Bathsheba and Nathan ensure Solomon's elevation to the throne.

542 BCE

Book of Joshua tells of the campaigns of the Israelites in Canaan, the destruction of their enemies and the division of the land among the Twelve Tribes, framed by two speeches, the first by God commanding the conquest of the Promised Land and the second by Joshua warning of the need for faithful observance of the law revealed by Moses.

541 BCE

Book of Isaiah promises judgment and restoration for Judah, Jerusalem and the nations. Isaiah speaks out against corrupt leaders and for the disadvantaged while promoting the righteousness of God.

540 BCE

Cyrus the Great, king of the Persian Empire, fought his way into the city of Babylon which had rebelled against his reign. He believed there was a way to allow his vassal states to experience their autonomy by channeling their national aspirations into their native cult. The king's proclamation of religious tolerance was welcomed throughout the empire but nowhere more so than in Judah. Cyrus set the Jewish exiles free and allowed them to return to their homeland. For those who returned to Jerusalem, they found the Holy City to be a pile of rubble. This experience drove Isaiah deep into himself, his heritage, and his worship. He was forced to rethink the relationship between Yahweh and the chosen people. Most important of all, he had to create another image of the nation in order for others to understand the mission of his people. He sketched a portrait of the servant figure, which embodied a higher, grander destiny for Israel than any Jew before him had ever envisioned. Judah was to be the servant through which all the nations of the world would be blessed, made whole, and set free. This task would be accomplished by accepting the afflictions of the powerlessness. If this role were too difficult for the nation of Judah to achieve, then perhaps one supreme son of Abraham might fill the role.

As the servant figure emerged in the writing of Second Isaiah, his task was seen to be that of going beyond the covenant people as an agent for bringing justice to Gentiles as well. He would be used by Yahweh to give light and salvation to the world (49:6), with his mission being universal, not nationalistic (49:6). His task was to express the tenderness of God for all humanity (42:6), to liberate the suffering (61:1), to guide the thirsty to water (44:22 f), to set human life free (42:7), to make human beings whole (55:1 f, 42:7), and to break the power of sin (53:12). He would impart God's law to the world (51:4); yet this law would not be forced on human family, it would be presented so that all would eagerly seek it (42:4).

537 BCE

Book of Leviticus consist of speeches in which God commands Moses to repeat to the Israelites. The story takes place after the Israelites leave Egypt and reach Mount Sinai. The book tells how Moses led the Israelites in building the Tabernacle with God's instructions.

One comment in Leviticus was made (18:22) that has given some modern readers a reason to give pause.

"Do not lie with a man as one lies with a woman, that is detestable."

Literary analysis of the original Hebrew language by scholars shows that the author of Leviticus was condemning same-sex rape (incest with a family member) with some modern translators making the translation as simple as possible which presents a reading that is not only harmful, but incongruent to the context of Leviticus. In sum, traditional English translations of Leviticus 18:22 are known to modern scholarship as "clobber passages" that condemn homosexuality using 18:22 as a weapon against all same-sex relationships which is not only unjust, but linguistically misguided.

Siddharta Gautama, better known as Buddha, left his family to become a mendicant ascetic because he had become appalled by the spectacle of suffering going on around him. He wanted to discover the secret of ending that pain. For six years he studied under Hindu gurus before he was able to put himself into a trance, gaining total enlightenment. Gautama had become the Buddha, the enlightened one. He believed in the existence of the gods, but he did not believe in them to be of much use to mankind because they were too caught up in the cycle of rebirth and would eventually disappear. He believed that the ultimate reality of *Nirvana* was higher than the gods, it was a blissful state where his disciples could save themselves. He taught that it was possible to gain relief from the sinful world by living a life of compassion for all living beings, speaking gently, and refraining from anything that could cloud the mind. He compares the process of rebirth to a flame that lights a lamp, from which a second lamp is lit, and so on until the flame is extinguished. If somebody is still aflame with earthly passion at death with wrong attitude, he or she will simply light another lamp. But if the fire is put out by having a correct attitude, the cycle of suffering will cease and *Nirvana* will be obtained with the word literally means "cooling-off" or "going-out," which is analogous to receiving the spirit of God.

536 BCE

Cyrus the Great of Persia, began construction on the second temple in Jerusalem.

525 BCE

Book of Micah defends the rights of the poor against the rich and powerful while looking forward to a world at peace centered in Zion under the leadership of a new Davidic monarch.

522 BCE

Zechariah, Haggai and Malachi prophesized in southern kingdom of Judah.

520 BCE

Book of Zechariah follows a series of eight visions, succeeding one another in one night, which may be regarded as a symbolic history of Israel intended to furnish consolation to exiles returning from Babylon and to stir up hope in their minds. The main purpose of the book is theological and pastoral. The book's focus is that God is at work and all his good deeds are accomplished "not by might nor by power, but by my Spirit" (4:6). Ultimately, God plans to live again with his people in Jerusalem. He will save them from their enemies and cleanse them from sin. However, God requires repentance, a turning towards faith in Him. God's greatest enemies are not fallen angles commanding armies of demons or even the gods of other nations, but, rather human beings. It isn't the devil that spreads evil across the face of creation – it is mankind. God is the Lord of justice, he is behind the good and the bad because it is he that gave human beings freedom of choice!

The Hebrew word *satan* occurs several times throughout the Hebrew Bible with the word being a job description rather than a proper name. During the "accusers" first appearance in book of Zechariah, his job entailed calling attention to the unworthiness of mankind. He was essentially the prosecuting attorney in the divine court of Yahweh, with his job collecting evidence to prove Yahweh's cases. It is difficult to determine at which point in history the accuser began to take on a much more sinister role or became the prince of darkness. It is perfectly clear that by the first century CE, Judaism developed a belief in the divine forces of "sons of light" doing battle against the "sons of darkness" - good vs evil. It is at this same time, that *satan* began to acquire various names and titles that have filled the writings of western civilization for 2000 years. The word *diabolos* in Greek from which the word *devil* arose is equivalent to the Hebrew word *satan*. Throughout the gospels,

Satan's "kingdom" was never considered to be a burning underworld full of the tormented dead, but rather, is equated to the bondage of sin brought upon humanity for acts of unrighteousness. Satan rebellion exemplifies the difficulty of mankind in choosing between true and false liberty. Everyone wants true liberty, but true liberty is based on justice, fairness to others, and fraternity. Liberty is self-destructive when it is thoughtless and uncontrolled. The growth of liberty follows the conquest of "self".

Early Christian writers such as Tertullian, Origen, and Augustine of Hippo began to apply the name "Lucifer" to the motif of a heavenly angle being cast down to the earth as being Satan. As a result, "Lucifer has become a byword for Satan in both the church and in popular literature, such as in Dante Alighieri's *Inferno*, Joost van den Vondel's *Lucifer*, and John Milton's *Paradise Lost.*

519 BCE

Book of Zephaniah focus is on God with his work and good deeds being accomplished "not by might nor by power, but by My Spirit." Yahweh plans to again live with his people in Jerusalem and will save them from their enemies and cleanse them from sin; however, He requires a turning away from sin towards faith in him.

516 BCE

Book of Haggai is filled with urgency for the people to rebuild the Jerusalem temple because Haggai attributes a recent drought to the people's refusal to rebuild, which he sees as a key to Jerusalem's glory. The book ends with a prediction of the downfall of the kingdoms with Zerubbabel, grandson of King Jehoiachin, being chosen by the Lord as leader of Judah.

515 BCE

Construction of the 2nd temple in Jerusalem completed.

458 BCE

Samarian exiles, from the northern kingdom, who returned to the southern kingdom of Judah, brought with them a Hellenized belief system whereby

Jews combined the Hebrew belief in Yahweh with Greek belief in divinity of kingship; deity intermarrying with an earthly woman; belief in immortality; and resurrection of the dead with the
Hebrew language and writing being replaced by Greek language, and philosophy.

455 BCE

Book of Jonah is about repentant hearts with Jonah being the central character. God commands Jonah to go to the city of Nineveh to prophesy against it but he refuses instead sailing to Tarshish. During the trip, a huge storm arises with the sailors, realizing that Jonah is to blame. Jonah admits this and states that if he is thrown overboard as a sacrifice, the storm will cease. As the storm subsides, the sailors offer sacrifice to God. Jonah was miraculously saved by being swallowed by a large fish in whose belly he spends three days and three nights. While in the great fish, Jonah prays to God upon which God commands the fish to vomit Jonah out. God then commands Jonah to travel to Nineveh to prophesy to its inhabitants with the people of Nineveh believing his word and proclaiming a fast. God seeing the repentant hearts of Nineveh spared the city.

450 BCE

Book of Psalms involves praise of God for his power and beneficence, for his creation of the world, and for his acts of deliverance for Israel. The book envision a world in which everyone and everything will praise God, and God, in turn, will hear their praise and respond.

441 BCE

Book of Malachi is about the social behavior of the Israelites. Although the prophets have urged the people of northern and southern kingdoms to see their exile as punishment for failing to uphold their covenant with God, it was not long after they returned to temple worship that their commitment to God, once again began to wane. Malachi reminds them that God is just, exhorting them to be faithful as they await his justice. The book concludes by calling upon the teachings of Moses promising that Elijah will return prior to the day of the Lord.

440 BCE

During the reign of King Artaxeres I, a high-ranking official from his court named Nehemiah, petitioned the king to go back to his ancestral city of Jerusalem and with the help of Ezra, who was both a priest and scribe, to rebuild the city which had languished.

Josephus discussed Ezra in *Antiquities of the Jews* with his account deriving from *1 Esdras*, where he says that Ezra is the one who restored the law that was destroyed with the burning of the first temple in Jerusalem. For scholars, it is fascinating to note that there is an ancient tradition about Ezra and the Torah of Moses that is preserved in a work titled *4th Book of Ezra*. Ezra said:

"The world lies in darkness, and its inhabitants are without light. For your law has been burned, and so no one knows the things which have been done or will be done by you. If then I have found favor before you, send the Holy Spirit to me, and I will write everything that has happened in the world from the beginning, the things which were written in your law."

In the fourth century, Jerome, noted Christian historian, commented:

"Whether you choose to call Moses the author of the Pentateuch or Ezra the re-newer of the same work, I raise no objection."

Yahwist belief system was transformed into today's modern Judaism.

427 BCE

Plato is viewed as being the founder of western philosophy. The most important aspect of Platonism on Christianity is his *Theory of Forms*. Plato ascribed importance to the form of *good* and the notion of *word*, through which the rationality of God is communicated and conceptualized. Theologians such as Justin Martyr (100 CE - 165), Irenaeus (130 CE - 200), Tertullian (160 CE - 225), and Origen (185 CE - 254) found his concept of *logos* immensely important, especially in dealing with doctrines of divine revelation and Christology.

410 BCE

Ark of the Covenant moved from Jerusalem to Elephantine Island in Egypt.

400 BCE

Book of Nehemiah tells a story about Jerusalem being without walls (spiritual protection) and, as such, Nehemiah returns and reforms the community according to the laws of Moses. After a time away, he returned to Jerusalem from Susa and found that the Israelites had been backsliding by taking non-Jewish wives.
399 BCE

Book of Ezra tells about the return of the exiles in the first year of Cyrus the Great's reign and dedication of the new temple in Jerusalem in the sixth year of the reign of Darius I. It is about the subsequent mission of Ezra to Jerusalem and his struggle to purify the Jews from marriage with non-Jews. Together with the Book of Nehemiah, it represents the final chapter in the historical narrative of Israel in the Hebrew Bible.

390 BCE

Hellenism is the word used to express the assimilation by the Jews, with Greek speech, manners, and culture, from the 4th century BCE through the first centuries of the common era. Post-exile Judaism of the northern kingdom was largely recruited from those returning exiles who regarded it as their task to preserve their religion uncontaminated. The Hellenic influence pervaded everything, and even in the very strongholds of Judaism it modified the organization of the state, the laws, and public affairs, art, science and religion affecting even the ordinary things of life and the common association of people.

355 BCE

Aristotle founded a school of thought in Athens known as the Lyceum. He studied under Plato and was a prolific writer who, with his idea of God, having an immense influence on later monotheists, particularly on Christians in the Western world. In the book *Physics,* he determined that in the world there was a hierarchy of existences, each one of which imparts change to the one below it, but that the emanations grew weaker the farther they were from their source. At the top of this hierarchy the "Unmoved Mover", which Aristotle identified as God was pure thinker and thought, engaged in an eternal moment of contemplation, the highest object of knowledge. Since matter is flawed and mortal, there is no material element in God. He causes all the activity in the universe since each movement must have a cause that can be traced back to a single source. He activates the world by a process of attraction since all beings are drawn toward believing.

350 BCE

Song of Solomon (Song of Songs) celebrates "the voices to two lovers" praising each other, yearning for each other. The two are in harmony. In Jewish tradition, it reads as allegory of the relationship between God and Israel. In Christian tradition, it describes the love of Christ for his church. In Ebonite tradition, it describes the relationship between Jesus and Mary Magdalene.

336 BCE

A young Macedonian king named Alexander, at age 18 years, took his army of 40,000 soldiers and invaded Persia. After defeating King Darius III at the Battle of Issus, he rolled inexorably forward first heading south into Syria, Phoenica, Judah, and Egypt, before turning east to capture Babylon, Susa, and Perepolis. When he conquered the Persian Empire, he carried the Greek civilization into the lands he conquered with many Jews replacing their Hebrew language with that of the Greeks who developed a worldview and system of education based upon logic and science. Greeks sought truth through human reason and the study of the natural world. Greek culture so attracted some Jews that they abandoned their own culture which began as a mutual admiration society between cultures with the Aramaic speaking Jews of Judah, who had not lived in exile, disapproving of most Greek institutions which they viewed as being dedicated to a way of life that was foreign to them.

As Alexander was plotting his next campaign into the Arabian Peninsula, he contracted a mysterious disease and after fourteen agonizing days, died in Darius's palace in Babylon. Because his death had come so suddenly no one had prepared for an orderly succession with this leading to a power struggle between his generals. In the end, each general chose a territory to which they had taken fancy. Ptolemy took Egypt; Seleucus took the heart of the Persian Empire while Cassander took Greece and Macedonia. Soon, these generals were at war with each other as they attempted to expand their territories.

Ptolemy, who was now being referred to as King Ptolemy I Soter, was founder of the Ptolemaic dynasty, which ruled over Egypt, Judah, and Phoenica from his capital in Alexandria. Seleucus became the head of the Seleucid dynasty, headquartered in Antioch, Syria with his control over Syria and Babylonia. After Jews from Jerusalem returned to Alexandria in 312 BCE, others followed with the new Egyptian capital becoming the crown jewel of the Ptolemaic Empire, a center of learning epitomized by the Library of Alexandria. Although Judah had enjoyed relative prosperity and religious freedom under the dynasty of Ptolemaic kings, things would change dramatically under the new "Seleucid" rules.

The outstanding intellectual of the Hellenistic world was Philo (20 BCE-50 CE) who was the Jewish religious leader of Alexandria at the time of Jesus. From Philo's writing scholars can see that Hellenism developed in its own way and was different from that of the Aramaic speaking Jews of Judah and Babylon. *On the Creation of the World # 69,* Philo interprets the divine image of God in mankind as "mind":

> Moses tells us that man was created after the image of God and in His likeness. Right well does he say this, for nothing earth-born is more like God than man. Let no one represent the likeness as one to a bodily form; for neither is God in human form, nor is the human body God-like. No, it is respect of the mind, the sovereign element of the soul, that the image is used; for after the pattern of a single Mind, even the Mind of the Universe as an archetype, was the mind in each of those who successfully came into being molded.

On the Virtues, Philo stated that the purpose of the laws of the Torah was to instill in society virtues defined by Greek philosophers:

> What our most holy prophet through all his regulations especially desires to create is unanimity, neighborliness, fellowship, reciprocity of feelings, whereby houses and cities and nations and countries

and whole human race may advance to supreme happiness. Hitherto,indeed, these things live only in our prayers, but they will, I am convinced, become facts beyond all dispute if God, even as He gives us the yearly fruits, grants that the virtues should bear abundantly.

Some Greeks adopted the Jewish belief in the one indivisible God. These Greeks were called 'God-fearers.' They worshiped the God of the Jews, but were not Jews as that identity was not based on just a God idea but on living by the Torah. God-fearers did not convert to the Jewish belief system because they wanted to continue as members of their own society – These were the first followers of Apostle Paul.

325 BCE

Chronicles 1 and 2 begins with Adam and Eve and is then carried forward through genealogical lists down to the founding of the first Kingdom of Israel. The remainder of Chronicles is concerned with the reign of King David, his son Solomon and with the Kingdom of Judah.

301 BCE

Palestine was placed under the rule of the Ptolemy's of Egypt.

298 BCE

The Stoic philosophy was found by Zeno (334 – 262 BCE) of Citium, Cypress. The philosophy teaches the development of self-control as a means of overcoming destructive emotions and understanding universal reason *(Logos)*. Stoicism's primary aspect involves the individual's ethical and moral well-being. The principle applies to the realm of interpersonal relationships, to be free from anger, envy, and jealousy.

284 BCE

Because Jews living in diaspora no longer spoke or read the Hebrew language , the Torah (Genesis, Exodus, Leviticus, Numbers, and Deuteronomy) was translated from ancient Hebrew into Greek and today is referred to as being the *Septuagint.*

255 BCE

Book of Esther is about a Hebrew woman living in Persia, born as Hadassah but known as Ester, who became queen of Persia and thwarted genocide of her people. The book is set in the Persian capital of Susa in the third year of the reign of king Ahasuerus. Festival of Purim is a Jewish holiday which commemorates the saving of the Jewish people living in Haman from royal vizier Ahasuerus who was planning to kill all Jews in Persia with his plans being foiled by Esther, his adopted daughter who would become Queen of Persia.

254 BCE

Book of Job is a defense of God's goodness and omnipotence in view of the existence of evil things happening.

253 BCE

Book of Proverbs raises questions of values, moral behavior, and the meaning of human life. Wisdom is praised for her role in creation. Wisdom, or the wise person, is compared and contrasted with foolishness or the fool, meaning one who is lacking in wisdom and uninterested in learning. "The fear of God is the beginning of wisdom" with the phrase implying submission to God's will.

249 BCE

Book of Jeremiah is a message to the Jews living in Babylon explaining that the exile was God's response to their pagan worship. The people are like an unfaithful wife and rebellious children, their infidelity and rebelliousness made judgment inevitable, although restoration and a new covenant are foreshadowed.

180 BCE

Book of Ecclesiastes is the musings of a King of Jerusalem as he relates his experiences and draws lessons from them. As king, he has experienced everything and done everything with the only good being to partake of life in the present, for enjoyment is from the hand of God. The world is filled with injustice which only God will adjudicate.

167 BCE

After capturing Jerusalem, King Antiochus IV of Syria (175-164 BCE), fearing the spread of Judaism, decided to convert the Jews to paganism by forbidding Jewish practices and destroying their scripture. Worst of all, Antiochus plundered the Jerusalem temple and erected a statue of the Greek god Zeus over the altar. He then pursued his goal of de-Judaizing Judah by moving into the countryside with troops under order to enforce his regulations against Jewish religious practices, with one of these units moving into the village of Modein in the foothills 6 miles northwest of Jerusalem.

An altar was set up in the village and before the assembled population, Mattathias a Jewish priest, was ordered to perform a sacrifice and eat of the pig's flesh. With him were his five sons: John, Simon, Judas, Elazar, and Jonathon. When Mattathias did not move from his spot, one of the assembled Jews moved forward to the altar to obey the order and perform the sacrifice. Mattathias, thereupon rushed forward in a fury, slew the traitor and killed the commander of the troops. His sons then led the villagers against the remaining Greek unit, killing them all; thus began the revolt of the Maccabees, which was the first battle in recorded history to be fought over the issue of religious freedom.

In 166 BCE, after Mattathias has passed, his son Judas took over command of the troops and was able to capture Jerusalem, cleansing the temple of all Greek idols and restoring the worship of Yahweh. Thus, 45 years after the capture of Jerusalem by Babylonian king Nebuchadnezzar, the Jews were once again free. During the next half century, the Maccabees' continued their struggle to liberate Samaria and Galilee with the Hasmonean Dynasty (167 to 63 BCE) being considered the most successful dynasty in the history of Israel. Leaders of the Maccabean Dynasty were:

Mattathias: 167-166 BCE
Judas Maccabeus: 166-160 BCE
Jonathan Maccabeus: 160-142 BCE
Simon Maccabeus: 142-134 BCE

John Hyrcanus I: 134-105 BCE
Aristobulus I: 105-103 BCE
Alexander Jannaeus:103-76 BCE
Salome Alexandra: 76-68 BCE
Hyrcanus II: 68-67 BCE
Aristobulus II: 66-63 BCE
Antigonus Mattathias: 40-37 BCE

When Salome Alexandra ruled the Hasmonean Kingdom during the last of the kingdom's golden days, women played a decisive role in Jewish history fighting for their country's freedom and peoples survival. When she died, a power struggle broke out between her oldest son Hyrcanus II and her younger son Aristobulus II because Hyrcanus favored the political faction of the Pharisees whereas Aristobulus favored the Sadducees. The result was a civil war which became a great concern to Rome because they feared that the turmoil would spill over into Egypt which supplied the empire with grain. Shortly after Roman General Pompey heard about the mayhem in Judah, he was invited by the Sadducees to intervene thereby adding the Hasmonean Kingdom to the Roman Empire.

165 BCE

Book of Daniel is a story about the God of Israel saving Daniel and his friends from their enemies during their time of oppression. Daniel was written during the Maccabean revolt using the figure Daniel as a way to reflect on the experiences of the Jewish people in the time of crisis.

106 BCE

One of the most influential figures in history was a Roman statesman, orator, essayist and philosopher named Marcus Tullius Cicero (106-43 BCE), a man who was never fully accepted by either the snobbish Senate elite or by the demagogic leaders of the masses, whom he despised. Toward the end of his life, he distinguished himself in his battle to save the Roman Republic by taking charge of the state during the months immediately following the assassination of Julius Caesar.

102 BCE

Julius Caesar (102 BCE - 44BCE) was born to Gaius Julius and Aurelia.

100 BCE

Book of Maccabee is considered by scholars to be the best history that has ever come down from ancient Israel. First book of Maccabees opens with a brief reference to Alexander the Great and to the Greek rulers who succeeded him. The history begins with Antiochus Epiphanes and the most important struggle the world had ever seen. It was fought not on the open battlefield but wherever in Palestine and the lands of the dispersion where the currents of ancient Jewish life and commerce met and mingled with the Greek culture. It details the history of the Maccabean Revolt against the Seleucid Empire as well as the founding and earliest history of the independent Hasmonean kingdom. It was the age-long conflict between Hellenism and Judaism that had long been maturing in the coast lands of the Mediterranean with Judaism representing the life and faith of the peasant people where Hellenism was born in the city, expressing Greek thought as an expression in civic life. Hellenism protested against the narrowness and intolerance of Jewish belief system whereas Judaism protested against the godlessness and immorality of Hellenism. For scholars the event that set things in motion was Antiochus IV failed invasion of Egypt in 168 BCE with his defeat allowing the Egyptian ruler Ptolemy VI to retake the southern Levant, a region that earlier Egyptian rulers regarded as their birthright. When a local uprising occurred in Jerusalem due to Antiochus IV raid on the temple, Ptolemy VI, king of the Ptolemaic Empire, saw it as a golden opportunity to foment destabilization deep in Seleucid territory.

Archaeological remains show a sudden wave of abandoned and destroyed sites across much of the region due to the Seleucid self-implosion which, not only the Hasmoneans took advantage of, so too did almost every major Levantine city from Cilicia in the south which achieved political autonomy including Tyre, Sidon, Akko-Ptolemais, Gaza, and Ashkeln.

80 BCE

Ark of the Covenant was moved down the Nile River from the isle of Tana Kirkos to the city of Aksum in Ethiopia were today, it is thought to be housed in Saint Mary of Zion cathedral.

79 BCE

Mount Vesuvius erupted burring the city of Pompeii, near Naples, under 18 feet of volcanic ash freezing a snapshot of Roman life in time.

73 BCE

Seventy gladiators, who were skilled fighters, broke out of their barracks at Capua in southern Italy because living conditions had become so unbearable. Upon news of the escape, other oppressed slaves from around the country fled to join Spartacus and his men. After their escape, it was to Spartacus's advantage that the Romans underrated the uprising and did little to respond. For over a year, Spartacus had more difficulty within his own ranks than he had with the Romans, as it was his intent to lead his men to freedom, while it was their intent to pillage and rob the north of Italy. Due to this lawlessness, Rome sent Marcus Licinius Crassus, in command of the eighth legion, to crush Spartacus's army with Spartacus being killed in battle. By the summer of 71 BCE, the Spartacus War had ended, with over 6,000 of his followers being crucified along the Appian Way.

70 BCE

Jacob-Heli, father of Joseph was born a descendent of King David through the priestly line of Nathan, his son. Because of Jacob's friendly relationship with Herod the Great, he was willing to help him in his plan to revive the messianic tradition which ended when the Maccabean nation fell due to political infighting. Jacob-Heli agreed to serve as third in a triarchy of Abraham, Isaac, and Jacob with Herod acting as the symbolic Abraham, father of Judaism, while Jacob-Heli agreed to serve as the symbolic 'David'. In this pre-Christian form of community, hierarchy was always thought of as being in groups of three because three was the number required to perform the central rite of atonement. For Jews, the individual representing Abraham was believed to have been called by God, justified by faith and living in fellowship with Him. The individual representing Isaac, his son, was believed to have inherited all promised blessings from his Father with Jacob, his son believed to have been chosen by God to experience the trials and tribulations of bringing God's blessings to Israel. *On the Life and Times of Jesus the Messiah*, Alfred Edersheim describes the role each of the three priests performed on the Day of Atonement. Herod's scheme of initiation into the new form of religion was immediately accepted by wealthy Jews living outside of the nation who were more than willing to come back home to join in this worldwide society by paying a half-shekel fee, which was about a day's income, as a ransom for one's soul.

69 BCE

Cleopatra was born, the third child of Ptolemy Auleyes, with her siblings being Cleopatra Tryphaena, Berenice, Arsinoe, Ptolemy XIII, and Ptolemy XIV. While Cleopatra was still a young child, Egypt became the focal point of Roman politics, as Rome was tempted to annex the country due to its vast real estate and extreme wealth. When Cleopatra became queen at age 18, she adopted her father's policy of collaboration with the Romans, as it was this policy that would assure the continuation of her family's reign since the independence of Egypt was her main goal. Paganism was very much alive as the Greco-Roman period held a passionate belief in the mystery religions, stressing initiation, purification, mystic communion, redemption in this world, and salvation next. It was the great age of ruler worship, as it was believed that the king of Egypt was the incarnation of the god Osiris and his queen was his partner on earth, Isis. This belief was passionately held by Cleopatra herself and provided the theological justification for the Ptolemaic institution of the marriage of kings to their sisters.

63 BCE

Because the Maccabean kingdom had all but fallen apart due to political infighting, Roman domination over Jerusalem began when the Pharisees, who were locked in battle with the Sadducees, invited Pompey to enter the city with his legions. By aligning Roman interests with those of the ruling class in the city, Pompey was guaranteed that local leaders remained wholly vested in maintaining the imperial system. All that Rome asked of Jerusalem was a twice-daily sacrifice on behalf of the emperor for his good health, keep up with the taxes and tribute, follow the provincial laws, and Rome was happy to leave you, your god, and your temple alone. What most puzzled the Romans about the Jews was not their strict devotion to their laws, but rather what the Romans considered their unfathomable superiority complex. For the Jews this sense of exceptionalism was not a matter of arrogance or pride it was a direct commandment from God who tolerated no foreign presence in the land he had set aside for his chosen people. In the years of tumult that followed the Roman occupation of Israel, the peasantry was not only obligated to pay taxes and tithes to the temple priesthood, they were now forced to pay a heavy tribute to Rome which, for farmers, amounted to nearly half their annual income.

61 BCE

From hiding places in caves and grottoes of the Galilean countryside, an entire crop of peasants, who found themselves stripped of their property with no way to feed themselves or their families, launching a wave of attacks against both the corrupt Jewish aristocracy and the agents of the Roman Republic. To the faithful, these peasant-warriors were nothing less than the embodiment of the anger and suffering of the poor which represented the first stirrings of a nationalistic resistance against Roman occupation.

54 BCE

When the Romans took over Jerusalem, they found the 2nd temple built by Cyrus the Great seriously damaged due to civil war which had taken place between the Pharisees and Sadducees.

52 BCE

After the death of Roman general and statesman Crassus fighting the Parthians, ill feelings began to surface between the Senate and Julius Caesar, as he was not willing to relinquish his role as governor of Gaul or give up command of his armies. It was also known to Caesar's enemies in the Senate that he had significant influence in the political arena and that he wanted to reform Senate activities, which had become overbearing and corrupt. Pompey, who had the Senate's support, wanted to become sole consul at the elections to be held even though it was Caesar's intent to run for the same office. To avoid civil war, Caesar sent Pompey a letter suggesting that both he and Pompey give up their military command, disband their armies, and run for office against each other in a peaceful manner with the followers of Pompey rejecting this plan, because they worried that they might lose the election and believed that Pompey's army could defeat Caesar.

49 BDE

Civil war broke out between the two leaders in Rome, with Julius Caesar being victorious over Pompey two years later. Within four days after the defeat of Pompey's army on Egypt's eastern border, Caesar arrived in Alexandria harbor with ten warships and a force of four thousand infantry and cavalry to claim possession of Egypt. For Cleopatra, she wanted a relationship with Caesar, as she liked his personality and knew that an association with such a man would further her policy of accommodation as other great dynasties, the Antigonids in Macedonia and Seleucids in Asia had each tried to fight Rome and lost. In Plutarch's book titled *Life of Antony*, he describes Cleopatra's personal attributes used to gain Caesar's attention:

> Her own beauty, so we are told, was not that incomparable kind which instantly captivates the beholder, but the charm of her presence was irresistible, and there was an attractiveness in her person and talk, together with a peculiar force of character which pervaded her every word and action, and laid all who associated with her under a spell. It was a delight merely to hear the sound of her voice.

47 BCE

Cleopatra traveled to Rome accompanied by an imposing entourage. The purpose of her visit was not only to continue her close relationship with Caesar but also to sign a new treaty that would safeguard her interests if there was an attempt by Rome to annex Egypt. After a short stay, she learned that she was pregnant with Caesar's child, a boy she named Ptolemy Caesar who was born in 46 BCE.

44 BCE

As emperor of Rome, Caesar planned to undertake an immense oriental operation on the scale of Alexander the Great years earlier to Parthia. Three days before his trip, conspirators at a meeting of the Senate assassinated him, terminating the most remarkable leader that Rome had ever known, at age fifty-eight.

It was proposed by Caesar's followers that at the upcoming Senate meeting to be held on March 15th , that he should be elevated from the status of consul to 'king' because of his godly qualities and worldly achievements with this move being more than some Senators could bear because it was a tradition of the Senate that after the fall of Lucius Tarquinius Superbus, the last king of Rome, that the empire would never again be ruled by a despot.

Superbus, king of Rome between 534 and 509 BCE, gained the throne through the murders of both his wife and his elder brother, followed by the assassination of his predecessor, Servius Tullius. He commenced his reign by refusing to bury the dead Servius and then putting to death a number of leading senators, whom he suspected of remaining loyal to Servius. By not replacing the slain senators, and not consulting with the Senate on matters of government, he diminished their authority. He judged capital crimes without the advice of counselors, causing fear among those who might wish to oppose him. From there, his policies on governance were not liked by the populous.

The plan to assassinate Caesar at the Senate meeting was supported by sixty Senators with its leader being Marcus Brutus. Caesar was warned by loyal supporters that he should provide himself with a body guard for the meeting but he refused. The Senate met in Pompey's curia where Vestricius Spurinna had prophesied that misfortune would befall Caesar on the Ides of March. Seeing Spurinna standing in the door of the Senate, Caesar smiled with an air of mocking superiority and said to him that the Ides of March had come and that nothing had happened to him. To that Spurinna replied, "They have come, but they are not yet over."

With that, Cleopatra had lost her lover, patron, and friend on whom the fulfillment of all her ambitions had depended. Two days after his assassination, his will was read and it became apparent to the citizens of Rome that neither Cleopatra or her son were mentioned and that the major ambitions that were rumored about her would never materialize, other than the renewed treaty of friendship between Egypt and Rome. Because she was not trusted by Roman politicians, she left the city and made her way back to Egypt.

43 BCE

Mark Antony and Octavian divided up the Roman World, Antony, like Caesar, selected the east due to its immense wealth. Due to the upcoming war with the Parthians, Antony needed Cleopatra's support, as well as Egyptian money. As their first meeting place, Antony selected Tarsus in Cilicia and had Cleopatra brought there from Alexandria. Determined, for the sake of her future and that of Egypt, she came from Alexandria to Cilicia sailing up the Cygnus to the ancient city of Tarsus. In Plutarch's *Life of Antony*, he describes her entrance:

> She relied above all upon her physical presence and the spell and enchantment which it could create. She came sailing up the river Cygnus in a barge with a deck of gold, its purple sails billowing in the wind, while her own rowers caressed the water with oars of silver, which dipped in time to the music of the flute, accompanied by pipes and lutes. Cleopatra herself reclined beneath a canopy of cloth made of gold, dressed in the character of Aphrodite (Venus) as we see her in paintings, while on the either side, to complete the picture, stood boys costumed as cupids, who cooled her off with their fans. Instead of a crew, the barge was lined with the most beautiful of her waiting women attired as Nereids and Graces, some at the rudders, others at tackle of the sails, and all while an indescribably rich perfume exhaled from innumerable censers wafted from the vessel to the riverbanks. Great multitudes accompanied this royal progress, some of them following the queen on both sides of the river, from its very mouth, while others hurried down from the city of Tarsus to gaze at the sight. Gradually the crowds drifted away from the marketplace, where Antony awaited the queen enthroned on his tribunal, until at last he was sitting quite alone, and the word spread on every side that Aphrodite had come to revel with Dionysus (god) for happiness of Asia.

In response to the assassination of Julius Caesar, his 18-year-old grandnephew and heir to the throne, Octavian, formed a triumvirate with Mark Antony and General Lepidus to bring the assassins to justice. The result of this endeavor was a civil war that would last for over a decade, and from which, Octavian would emerge victorious. He then founded the Roman Empire, and ruled as emperor Augustus from 27 BCE to 14 CE. In *Embassy to Gaius*, Plato described Augustus:

This ruler, Augustus, who truly deserves the title of 'Averter of Evil,' is the Caesar who lulled the storms which were crashing everywhere, who healed the sickness common to Greeks and barbarians alike…This is he who cleared the sea of pirate-ships and filled it with merchant-ships. This is he who set every city again at liberty, who reduced disorder to order, who civilized all the unfriendly savage tribes and brought them into harmony with each other…This is he who safeguarded peace, gave each man his due, distributed his favors widely without stint, and never in his whole life kept any blessing or advantage back.

Roman Republic system of government featured an elected consul to serve as both civil and military leader, a senate and government bodies empowered with voting rights. In 42 BCE, after Caesar's death, the new regime of Octavian, Mark Anthony and Lepidus formally deified Caesar authorizing a temple be built in recognition of his divinity with the temple being placed on the spot where Caesar's body was cremated after Octavian had defeated Mark Anthony ten years later after assuming sole ruler-ship of the Roman world.

Joseph (44 BCE - 23 CE), father of Jesus, was born eldest son of Jacob-Heli.

From *Essenes Children of the Light* by Stuart Wilson and Joanna Prentis, Joseph, father of Jesus, is described:

Joseph is a great friend and a wise man, but also a man who is careful in his speech. He is quite strong physically, and there is a calmness and balance about him which impresses people. He listens to people, and has a quiet charm and a keen sense of humor, but that is deceptive. He's really quite a clever man, but he hides his gifts.

42 BCE

Whatever happened to the Jews in the contemporary world was viewed by them as being God's punitive design. This applied to the Romans just as much as it had earlier to the Egyptians, Assyrians, Babylonians, Persians, Greeks, and Syrians. As discrimination, cultural domination, and imperial oppression became more severe, the oppressed became desperate with many hoping for divine intervention that would bring heaven down to earth.

37 BCE

Before ruling Palestine, Herod the Great spent time in Rome alongside Octavian and Mark Anthony under the rule of Julius Caesar. After helping the Romans retake Jerusalem from king Antigonus II, the last of the Hasmonean Dynasty fell with Mark
Antony installing Herod vassal king of Palestine. He was gifted, extravagant, and became the stimulus for a mission to bring Jews living in exile home into a world-wide society that would have significant political power.

At the time Herod assumed the kingship, a great opportunity arose for the Jews due to his world plan which could be fulfilled by Jews who were living in exile. He believed that if he could bring them back home to enter a New Covenant, they would bring with them income for the impoverished homeland. Having an association with the Essene, Herod knew of the Jews long-standing support of the David family and their dream to restore the Jewish society of old including the high priests of the family of Zadok. Upon becoming king, Herod agreed that a David could have power in the empire but only as a subordinate to him acting on behalf of Rome. From *Antiquities of the Jews,* Josephus describes the administration of Herod the Great:

> In his administration of the state, the king, in an earnest effort to put a stop to the successive acts of injustice committed both in the city and in the country, made law for the punishment to be made severe and unlawful, as was then determined seemed the part of arrogance, and his decision to impose the penalty was not an act of a king by a tyrant and one who held the public interests of his subjects in contempt. Accordingly, this action, which was similar to the rest of his behavior, was partly responsible for the charges made against him and the dislike felt for him.

During the reign of Herod, Judah and Samaria had an unprecedented level of building activity that would change the face of Roman Palestine forever with economic as well as political considerations prompting much of this. Galilee, however, did not benefit from this modernization. Instead, Galilee was ruthlessly taxed to finance much of the building activity in the south, which explains the ill feelings that many of Jesus' contemporaries had toward tax collectors. In an effort to placate his observant Jewish subjects, Herod embarked on a project to enlarge and repair the temple in Jerusalem into one of the largest sanctuaries in the entire Roman world. Because the temple was built on a hill, Herod created a vast floating esplanade with strong supporting walls with one of these having survived to modern times and is revered today as the Western Wall, the holiest location in Judaism. Upon his death – Judah, Idumea, and Samaria would henceforth be ruled by his son Archelaus; the territory of Galilee and Peres would be ruled by son Herod Antipas , while the territory northeast of the Sea of Galilee including Gaulanitis would be given to his son Phillip. Finally, the coastal region of Azotus (today's Ashod), as well as the region around Jabneh and Phaesalis, were given to Herod's sister, Salome.

33 BCE

As civil war was ending between the forces of Octavian and Mark Anthony, Octavian's forces entered Alexandria's eastern suburb of Canopus. Due to the threat posed, Mark Anthony committed suicide at Cleopatra's palace by plunging a sword into his body while, Cleopatra committed suicide (age 36) by means of a poisonous snake at her mausoleum nearby.

In 1992, Frank Goddio, President of the European Institute of Underwater Archaeology and his team, discovered the sunken island of Antirhodos in a small harbor off the coast of Alexandria under 10 meters of murky water. While exploring the island, divers found the foundation of Cleopatra's palace, Cleopatra's shrine/ temple with a statue of her high priest guarded by two sphinxes, remains of ancient ship docks on the east side of the island, the wreck of an ancient cargo ship of more than 30 meters (98') in length containing jewelry, pottery, and glass cups, and a series of giant pillars made of red Egyptian granite.

27 BCE

Gaius Octavius (Augustus Caesar) became 1st emperor of Rome (27 BCE - 14 CE).

Mary, mother of Jesus, was born. Mary's parents were Joachim and Anna with her father being a member of the Levi tribe. Her sisters were Elizabeth, mother of John the Baptist, and Salome wife of Zebedee, are found in second century *Protoevangelium of James* and in third century *Bodmer Papyrus*. In *Gospel Birth of Mary*, we learn that Mary's father was a high priest and a member of the Levi tribe; from *Protevangelion* we learn that he "being very rich, made double offerings to the Lord" and that Mary, as a young girl, was pledged in marriage to a local artisan named Joseph at the age of fifteen. In *Did Our Lord Visit Britain as They say in Cornwall and Somerset*, we learn the historical background of Anna, mother of Mary:

> Anna was born in Cornwall, England of royal blood. Brutally treated by a jealous husband, when with child, she fled towards the sea: an angel caused her to enter a vessel, and took her to Asia and then to Jaffa, where she landed, and whence she reached Nazareth. There she gave birth to a little girl, whom she named Mary. When the child was fifteen years old, she was married to a carpenter, named Joseph, and Anna then prayed to God to take her back to Cornwall. The same angel again took her over the waves.

In *Essenes Children of the Light*, Anna is described:

> A princess from a Celtic family in Britain. She was a very wise and graceful person, but also a person of authority. We recognize her as someone of real ability, a high initiate. When she came to our land from Britain, Anna made a big effort to adopt to our customs and ways, so as to become one of us – but her blue eyes and hair that had a reddish tinge in it, she would never look entirely Jewish.

Joseph of Arimathea, younger brother Mary's father Joachim, owned a palatial home in Jerusalem, a country residence just outside the city and a spacious estate at Arimathea located 8 miles north of Jerusalem. As a legislative member of the Sanhedrin Council, he earned great respect among its members due to the tin mining operations he owned in England which were crucial to the manufacture of weapons used by the Roman Empire. As owner of one of the largest shipping fleets in the world, Joseph would regularly travel between England and the many harbors of the Roman Empire. From *Lost Ten Tribes of Israel*, by Steven M. Collins, we learn that Joseph of Arimathea acted as a father figure to Jesus between the ages of twelve and thirty with scholars agreeing that Joseph, Jesus earthly father, died in a construction accident when he was still relatively young. From the book *The Drama of the Lost Disciples* written by George F. Fowler, we learn that Joseph took Jesus on trips to Europe between I CE and 37 CE.

19 BCE

Repair and enlargement of the 2nd temple in Jerusalem began under Herod the Great.
Mary (age 15), mother of Jesus, was pledged in marriage to Joseph (age 35).

From *Urantia Revelation* we learn that eight children were born to Joseph and Mary: Jesus (5 BCE), James (3 BCE), Joseph (1 CE), Simon (2 CE), Jude (5 CE), Esther, Martha, and Salome. We also learn that Mary and Joseph were considered to be extra-ordinary – they were well educated with Joseph having a thorough knowledge of Jewish ceremonial procedures because both he and his father, Jacob-Heli, were priests themselves. Joseph was of a melancholy disposition, but thoughtful and spiritual. Mary was very cheerful. She was a devoted homemaker. Joseph and Mary married after a two-year courtship. They lived in a one-room stone house with a flat roof that Joseph had himself built at the foot of the highest hill in Nazareth at the edge of town. An adjoining building housed the animals. The house had a low stone table, earthenware pots, a lamp stand, stools, and mats for sleeping on the stone floor. In the courtyard was found an oven and mill for cooking and grinding grain.

9 BCE

According to Jerome, in *De Virus Illustribus*, Apostle Paul was born in Gischala in Galilee, a Jewish town about twenty-five miles north of Sepphoris. He was a member of the order of Benjamin, an order of Pharisees who adopted an ascetic discipline while remaining in public life. When revolts broke out following the death of Herod in 4 BCE, Paul and his parents were captured, and, as part of a large-scale exile of Galilean inhabitants from Palestine, were sent to Tarsus in Cilicia. Upon reaching manhood, Paul was instructed in Jerusalem by Gamaliel I studying theology. He was a fervent nationalist, holding the ***eastern Hebrew party*** view which was opposed to Jesus being the David due to his unusual birth date. He enjoyed Roman citizenship inherited from his father, who was a committed Pharisee. He was a tent maker by trade who spoke Aramaic with modern scholarship suggesting that Koine Greek was his first language. His letters drew heavily on his knowledge of Stoic philosophy using Stoic terms and metaphors.

6 BCE

Israel was annexed into the Roman Empire marking the beginning of oppression of the Jews.

5 BCE

John the Baptist, heir to the Zadok dynasty of priests, was born to Zechariah, a priest of the eighth of the twenty-four courses and Elizabeth, a descendent of Aaron six months prior to his cousin Jesus in the small hamlet of Ein Kerem which was nestled in the hill country just west of Jerusalem. John was an intense personality with a strong sense of impending doom. He chose political activity but only as one who worked to earn heaven's intervention at the time appointed by prophecy. He lived as a hermit, enduring self-imposed hardship as a way of gaining merit. John was called the "Teacher of Righteousness" by ascetics at Mird and Qumran. His ministry began in the desert which is viewed by scholars as being a transitional place. It is the place where prophets like Moses and Elijah went to pray and regroup. A place where Satan tests the stoutest of hearts as he tempted Jesus in the desert. For modern scholars, the inner turmoil facing Jesus centered on the decision he was being forced to make – should he be a spiritual leader of the people or take up the role of military leader of an army that could easily be assembled.

In 1973, archaeologists discovered the cave in which John the Baptist lived located eight miles west of Jerusalem in an isolated desert area.

Jesus was born March 2 in a small village called Bethlehem in Galilee. Within a year of his birth, his family moved to Nazareth with a population thought to be as small as 200 people. Four miles away, stood the large Greek city of Sepphoris, with a population of 40,000 in which Herod Antipas lived. Because Jesus birth fell at an incorrect time of the year, it meant that the strict Nazorean rules of dynastic wedlock found in Dead Sea Scrolls were infringed as the future David must be born in the atoning month of

December. For the conservative Jews of the **eastern Hebrew party**, Jesus questionable birth meant that James, his brother, should be the rightful heir to the throne of David and not Jesus. For the more liberal Jew of the **western Hellenist party,** who had been exposed to the Greek gods, being oldest son of Joseph easily qualified Jesus to be the heir to the throne of David.

The term Nazarene, which is often used in reference to Jesus, is a title which, if used properly, describes a person consecrated by God either from birth or by taking special vows of dedication – it does not refer to the hometown where a person lives. In the book *Jesus the Man*, scholar Barbara Thiering gives meaning to the "virgin birth" story based upon her study of the Dead Sea Scrolls:

> Once it is known that Jesus was connected with the Essenes, an explanation of the virgin birth comes to light. For the Essenes, celibacy was the highest way of life. Marriage and sex were considered to be unholy, and the aim of the higher members was to be perfectly holy in order to be pleasing to God. But some recognized that if they did not marry and have children, their race would not continue. They were members of the great dynasties, the Zadoks and the Davids, who had been the high priests and kings of Israel before the fall of Israel before the fall of the temple in the sixth century. The men of these families, potential priests and kings, wanted to live a perfectly holy life, and believing that sex was defiling, they practiced it only for the sake of having children, putting the most severe restrictions on themselves and their wives. For the most part they lived apart from their wives, like Monks in a monastery. But when the rules required that they continue the family line, they left the monastery and prepared for marriage.

In 1885, the childhood home of Jesus was discovered under the Sisters of Nazareth convent in central Nazareth but it wasn't until 2006 that archaeologists Ken Dark, a professor at the University of Reading in the United Kingdom, confirmed it as being the place where Jesus lived as a child. Said Dark, "Whoever built the house had a very good understanding of stone-working which would be consistent with the sort of knowledge we would expect of someone who might be called a tekton," the ancient Greek work for craftsman that was used when referring to Joseph.

4 BCE

When Herod the Great passed away, Caesar Augustus split his kingdom among his three sons which proved to be a disaster for Rome because of the resentment that had been building during Herod's oppressive reign that his sons could hardly contain. It was around this same time that a fearsome group of patriots arose in Galilee, led by an inspired revolutionary known as Judas the Galilean. He was the son of Hezekiah, a failed 'messiah' whom Herod had captured and beheaded thirty years earlier as part of his campaign to clear the countryside of the bandit menace. The Zealot movement began within the Essene community in Qumran with zealots being political activists who sought the over-through Roman occupation by the use of military force. They viewed themselves as being a holy army of God with the forces of good taking on the forces of evil. They were looking for a secular leader like King David who would rise-up and lead them in battle; they were looking for a messiah figure.

In 1953, archaeologists discovered an elaborate monastery with a series of aqueducts lined with a ceramic coating to prevent leakage, supplying the Essene at Qumran abundant water from springs in the surrounding hills. The water not only provided necessities of life, but was essential for the religious practices of the monastery. Large rectangular depressions were found, which were used for communal baths for ritual cleansing. The main feature of the site was a three-story tower that overlooked a central courtyard, surrounded on all sides by buildings of considerable size used for community gatherings, meals, and a scriptorium where the Dead Sea Scrolls were written. The people of Qumran were called the "people of the Light" and were a select group who lived their lives in continual preparation for the messiah's arrival with Judas Iscariot being leader of the sect at the time of Jesus. From *Antiquities of the Jews*, Josephus describes the final days of Herod the Great:

> But the disease of Herod became daily more virulent, God inflicting punishment for his crimes. For it was a slow fire, not only exhibiting to those who touched him a heat in proportion to the internal wasting of his body, but there was also an excessive desire and craving after food, while no one dared to refuse. This was attended

with swellings of the intestines, and especially excessive pains of the colon. A moist and

transparent humor also covered his feet. Similar also was the disease about the ventricle, so that the corruption causing worms in the lower part of the abdomen, there was an increased violence of breathing, which, of itself very offensive; both on account of the disagreeable effluvia, and the rapidity of the respiration. He was also so convulsed in every part of his body, that it added an almost insuperable strength. It was said, therefore, by those who are conversant with divine things, and to whose wisdom it appertained to declare such things, that God inflicted this punishment upon the king an account of his great impiety.

In 2008, archaeologists discovered the tomb of Herod the Great at Herodium, where his hilltop fortress once stood, seven miles outside of Jerusalem.

The Hellenistic world in which Jesus and John the Baptist were raised, was a Greek speaking world that was created after the conquest of the near east by Alexander the Great at the end of the fourth century BCE. Philo of Alexandria (30 BCE - 50 CE), the leading Jewish philosopher and scriptural interpreter at the time of Jesus is an example of the intense Hellenization of the Jewish belief system as he tried to establish a relationship between Hebrew scripture with the philosophy of Plato. For instance, in saying that the 'word of God' is divine reason he interpreted the word *logos* as meaning the 'mind of God.' As this thinking was developing, the rationality of the world was being taken over by the Stoic idea that reason constitutes the inner working of the world with both of these strands of Hellenistic tradition having a significant impact on Christian theology of a later generation as it tried to make sense of Jesus *being* and his teaching within the broader framework of Greek and Roman polytheistic culture where there was a growing appreciation for the unity of the divine and notion that there was a single divine principle underlying all things.

3 BCE

James, brother of Jesus was born to Joseph and Mary.

2 BCE

Miriam, sister of Jesus, was born to Joseph and Mary.

1 CE

Joseph, brother of Jesus, was born to Joseph and Mary.

Mother Mary, along with her children Jesus, James, Miriam, and Joseph plus Joseph of Arimathea, travelled to the British Isles. *(Protoevangelium of James; Bodmer Papyrus).*

Jesus and John the Baptist attended school together at Mt Carmel.

2 CE

Simeon, brother of Jesus, was born to Joseph and Mary.

3 CE

Martha, sister of Jesus, was born to Joseph and Mary.

4 CE

In the book *Jesus and the Essenes,* Dolores Cannon gives Essene Suddi Benzahmare's impression of Jesus as a young adult:

> He was born wise, but he was not born with all of the knowledge that he amassed in his lifetime. He was taught in many schools. Among them, those known as the community of the Essenes. There were many lands and many teachers that he sat at their knees and listened and learned. He was shown many different ways and paths. And in turn he showed other the right ways upon their paths. Benjoseph (Jesus) never had to argue. He just looked at you. If he felt that you weren't understanding, perhaps, his point of view on a certain thing, and he had gone over it several times, he would just look at you with those soulful eyes. And it was just like he was saying that, "Even though I know you do not understand, I forgive you anyway."

John, the evangelist, was born to Salome and Zebedee a wealthy fisherman who had business partners Simon Peter and Andrew. Salome, who was mother of John and James, was sister of Elizabeth, mother of John the Baptist and Anna, grand-mother of Jesus on his mother's side. James of Zebedee, who had been a follower of John the Baptist, joined Jesus mission preaching in Judah and later traveling to India and Spain while his brother John, fulfilled his mission in Asia Minor preaching to the Parthians who lived on the borders of what is now Russia and Iran near the eastern region of Turkey.

5 CE

Jude, brother of Jesus, was born to Joseph and Mary.

6 CE

When Judah officially became a Roman province, Quirinius called for a census to register and properly tax the people in the newly acquired region with Zealots seizing the opportunity to make a final appeal to the Jews to stand with them against Rome. Zealots argued that by paying taxes to Rome, Jews were admitting that the land did not belong to God and that they were not the chosen people.

Annas ben Seth was appointed high-priest in Jerusalem by the Roman legate Quirinius. He officially served as high priest for ten years (6 -16 CE), when at the age of 36 he was deposed by procurator Valerius Gratus for treating the Jews poorly. Even though he had been removed from office, Annas remained one of the nation's most influential individuals aided by his five sons and son-in-law Caiphas who also acted as high priest in Jerusalem. Annas' family members who served as high priest in Jerusalem:

-   Eleazar ben Annas (16 -17 CE).

-   Caiaphas (18 – 36 CE).

-   Jonathan ben Annas (36 - 37; 44 CE)

-   Theophilus ben Annas (37 – 41 CE).

- Mattias ben Annas 4(2 – 43 CE).

7 CE

Amos, brother of Jesus, was born to Joseph and Mary.

8 CE

Luke, the evangelist, was born in Antioch, Syria. He is thought to have been a physician, disciple of Apostle Paul and a Hellenistic Jew.

Mary Magdalene was born in Heliopolis which is located in the northeastern part of modern-day Cairo. Her father, Syro the Jairos, was a member of the royal house of Cyrus the Great. In government he was responsible for the movement of commerce throughout the Persian Empire and the administration of northern Galilee. He was high-priest at the temple of Onias which worshipped the pagan goddess Isis. At a young age, Mary and her family migrated from Egypt to Phoenicia which was located on the Mediterranean in what is today called Lebanon. After a short time the family moved to Magdala by the Sea of Galilee. There, at the age of 18 years, Mary took up her priestly calling. Her family belonged to the priestly Hasmonaean house of the Maccabees which reigned in Israel between 167 - 63 BCE. Her family belonged to the order of Dan were young women were referred to as being 'virgin' until such time as they married. Mary was sister of Martha, Lazarus, and Nathan. For scholars, Mary "being raised from eternal darkness" symbolically refers to her elevation in status within the Nazarite order to senior bishop which allowed her to wear the black robe of the Egyptian goddess Isis. Mary exhibited exceptionably high qualities of spiritual development: faith, knowledge, self-restraint, simplicity, innocence, reverence, and love. She was a forceful personality with strong opinions and a commanding presence. She was seen by her followers as being the incarnation of the goddess Artemis. She was a woman of stature and wealth, heiress to the land bordering Jerusalem, born of the lineage of King David, a woman at the foot of the cross, the woman who arrived first at the tomb on resurrection morning, and the woman thought to be consort of Jesus by her peers and leader of his apostolic network where she was referred to as being the women who knew "All." She was the apostle endowed with knowledge, vision, and insight far exceeding all others. Because of her closeness to Jesus and association with the goddess Isis, she was constantly at odds with Peter and Andrew. Her brother Lazarus was tribal leader of the Magians of West Manasseh, a priestly caste of 52,000 Samarian philosophers who supported the legitimacy of Jesus as the Messiah. He was a man of extraordinary personal gifts who could attract followers to his vision of the doctrine, an amalgam of liberalized Judaism and Greek philosophy. He was a Jew who married a Gentile thus becoming referred to as a Samarian.

Samaria is the name given to a mountainous region of the Eastern Mediterranean. To the north, Samaria is bounded by the Jezreel Valley; to the east, by the Jordan Rift Valley; to the west, by the Carmel Ridge and the Sharon plain; to the south, by the Jerusalem Mountains. Since 1967, the name Samaria has been used by Jewish officials to refer to the West Bank region with the ancient capital city called Samaria being located 30 miles north of Jerusalem. From *Essenes Children of the Light,* Essene David Benezra describes Mary Magdalene:

> Mary was a high being, an advanced being, but she was much misunderstood. Her difficulty was that she had gained much experience and training in Egypt. She had been a priestess of Isis, and that was a problem for some of the narrow-minded ones who gathered themselves around Jesus. Indeed that would have damned her in the eyes of most conventional Jews. For the Essene it was not an issue as we had great respect for the Isis tradition in Egypt and for most of the disciples it was not a problem, although one or two had reservations about her, and it caused ripples in the larger group around Jesus.
>
> Jesus and Mary would have many deep and profound conversations, and this made some of the disciples feel uncomfortable, especially those who could not keep up with what was being said. Some of the disciples were quite traditional in their ways, and were not eager to see women have this kind of power. Mary understood the kingdom of God better than any of the disciples – far better in fact, for the only one who remotely approached her in understanding was John. He knew how advanced Mary Magdalene was,

and was glad to have her counsel. Mary was in truth the supreme disciple, who became the teacher of the teachers, for she understood the path to the Light so well. She came into her own after the crucifixion.

Before the *Nag Hammadi Codex* discovery in the mid-1940s, several other first- and second-century texts had been discovered in the eighteenth, nineteenth, and early twentieth centuries that mention Mary Magdalene: *Pistis Sophia, Dialog of the Savior, Sophia of Jesus Christ, Gospel of Thomas, Gospel of Peter, Gospel of Mary Magdalene, Gospel of Philip, Psalms of Heracleides, Epistula Apostolorum, Apostle Church Order, Acts of Philip,* with all being used by scholars to add to their knowledge. In the book *The Resurrection of Mary Magdalene,* Jane Schaberg points out that all gospel stories written about Mary Magdalene have the following points in common:

- She was prominent among the followers of Jesus.

- She was a teacher and evangelist in her own right.

- She spoke boldly.

- She played a leadership role vis-à-vis the male disciples.

- She was a visionary.

- She was praised by Jesus for her superior understanding.

- She was identified as the companion of Jesus.

- She was in open conflict with Peter and Andrew who were jealous of her position, understanding and rank.

- She was defended by Jesus when attacked by Peter.

- She was the disciple Jesus loved most.

In *Mary Magdalene the First Apostle,* scholar Ann Graham Brock points out that when scholars study the comparative ranking of the followers of Jesus for their importance in terms of being an authority figure, Christian texts are examined and compared. Scholars look to which disciple's name appears most often; they look to see who the primary witness is to the resurrection; they look to see who is commissioned by Jesus to deliver the Good News; they look to see who is given the most speaking parts in the storyline, and they look to see who appears to be closer to Jesus in some capacity with all of the criteria noted, suggesting that ancient authors of scripture would feel most inclined to focus on the individual who is of most importance in the Christian movement next to Jesus himself. In sampling of scripture, Mary Magdalene is by far the most dominant individual mentioned with Peter finishing in a distant second place.

9 CE

Jesus visited the British Isles with Joseph of Arimathea to study with the Druids. They stayed at Isle of Avalon, modern day Glastonbury, England *(Protoevangelium of James, Bodmer Papyrus).*

Ruth, sister of Jesus, was born to Joseph and Mary.

10 CE

Life of Saint Issa: Best of the Sons of Men, was written between 31-54 CE tracing the travels of Jesus between his temple appearance with the scribes through the time he was baptized by John the Baptist - a period referred to by scholars as being the "lost years of Jesus". Leaving his family at age fourteen, he explored the world around him. He first traveled to Turkey and studied with Persian and Arab scholars at Byzantium (modern-day city of Istanbul, Turkey). From there he went on to Mesopotamia (land that lies between the Tigris and Euphrates Rivers in Iraq) to the city of Babylon and then on to Persia (modern-day countries of Pakistan, Afghanistan, Iran, and Iraq) finally arriving in India. He spent several years in Kashmir and Tibet, studying the Hindu religion of wisdom and the teaching of peace. This memoir concerning Jesus was housed in Lhasa in the capital city of Tibet located high in the Himalayan Mountains. The memoir was written by Brahmin historians and Buddhist monks with the story being recorded in the Pali tongue, which is a form of Arabic with the name *Issa* being equivalent to the name Jesus. The story was recorded by merchants who traveled between India and Egypt, going through Jerusalem. The story begins by announcing that, in the very year of the crucifixion of Jesus, a few merchants had just returned from Judah to Asia and had brought back information that Jesus, after being acquitted twice for sedition was then put to death at the instigation of Roman governor Pontius Pilate, who feared that Jesus would take advantage of his popularity and re-establish the kingdom of Israel and expel the Romans from his land. The following information is learned from the Buddhist monks:

- Pharaoh had two sons, the youngest was named Moses (2.7).

- Pharaoh ordered Moses to lead the Jews out of the capital city and to establish a new Jewish city nearby (2.15).

- Eternal Spirit detached itself from God and entered Jesus (4.2) to demonstrate by example how man may attain moral purity implying that God and Jesus are two distinct beings (4.3).

- Parents of Jesus were of a priestly class and wealth (4.6).

- Israelites believed the Eternal Spirit dwelt in Jesus (4.9).

- Jesus started his worldly travels in 10 CE (4.10)

- Mary and Joseph's house was a meeting place for those who wished for their daughters to have Jesus' hand in marriage (4.11).

- Jesus declared that only the commandments of God are sacred (5.12).

- Salvation lies in helping the poor and assisting the weak (5.27).

- God has shared the world with no one nor has he confided his intentions with anyone (6.10).

- Jesus declared himself to be a prophet (8.8).

- Jesus returned to Israel in 26 CE (9.1).

- The temple of God is the human heart illuminated with good thoughts, patience, and unflinching faith placed in the Father (9.11).

- Jesus endeavored to establish Jewish law in the hearts of men (10.21).

- After God, best thoughts should belong to wives (11.18).

- Jesus is the best of mortal man (12.4)

- The 'soul' of Jesus left his body and was absorbed in divinity (14.3).

- Pilate gave the body of Jesus to a family member who buried him (14.5).

- Three days after the crucifixion, Pilate sent soldiers to the tomb so that the body of Jesus could be taken and buried elsewhere (14.6).

Discovered documents that refer to Jesus's extended education and traveling included letters written by Joseph Caiaphas, Herod Antipas plus accounts recorded in: *Humane Gospel of Christ, Gospel of the Holy Twelve, Aquarian Gospel of Jesus Christ* and *Nine Faces of Christ.*

11 CE

Joseph of Arimathea, accompanied by Jesus, travelled to the British Isles *(Protoevangelium of James; Bodmer Papyrus).*

12 CE

Amos, brother of Jesus, passed due to illness.

John Mark was born in Cyrene, in the Pentapolis of North Africa. He departed for Alexandria in the third year of emperor Claudius. In 49 CE, he founded the Church of Alexandria and became its first bishop. He recorded the sermons of Peter and is founder of the Christian religion in Africa.

14 CE

Tiberius, son of Tiberius Claudius Nero and Livia, distinguished himself in military campaigns while proving himself an able administrator. Upon the death of his father, his accession was welcomed by Herod Antipas whose relationship with Claudius was strained. Suetonius describes Tiberius, 2nd emperor of Rome (14-37 CE), in his book titled *Tiberius*:

> He possessed a most peculiar nature. He never let what he desired appear in his conversation, and what he wanted he usually did not desire at all. On the contrary, his words indicated the exact opposite of his real purpose; he denied all interest in what he longed for and urged the claims of what he hated. He would exhibit anger over matters that were very far from arousing his wrath and make a show of affability where he was most vexed. He would pretend to pity those whom he severely punished and would retain a grudge against those whom he pardoned.

17 CE

Jacob-Heli, grandfather of Jesus, passes in old age with his son Joseph, inheriting the title 'David.'

18 CE

Joseph Caiaphas was appointed high priest in Jerusalem (18 – 36 CE) following in the foot-steps of his father-in-law, Annas ben Seth. A rabbinic text found in *Babylonian Talmud Pesahim: Tosephta Menabot* laments the abuses of this priestly family saying:

> Woe to me because of the house of Hanin [Anannus ben Seth]; Woe to unto me for their calumnies; Woe to me because of the House of

Kathros [Joseph Caiaphas]; Woe is me because of their pens for they are the High Priests, and their sons are treasurers, and their sons-in-law are trustees, and their servants beat the people with staves.

20 CE

Apostle Paul began his study of the Torah in Jerusalem under Gamaliel I who was the son of Simeon ben Hillel and grandson of Hillel the Elder. In the *Talmud*, Gamaliel I is described as being the president of the Sanhedrin and holds the reputation in the *Mishnah* for being one of the greatest teachers of all times in the annals of Judaism. In *Archko Volume*, Rabbi Gamaliel I gives his impression of Jesus:

> While he is nothing but a man, there is something about him that distinguishes him from every other man. He is the picture of his mother, only he has not her smooth, round face. His hair is a little more golden than hers, though it is much more sunburn as anything else. He is tall, and his shoulders are a little dropped; his visage is thin and of swathe complexion, though this is from exposure. His eyes are large and of soft blue, and rather dull and heavy. The lashes are long, and his eyebrows very large. His nose is that of a Jew. In fact, he reminds me of an old-fashioned Jew in every sense of the word. He is not a great talker, unless there is something brought up about heaven and divine things, when his tongue moves glibly and his eyes light up with a peculiar brilliancy; though there is this peculiarity about Jesus, he never argues a question; he never disputes. He will commence and state the facts and they are on such solid basis that nobody will have the boldness to dispute them. He has no pride in confuting his opponents, but always to be seems sorry for them. His strongest points are in the spiritual power of the law and the intentions of the prophets.

Greek speaking Jews were very comfortable in the Greek world of thought. Their leaders came to believe that the Torah was a book of Jewish philosophy. They interpreted the Torah allegorically finding in it lessons learned from Plato and Aristotle long before. The outstanding intellectual of the Hellenistic Jewish world was Philo Judaeus (20 BCE - 50 CE) of Alexandria, Egypt, a contemporary of Jesus. Philo identified the biblical God with the "Form of Good" as the ultimate source of all being and knowledge. He distinguished between the literal and allegorical meaning of biblical texts and in many cases ignored the literal meaning altogether. Philo believed that man cannot attain virtue alone but only through contemplation of God. He described God as an exalted being known only to himself. Philo saw God as the architect of the world, molding matter into our universe. Because matter was essentially imperfect and evil, God's interaction with the world is an indirect affair where he creates our world according to an ideal pattern using *logos* as an intermediary.

21 CE

Joseph's family moved from Nazareth to Tiberius traveling north along the Sea of Galilee through the towns of Magdala, Bethsaida and Capernaum. While in Bethsaida, Jesus met-up with his uncle Zebedee who hired him to build boats for his fishing fleet. Salome, who was Zebedee's wife, sister of Anna, and cousin of Annas ben Seth, had seven children including evangelists John and James with brother David's messenger corps helping to make Jesus' ministry possible.

In 1838, archaeologists discovered a complex know as Tell Hum, the city of Capernaum where Peter, Andrew, and Matthew lived and Jesus centered his ministry. Unearthed also was a magnificent limestone synagogue which is thought to be the place where Jesus taught and performed at least one miracle.

22 CE

Jesus and brother James travelled to Egypt to study the Egyptian and Persian mystery religions *(Protoevangelium of James, Bodmer Papyrus).*

23 CE

Joseph, father of Jesus, died due to a fall from a construction crane in Sepphoris with Jesus, inheriting the title 'David.'

24 CE

John the Baptist, heir to the Zadokite dynasty of priests, began his ministry in the hills of Judah. He warned that the nation's neglect of the Jewish law would invite the wrath of the Lord who would send a fearsome, divinely appointed messiah to eject foreign occupiers and install a true reign of God. John coming to the Jordan was to preach to the people of Israel to repent of their sinful ways and to prepare for the return of the prophet Elijah. John's mission was to baptize people who were self-confessed sinners, who had seen the error of their ways and were prepared to change their lives with his practice of immersion being an act of forgiveness whereby past deeds were washed away in exchange for the sinner's determination to repent.

Under the Baptist, two political parties were formed. The conservative **eastern Hebrew party** that used the Hebrew language in worship and followed Jewish social customs. They belonged to the Palestinian Essenes who were an ascetic coalition made up of John the Baptist himself, Agrippa I, James, brother of Jesus, Thomas Didymus, and temple high priest Joseph Caiaphas with their moral view denying the legitimacy of Jesus as being the David due to his untimely birth date.

The liberal **western Hellenist Jews** living in Diaspora used the Greek language in worship, the Old Testament written in Greek, and followed Hellenized ways. As a Hellenist, Joseph chose to continue with his marriage to Mary knowing the problem her untimely pregnancy would cause under a temple high priest practicing the doctrine of the eastern Hebrews. He also knew that under a temple high priest holding the liberal view of the Hellenists, Jesus could act as the David.

25 CE

Peter married Priscilla, daughter of Aristobulus IV with Aristobulus being grandson of Herod the Great. Priscilla gave birth to a daughter named Petronilla and a son who died at a young age.

Biblical Archaeological Review (BAS) announced in 1966 that archaeologists excavating an unusual octagonal church in Capernaum found the ruins of a much older building underneath. The house was simple with coarse walls and a roof made of earth and straw. It consisted of a few small rooms clustered around two open courtyards. Based on inscriptions found on the walls, the function of the house changed dramatically, it no longer functioned as a private dwelling but as a place for communal gatherings with Greek, Syriac and Hebrew writing on the walls saying "Lord Jesus Christ help thy

Servant" with Peter's name mentioned many times leading archaeologist to believe this was the original house in which Peter lived at the time of Jesus.

Scholars believe that Jesus met Mary Magdalene at the well with Mary being a Samaritan priestess of Isis and Hellenized Jew. As a Samarian, she was not bound by the Jerusalem temple meaning she did not worship the god Yahweh with Deuteronomists saying God's chosen people in the northern kingdom had gone astray by worshipping pagan deities. In John 4:17-18, Jesus engages in a most unusual conversation with the woman at the well.

> "Jesus said to her, 'You are right when you say you have no husband (Yahweh). The fact is, you have five husbands (Samaritan beliefs), and the man you now have (Canaanite high-god Elyon) is not your husband (true belief). What you have just said is quite true.'"

Five husbands were Samarian beliefs that were uncommon to Galileans of the southern kingdom:

-   They only accepted the Pentateuch as Holy Scripture rejecting other prophets sent by God as well as rejecting the Talmud.

-   They made their sacrifices and celebrated their high holy days on Mt. Gerizim rather than in the temple in Jerusalem.

-   They considered Levite priests to be the highest religious authority in the land rather than temple priests being their interpreters of the law.

-   They rejected the idea of resurrection after death because it was not written in the Pentateuch.

-   They awaited a prophet who would establish a period of peace and justice on earth whereas the Judeans of the southern kingdom awaiting a messiah that would militarily overthrow the Romans.

For scholars, Jesus' conversation at the well bears all the marks of deep theological engagement on both sides. The woman knows that according to tradition, Jesus, as priest, would be ritually contaminated if he were to associate with a Samaritan. However, he gladly stayed with her to discuss the nature of worship, salvation, and concept of messiah with the initial tension soon being broken resulting in Mary Magdalene, as a high priestess of Isis, testifying to her village about Jesus..

26 CE

For scholars, Jesus' life began not with his miraculous birth but at the moment he met John the Baptist at the Jordan River. If John's ceremony was an initiation rite into his movement, Jesus was being admitted as a disciple. Josephus wrote in *Antiquities of the Jews* that John's baptism was "not for the remission of sins, but for the purification of the body" meaning John was establishing a New Israel based upon the commandments of the Lord. Jesus' mission would not mimic John's as his message was far more revolutionary as his concept of "Kingdom of God" was more dangerous than anything John could have conceived as the forerunner. Jesus's kingdom was in the 'here and now' not in some future place as was John's. Jesus would baptize with the Holy Spirit as his message was designed to be a direct challenge to the wealthy and powerful. His message was simple – God had seen the suffering of the poor; he has heard their cries of anguish – It is time for change!

Parables of Jesus are located in the gospels of Mark, Matthew and Luke. They represent a key part of the teachings of Jesus, forming approximately one third of his recorded teaching. Jesus' parables, while they seem like simple stories convey deep messages that are central to his teaching. Many of Jesus' parables refer to simple everyday things, such as a woman baking bread, a man knocking on his neighbor's door at night, or the aftermath of a roadside mugging; yet they all deal with major religious themes, such as the growth of the "Kingdom of God" within oneself, the importance of prayer, and meaning of love. Gospel of Luke contains 24 parables; Matthew contains 23; and Mark contains 8 while Gospel of John is thought to contain none. In total there are 55 parable stories attributed to Jesus. Parables noted below are examples of the deep meaning being conveyed by Jesus through a simple story:

Parable of the Workers in the Vineyard

The object of this parable is to show that even though the Jews where first called to the vineyard *(Jerusalem-church)*, the gospel should also be preached to the Gentiles and that they in turn, should receive equal privileges and advantages as the Jews as there is no different between mankind before the eyes of God. The parable also shows that: many who begin last, and promised little sometimes, by the blessing of God, achieve knowledge, grace and usefulness; that the recompense of reward will be given to the redeemed, but not according to the time of their conversions as all are deemed equal.

The parable describes the state of the visible church, and explains that the last redeemed shall be as cherished as the first redeemed. Until we are hired *(transformed)* into the service of God, we are standing all day in a sinful state. Gentiles came into the church at the eleventh hour because the gospel message had not yet reached them because God's word first came from the Jerusalem-church of James, Peter, and John and then moved on to the followers of Apostle Paul at a later date.

Mathew 20:1-16 (NIV)

"For the kingdom of heaven *(Truth, mercy, and justice for all)* is like a landowner *(God)* who went out early in the morning to hire *(spiritually transform)* workers *(those the Spirit called to do God's work)* for his vineyard *(the visible church)*. He agreed to pay them a denarius *(price for redemption in the kingdom of Heaven)* for the day and sent them into his vineyard. "About nine in the morning he went out and saw others *(those living in a sinful state)* standing in the marketplace *(the world)* doing nothing. He told them, 'You also go and work in my vineyard, and I will pay you whatever is right.' So they went. "He went out again about noon and about three in the afternoon and did the same thing. About five in the afternoon he went out and found s till others standing around *(not doing the Lord's work)*. He asked them, 'Why have you been standing here all day long doing nothing?' "'Because no one has hired us,' *(the Gentiles had not yet received the word of God through Jesus)* they answered. "He said to them, 'You also go and work in my vineyard *(all are welcome).*' "When evening came, the owner of the vineyard *(God)* said to his foreman *(Jesus)*, 'Call the workers and pay them their wages *(price for redemption)*, beginning with the last ones hired *(those who received the Word later in life)* and going on to the first *(those who received the word in their youth).*' "The workers who were hired about five in the afternoon *(later in life)* came and each received a denarius *(price for redemption)*. So when those came who were hired first, they expected to receive more. But each one of them also received a denarius *(price for redemption)*. When they received it, they began to grumble against the landowner *(God)*. 'These who were hired last worked only one hour,' they said, 'and you have made them equal to us who have born the burden of work *(spreading the Gospel message)* and heat of the day *(receiving persecution)*.' "But he *(God)* answered one of them, 'I am not being unfair to you, friend. Didn't you agree to work for a denarius *(price of redemption in the kingdom of Heaven)?* Take your pay and go. I want to give the one who were hired last the same as I gave you *(all men are equal regardless of when they received the Word)*. Don't I have the right to do what I want with my own money *(eternal life)*? Or are you envious because I am generous *(receiving all without precondition)*?' "So the last will be paid first, and the first will be last."

Parable of the Good Samaritan

Origen (185 CE - 254), the great Christian theologian of the third century, describes this parable as an allegorical reading that was taught universally throughout early Christianity.

Samaritans were/are Jews who live in the West Bank area near Jerusalem. They did not worship in the Jerusalem temple nor fall under the jurisdiction of the temple priests. They were worldly Greek speaking Jews who had ancestors dating back to King Nebuchadnezzar of Babylon. For the most part, they worshipped Elyon and his consort Asherah and were despised by the conservative 'home-grown' Hebrew speaking Jews who worshipped Yahweh. Samaritans because of their more worldly background, looked down on the home grown Jews as being nothing more than a bunch of uneducated peasants. Mary Magdalene, companion of Jesus, was not only a Samaritan, she was a high-priestess of Asherah which caused a certain amount of conflict with Peter and several other conservative disciples.

Luke 10:25-37:

And behold, a certain lawyer stood up and tested Him, saying, "Teacher, what shall I do to inherit eternal life?" He said to him, "What is written in the Law? What is your reading of it?" So he answered and said, "You shall love the Lord your God with all your heart, with all your soul, with all your strength, and with all your mind,' and your neighbor as yourself.'" And He said to him, "You have answered rightly; do this and you will live," But the lawyer, wanting to justify himself, said to Jesus, "And who is my neighbor?" Then Jesus answered and said: "A certain man *(Adam)* went down from Jerusalem *(paradise)* to Jericho *(the world)*, and fell among thieves *(hostile powers)*, who stripped him of his clothing *(humanity)*, wounded him, and departed, leaving him half dead *(in a sinful state)*. Now by chance a certain priest *(Jewish Law)* came down that road. And when he saw him *(a Gentile)*, he passed by on the other side. "Likewise, a Levite *(Pharisee priest)*, when he arrived at the place, came and looked, and passed by on the other side. "But a certain Samaritan *(Jesus who believed in a liberalized interpretation of the Law)*, as he journeyed, came where he *(Gentile)* was. And when he saw him, he had compassion. "So he went to him and bandaged his wounds *(shared the Word of God)*, pouring on oil and wine *(love and compassion)*; and he set him on his own animal *(the sacrificed body of Christ)*, brought him to an inn *(the church)*, and took care of him. "On the next day, when he departed, he took out two denarii *(a double dose of redemption)*, gave them to the innkeeper *(leader of the Church)*, and said to him, 'Take care of him; and whatever more you spend, when I come again *(the Samaritan promised the second coming of the Savior)*, I will repay you.' "So which of these three do you think was neighbor to him who fell among thieves?" And he said, "He who showed mercy on him." Then Jesus said to him, "Go and do likewise."

The Parable of the Prodigal Son

This is Jesus' response to the Pharisees' complaint about him when they said: "This man welcomes sinners and eats with them." Luke 15:11-32

Jesus tells the story of a man who has two sons. The younger son *(selfish, immature, and rebellious)* asks his father *(God)* to give him his portion of the family estate *(salvation)* as an early inheritance. Once received, the son promptly deserts the family *(lives in a sinful state)* and sets off on a long journey to a distant land *(Hades)* and begins to waste his fortune *(salvation)* on wild living. When the money runs out, a severe famine hits the country and the son finds himself in dire circumstances. He takes a job feeding pigs *(an unclean animal no devote Jew would get near)*. He is so destitute that he even longs to eat the food assigned to them.

The young man finally comes to his senses *(is touched by the Spirit)*, remembeing his father *(God)*. In humility, he recognizes his foolishness

(transformation), decides to return to his father and asks for forgiveness and mercy *(repentance)*. The father *(God)*
who had been watching and waiting receives his son back with open arms and compassion.

Meanwhile, the older son *(a Pharisee who is self-righteous, and hypocritical who forgets to rejoice when a sinner returns to God)* is not one bit happy when he comes in from working the fields *(resentment keeps the Pharisee from forgiving)* and discovers a party *(treasure the family enjoys through a constant relationship with the father)* going on to celebrate his younger brother's return. The father tries to dissuade the older brother *(a Pharisee)* from his jealous rage explaining, "You are always with me *(be not judgmental)*, and everything I have is yours."

As governor (26 – 36 CE), Pilate's most important task to manage the civil and economic affairs of Judah while ensuring the uninterrupted flow of tax revenues back to Rome. To do so, he had to maintain a functional relationship with the temple high priest who maintained the Jewish cult. From *Ecclesiastical History of the Church,* Eusebius describes Pilate:

> Pilate himself, the governor in our Savior's day, was involved in such calamities that he was forced to become his own executioner and to punish himself with his own hand: divine justice, it seems, was not slow to overtake him. The facts are recorded by those Greeks who have chronicled the Olympiads together with the events occurring in each.

Caiaphas was appointed to the office of high Priest not because of his own merit but through the influence of his father-in-law Annas ben Seth, a larger-than-life character who managed to pass the position of high priest on to five of his sons while remaining a significant force throughout their tenure. Part of the reason Caiaphas was able to hold his position as high priest for an unprecedented eighteen years was due to the close relationship he forged with Pontius Pilate. The two men worked together well with their combined rule, between 18 – 36 CE, being the most stable period of Judah in the entire first century. Together they managed to keep a lid on the revolutionary impulse of the Jews by dealing ruthlessly with any hint of political disturbance no matter how small.

After several months serving in John's ministry, Jesus departed to begin his own ministry. That calling is confirmed in a scene in which Jesus prepares to launch his ministry in the synagogue of Capernaum. Choosing a verse from the Book of Isaiah, he read:

"The Spirit of the Lord is upon me, because he has anointed me to bring good news to the poor. He has sent me to proclaim release to the captives and recovery of sight to the blind, to let the oppressed go free, to proclaim the year of the Lord's favor" (Isaiah 61:1).

In *What Did Christ Really Look Like,* Jack Anderson features a letter discovered in the Vatican Archives written by Roman Senator Publius Cornelius Lentulus (15 BCE – 52 CE) which describes Jesus:

> This is a man of noble and well-proportioned stature, with a face full of kindness and firmness, so that the beholders both love him and fear him. His hair is the color of wine and golden at the root – straight and without luster – but from the level of the ears curling and glossy, and divided down the center after the fashion of the Nazarenes. His forehead is even and smooth. His face without blemish and enhanced by a tempered bloom; his countenance ingenuous and kind; his beard full, of the same color as his hair, and forked in form; his eyes blue and extremely brilliant. In reproof and rebuke he is formidable; in exhortation and teaching, gentle and amiable of tongue. None have seen him to laugh, but many, of the contrary, to weep. His person is tall; his hands beautiful and straight. In speaking he is deliberate and grave and little given to loquacity; in beauty surpassing most men.

In *Antiquities of the Jews,* Josephus gives his interpretation of the central theme of Jesus' "Kingdom of God" movement:

> God reigns in heaven and that the Kingdom exists there; that God has allowed human history to run its course with little interference but at a future time God will bring normal history to an end, and God will come down and govern

the earth perfectly; that those who heard God's word and accepted his teaching would strive to be upright people in preparing for the Kingdom and that upright people who cared about their fellow man would influence society in a positive way for those who have the upright status due to the Word, the Kingdom is in heaven and on earth now and forever.

Marcus Borg, in his book titled *Jesus,* states that "on historical grounds, it is virtually indisputable that Jesus was a healer and exorcist." Scholar John Dominic Crossan comments saying: "Throughout his life, Jesus performed healings and exorcisms for ordinary people" with Josephus saying that Jesus was widely known as being "a doer of amazing deeds – a teacher who won over many Jews and many Greeks." As for the *Babylonian Talmud:* "On the eve of Passover, Yeshu was hanged because he has practiced sorcery and led Israel astray." (Talmud, b, Sanh 43a)

In *Talmud 27 B* is found a letter written by a man named Massalian who had been a close friend of Jesus with the letter telling about Jesus' plan for mankind:

He makes all nature preach the doctrine of trust in the divine Fatherhood. He speaks of the lilies as pledges of God's care, and points to the fowls as evidence of his watchfulness over human affairs. Who can measure the distance between God and the flowerof the field? What connection is there between man and the lily? By such illustrations he creates solitude in man that seems to awe him into reverence, and he becomes attracted toward heavenly thought, and feels that he is in the presence of one that is superior. In this talk he brings one to feel he is very near the presence of God. Thus by beginning with a flower he reasons upward to the absolute, then descends and teaches lessons of trust in a loving Father.

Jesus in his talks brings all illustrations to make man feel his nearness to his kindred, man, teaching also their relation to and dependence upon God. He teaches that man and the flowers and birds drink from the same fountain and are fed from the same table. Through Jesus, in his teachings, we learn that God is Spirit, and God is Father and he says these are the only two things that are essential for man to know. Then he illustrates this to the parents, and asks them what they would do for their children. All his ideas refer to the future; like the parent helping the child with his burden of today, by telling of the blessings of tomorrow; and by making today the seed-corn of tomorrow; keeping the action of today under moral control by making the morrow the day of judgment.

In *Ecclesiastical History of the Church*, Eusebius writes the following about the first followers of Jesus:

> They regarded him as ordinary, a man esteemed as righteous through growth of character and nothing more; the child of a normal union between a man and Mary, and they held that they must observe every detail in the law by faith in Christ alone and a life built upon that faith or they would never win salvation…. They also observed the Sabbath and other discipline of the Jews just like them, but on the other hand, they also celebrated the Lord's days very much like us in commemoration of his resurrection.

Scholars believe that the Temptation story is a genuine event. The temptation of Jesus revolved around the question uppermost in the minds of his countrymen: What should the messiah look like? Should the messiah stand tall at the lofty pinnacle of the temple? Should the messiah be a militant leader like King David and rule over all kingdoms of the world? Judas Iscariot, as zealot commander in the personification of Satan, confronted Jesus giving him the chance to be the thundering Messiah, the mighty warrior that everyone had wanted him to be. They wanted Jesus to lead a military uprising against Rome. When he refused – Judas Iscariot viewed Jesus as being a traitor.

Jesus was not in Capernaum long before he began gathering around himself a group of like-minded friends and relatives. It was this gathering that was done to prepare for the unavoidable consequences of establishing the "Kingdom of God" that he handpicked twelve male apostles. Designation of the twelve, if not a call to war with Rome, was an admission of its inevitability which is the reason Jesus expressly warned:

> "If anyone wishes to follow me, let them deny himself and take up his cross and follow me" (Mark 8:34).

For scholars, this was not a statement of self-denial or symbol of self-abnegation as proclaimed by the church of Constantine in 337 CE; the cross represented punishment for sedition. Jesus was warning his disciples that their status, as the embodiment of the twelve tribes to throw off the yoke of occupation, would be understood by Rome as treason and inevitably lead to crucifixion. Jesus therefore chose to hide his "Kingdom of God" message in parables that were nearly impossible to understand. "The secret of the Kingdom of God has been given to you to know," Jesus tells the disciples. "But to outsiders, everything is said in parables so that they may see and not perceive, they may hear and not understand" (Mark 4:11-12). For scholars, "Kingdom of God" is not a celestial kingdom which exists on a cosmic plane as some would believe when Jesus tells Pilate in John 18:36:

"My kingdom is not of this world."

When John 18:36 is an correct translation from the Greek to English, the phrase *ouk estin ek tou kosmou,* actually means:

"My kingdom is not a part of this system."

Jesus was not claiming that the "Kingdom of God" is unearthly, he was declaring that God's kingdom is incompatible with the Roman government that currently exists on earth. Simply put, "Kingdom of God" was short-hand for the idea of God as sole ruler over the entire world with the implication of these words being – God's restoration cannot happen without first destroying the present order – Rome. For the Romans, Jesus' celestial kingdom was a clear call for revolution.

The most accurate list of Jesus' disciples is given in Gospel of Mark 6:1-7:

- *Simon Peter* was born in Bethsaida, Gaulanitis, Syria in 1 CE; was business partner of Zebedee in his fishing business. He was a married village Essene of the order of Naphtali. He travelled throughout Israel, Turkey, Greece, Syria, Iraq, Iran, and India going as far as China. Antioch, in Syria, was home base for his ministry. He recommended that Matthias, brother of Jesus, replace Judas Iscariot on the Council of Twelve. He has been identified by scholars as belonging to the **eastern Hebrew party** within the Christian movement.

- *James, the Greater* son of Zebedee and Salome was born in Bethsaida, Gaulanitis, Syria in 5 BCE. He first preached the gospel in Judah later travelling to India and Spain. He has been identified by scholars as belonging to the ***eastern Hebrew party*** within the Christian movement.

- *John,* son of Zebedee, was born in Bethsaida, Galilee in 6 CE. He was leader of the 5,000, that is, married uncircumcised Gentiles of the Order of Asher. He fulfilled his ministry in Asia Minor preaching to the Parthians. He was exiled to the Island of Patmos later dying of natural causes in Edessa. Scholars have identified John as belonging to the ***eastern Hebrew party*** within the Christian movement.

- *Andrew,* brother of Simon Peter, was born in 5 CE in Bethsaida, Galilee son of Jonah. He was a business partner of Zebedee in the fishing business. He was a married village Essene of the order of Naphtali. He preached in Turkey, Greece, and southern Russia. Scholars have identified Andrew as belonging to the ***eastern Hebrew party*** within the Christian movement.

- *Philip* was born in Bethsaida, Galilee in 4 CE. He was leader of the uncircumcised Gentiles who were referred to as order of Shem. He was an official of the Egyptian Therapeutate the healing community of Qumran. He preached in Hierapolis. Scholars have identified Philip as belonged to the ***eastern Hebrew party*** within the Christian movement.

- *Bartholomew* born 1 CE in Cana, Galilee. was son of Talmai, king of Geshur. He was leading Gentile proselyte meaning he was leader of those who were accepting of some Jewish ritual law while rejecting others. He became sponsor of John's gospel, which represented his outlook. He preached in Egypt, Ethiopia, Libya, Mesopotamia, Arabia, Parthia and Persia. Scholars have identified Bartholomew as belonged to the ***eastern Hebrew party*** within the Christian movement.

- *Matthew,* also called Levi, was son of Annas ben Seth. He was a Levitical bishop for five provinces of Asia Minor and was sponsor of Gospel of Matthew which was attributed to him. He has been identified by scholars as belonging to the ***western Hellenist party*** within the Christian movement.

- *Thomas*, also known as Crown Prince Philip, husband of Herodias, brother of Herod Antipas, was born in 1 CE. Gospel of John refers to him as "doubting Thomas" implying that he did not believe in the bodily resurrection of Christ when, in fact, he held the view of the ***eastern Hebrew party*** which did not believe that Jesus was messiah but then change his opinion about believing Jesus to be the rightful heir to the thrown. Thomas ministered in Israel, Parthia, Tibet, and India.

- *James, the Less,* brother of Jesus, was born in 3 BCE and first bishop of the Jerusalem church. He believed that Gentiles need not be circumcised but that they must keep certain aspects of the ritual law as professed by Jesus. Scholars have identified James as belonging to the ***eastern Hebrew party*** within the Christian movement.

- *Thaddaeus* was head of the Egyptian Therapeutae, a moderate nationalistic group of Alexandria. He was an influential leader of the community and a zealot commander. Scholars believe that Lebbaeus whose surname was Thaddaeus is none other than Judas born 5 CE, who was younger brother of Jesus. Jerome refers to Judas as "Trionius" which means, the man with three names. In Gospel of Matthew (10:3) he is called "Lebbaeus, whose surname was Thaddaeus". In Gospel of Mark (3:18) he is called Thaddaeus. In Gospel of Luke (6:16) he is called the "brother of James" as translated in the Catholic version of scripture and in Acts of the Apostles (1:13) he is referred to as "Judas the son of James" which translates to mean 'younger brother'. In Epistle of Jude (1:1), the author speaks of himself as being the "brother of James" (1:1) who, for scholars, is also the brother of Jesus. The Gospel of Ebonite's states that Jude was among the first who received the call to follow Jesus; in

Genealogies of the Twelve Disciples, Jude is declared of the house of Joseph implying that Jesus' father was also his. In *The Belief of the Blessed Judas the Brother of Our Lord Who was Surnamed Thaddaeus*, Eusebius pronounces Judas as one of the twelve. Scholars find that Thaddaeus tended to fluctuated between the **eastern Hebrew party** and **western Hellenist party** in the early Christian movement.

- *Judas Iscariot* was leader of the Essene at Qumran with the Dead Sea Scrolls written under his tutelage and that of his predecessor, Judas the Galilean, founder of the Zealot movement. Aside from his academic prowess, Judas was tribal leader of East Manasseh half-tribe, a fervent militant nationalists group. Although placed at the end of the apostolic list, Judas was politically second in seniority among the disciples only to Lazarus, brother of Mary Magdalene. He is the one who is referred to as 'Satan' in the temptation story because it was Judas who confronted Jesus in the desert demanding that, as Messiah, he must lead a military uprising against Rome. Judas has been identified by scholars as belonging to the **western Hellenist party** in the early Christian movement.

According to Gospel of Matthew 26:15, Judas betrayed Jesus in exchange for 30 pieces of silver which for biblical scholars is a contrived story used to blame the Jews for the death of Jesus rather than the Romans.

- *Simon the Zealot* was a towering figure in history and the most major player next to Jesus and Mary Magdalene in his movement. He was a gnostic, self-styled miracle worker, head of the West Manasseh Magians, a group of Diaspora Essene who were a priestly caste of scribes, philosophers, an amalgam of liberalized Judaism, Greek philosopher, and scientist who supported Jesus as being the David. His home base was the land immediately north of the tribe of Ephraim. Also known as Lazarus, older brother to Mary Magdalene, he was a Zealot commander who held an extreme nationalistic view believing that the Romans must be driven out of Palestine. He has been identified by scholars as being a leader of the **western Hellenist party** in the early Christian movement. Because of Lazarus's many talents, he is referred to in the Bible as being:

Alexander the Coppersmith as adversary to Agrippa I.

Beelzebul when opposed to the teaching of Apostle Paul.

Demetrius the Silversmith when bishop of Ephesus.

Lightening when describing his fierce personality.

Lazarus as brother to Mary and Martha.

Magus because of his many unusual talents including the power to heal by use of medicines with the word "Magus" in Greek being equal to magician.

Simon Magus as head of the Magians of West Menasseh.

Simon the Leper when apposed to the teaching of Apostle Paul.

Simon the Cannite so named as a Samaritan.

Simone Cananios a variation of Cannite.

Simon the Zealot so named as Zealot commander.

Helena, who was the companion of Lazarus, joined the Jewish religion in its early Herodian form which supported bringing back the David line and Zadok priests. She was a woman of high discipline, prayer, and good works as mandated by God for women of high rank holding significant material wealth. Her order based in Tyre was called the "harlots" because it was not faithful to any one spiritual belief but chose from various points of view. Because of her association with Simon, she was referred to as being "a whore from the brothel in Tyre." As female cardinal in Ephesus, she was spiritual mother of the Gentiles, where she was referred to as "prophetess Jezebel." She accepted Jesus as being the David and the view that

Jewish laymen could act as a Levite priest but not Gentiles because they were not of Jewish ancestry. Contrary to Lazarus, she favored peace with Rome. She and Lazarus were believed by their Hellenist followers to be the incarnation of deities.

- *Mattias* is also referred to as Jose, brother of Jesus, in *Antiquities of the Jews* (1:23-26) and as Barnabus in *Clementine Recognitions* (1:60). He was born in 1 CE and is identified by scholars as belonging to the **eastern Hebrew party** in the early Christian movement.

28 CE

When John the Baptist was imprisoned, it caused Jesus role as a social worker and charismatic healer to change. Rather than merely ministering to the sick and the poor, he began to formulate a vision that would rectify the great social injustice he was witnessing. From *The Historical Jesus: The Life of a Mediterranean Jewish Peasant*, John Dominic Crossen writes:

While in prison, John's anger towards Jesus began to grow because Jesus had turned away from John's conservative teaching, ushering in his own liberal religious thoughts and practices. John's vision was one of awaiting the apocalyptic God as a repentant sinner, while Jesus deemed that theology as being inadequate, as it was not enough to await the future kingdom because one must enter a present kingdom that exists on earth *here and now* by loving God above all else and helping mankind find fulfillment.

The missions of John and Jesus were similar in that they gave the masses access to God directly without the usual trappings of the temple administrated to by priests or the need to follow rituals. Jews who were familiar with the Hebrew Bible expected the ministry of John to pave the way for the appearance of the Messiah when seven centuries earlier, Isaiah proclaimed that "one would prepare in the wilderness the way of Jehovah,"(Isaiah 40:3). For followers of Jesus, who viewed him as Messiah, the word 'messenger' represented John the Baptist while 'messenger of the covenant' came to represent Jesus. The power of John's preaching, together with the spiritual void left in Israel's heart due to years of oppression, were a winning combination as John's mission can be summed up by one word—'preparer.'

John's preaching was about the coming kingdom and need to repent. His message of repentance entailed recognition of the offense to God within the sinner's heart, and need for transformation. When John saw the Jews submitting to his baptism, void of any change in their behavior, he rebuked them by saying: "You offspring of vipers" (Matthew 3:7). In *Antiquities of the Jews*, Josephus said several things were required of those submitting to John's immersion in order for the rite to have validity.

- The candidate must believe in the messianic message of the Hebrew Bible.

- Baptism was one of repentance which would motivate radical change in a persons' disposition.

- Baptism involved a confession of sin with the purpose of immersion being for forgiveness of sins.

When these requisites were satisfied, the individual received pardon, hence, was a part of the people who were prepared for the Lord (Luke 1:17). Josephus describes John's baptism ceremony in *Antiquities of the Jews:*

The people who were being baptized must first listen to John's sermon to cleanse their soul and purge their sins. After that, the people were immersed in the Jordan in mass in order to purify their flesh from pollutants. After emerging from the Jordan, John would again call the name of God and ask that the Holy Spirit descend upon the crowd. At the end of the ceremony, doves were released from cages as being a symbol of the special relationship that God had with his chosen people.

29 CE

In *Antiquity of the Jews,* Josephus describes the reason for John the Baptist being put to death:

For Herod had put him to death, though he was a good man and had exhorted the Jews to lead righteous lives, to practice justice toward their fellows and piety toward God, and so doing to join in baptism. In his view this was necessary preliminary if baptism was to be acceptable to God. They must not employ it to gain pardon for whatever sins they committed, but as a consecration of the body, implying that the soul was already thoroughly cleansed by right behavior. When others too joined the crowds about him because they were aroused to the highest degree by his sermons, Herod became alarmed. Eloquence that had so great an effect on mankind might lead to some form of sedition, for it looked as if they would be guided by John in everything that they did. Herod decided therefore that it would be much better to strike first and be rid of him before his work led to an uprising than to wait for an upheaval, get involved in a difficult situation, and see his mistake.

The ending of John's ministry coincided with Herod Antipas marrying Herodias in violation of Essene law. Antipas, who was married to Phasaelis, daughter of king Aretas of Nabataea, divorced her to marry Herodias wife of his brother Philip, while Phasaelis was still alive which was in violation of Essene law. Worse than that, he was marrying his niece the daughter of his brother, Aristobulus. With this unholy union, John did not hesitate to publically proclaim that it was not right for Antipas "to have your brother's wife" citing Leviticus 18:16 with this criticism not being tolerated for long.

John's death marked the beginning of Jesus' career as a solo prophet. By inheriting some of John's followers, Jesus increased the influence of his teachings while making himself a political enemy of Rome. Other followers of John, who chose not to follow Jesus, moved in their own direction with both parties rivaling each other until well into the second century.

The conservative teaching of John focused on an apocalyptic message with baptism as an initiation, while the liberal ministry of Jesus focused on the reality of a non-judgmental God reigning as Jesus would dine with all and eat and drink whatever was available in the name of fellowship. For scholars, John the Baptist is viewed as being the last prophet of the Old Testament period and bridge to Jesus who was messenger of the 'new' covenant in the New Testament era.

Upon a careful look at the New Testament, you will find that it is a battleground. We find that Jesus criticized the high priests, scribes and hypocrites everywhere. He showed distain for Hebrew law in one place while asserting perfect adherence to it in another place as the only way to salvation. His disciples fight over who should be in charge under him while twisting his words to suit themselves. Jesus advocates poverty as a cure for the rich, not riches as a cure for the poor, confounding expectations on all sides.

During his lifetime, Jesus had to deal with the following political and religious groups which, in most cases, held views contrary to one another:

Galileans were a nationalistic sect which rebelled against all foreign elements advocating Israel return to a theocratic form of government whereby it is divinely guided.

Herodians believed that Israel's only chance of survival was under Herod the Great.

Levites were in charge of the Temple.

Pharisees were guardians of Israel's written and oral traditions which were popular with the people.

Publicans were tax collectors for the Empire with their view being anti-Galilean.

Sadducees were aristocrats who held most of the seats in the Sanhedrin accepting only the written Law.

Samaritans were Jews of the northern kingdom who were taken into exile under the reign of Assyrian kings. They intermarried with foreigners making them a separate race – neither Jew nor Gentile. They were held in contempt by the Jews of the southern kingdom of Judah for their seemingly pagan ways.

Sanhedrin was the Supreme Court of the Jews for both religious and legal matters. It had seventy-one members which included the high priest.

Scribes were the interpreters of the Hebrew scriptures. They had great power in Jewish society and were often called upon to settle disputes.

Eastern Hebrew Party was made up of Jews from the southern kingdom of Judah who favored peace with Rome. They did not accept Jesus as messiah because of his untimely birth; they favored James, brother of Jesus, as messiah.

Western Hellenist Party was primarily made up of Samaritans from the northern kingdom of Israel who favored war with Rome advocating Jesus as rightful heir to the throne of David.

In *Urantia Revelation*, we find that Jesus commissioned a corps of twelve women disciples to minister to women and children. They were:

Suzanna, daughter of Chazen, from the Nazareth synagogue.

Joanna, wife of Chazen, steward of Herod Antipas.

Elizabeth, daughter of a wealthy Jew from Tiberius and Sepphoris.

Martha, elder sister of Peter and Andrew.

Rachel, sister-in-law who was married to Jesus' brother Jude.

Nasantia, daughter of Elman, a Syrian physician.

Milcha, cousin of Apostle Thomas.

Ruth, eldest daughter of Matthew Ananas.

Celta, daughter of a Roman centurion.

Agaman, widow living in Damascus.

Rebecca, daughter of Joseph of Arimathea.

Mary Madgalene

Jesus led a band of two hundred followers into Jerusalem during Sukkoth Feast of Booths in September where they attacked the temple priests, overturning the tables of the money changers, assaulting some, and breaking free the sacrificial animals from their cages with this attack being described in *Urantia Revelation*:

> In mid-September, Jesus and thirty of his followers walked to Jerusalem by way of Bethany in the early morning hours to attend the Sukkos Feast of Booths. By advanced agreement, he met others at Zion's immersion pools. Most of his two hundred supporters had taken up positions inside the great court at the temple to assure that Jesus would not be harmed. He went to the speaker's platform and was about to speak when he was interrupted by a loud altercation between a money-changer and a customer who had been cheated. In a fit of indignation Jesus suddenly stepped down from the speaker's dais to address the issue. His followers moved in squads. They overturned the vendors' tables, released the birds, untethered the animals used for sacrifice and drove them out of the ceremonial gate on the west side of the temple. The vendors yelled and shouted in outrage and horror. Some were pushed and dragged out of the temple by his followers. Others were beaten, punched and kicked. There was at least one murder of a vendor by Barabbas, one of the many violentmilitants who had attached themselves to Jesus. With all haste the mob left Jerusalem with the temple being left in shambles.

> A few months later, after things had quitted down, Jesus announced that after completing their tour of southern Perea that the group would go up to Jerusalem for Passover.

Authorities were irate about the attack because it represented an attack on Rome itself. Jesus was captured seven months later during the Passover Festival in Jerusalem and sentenced to death by crucifixion with the authors of the New Testament condensing this event into a one week period for theological reasons. For scholars, Jesus was crucified by the Romans for sedition.

Many scholars believe that the wedding feast at Cana actually describes the betrothal of Jesus to Mary Magdalene following dynastic rules found in the Dead Sea Scrolls. A second wedding service was held at Ain Feshkha at the house of Lazarus – brother of Mary Magdalene. By Jewish custom, as formal host of the wedding, Jonathan Annas, as Zadok priest, acted as Lord following the death of John the Baptist, was in full charge as Ruler of the Feast while the secondary authority rested with the bridegroom, who was in charge of the wine offering. The communion, equivalent to a modern engagement party, with Mary Magdalene acting as the bride of Solomon, took place on March 18, three months after Tamar-Sarah was conceived with Mary anointing Jesus' feet signifying such an event. For scholars, six pots of wine containing 20 to 30 gallons apiece, indicates that at a minimum of 2500 guests attended this royal engagement party based upon the normal amount of wine consumed by a present day guest. The sacred meal was held between six and ten p.m.

Scholars agree that New Testament evidence for Jesus's celibacy has been weighed and found wanting. Apostle Paul, who provides the earliest canonical record of Jesus, did not point out Jesus as being a model for the unmarried. In 1 Corinthians, Paul explicitly states that he knew nothing about Jesus's position of celibacy (7:25) and goes on to say that wives accompanied their traveling husbands as they spread the Good News which was standard practice (9:5). In addition to that, *Anti-Nicene Fathers Library* makes reference to the fact that all the apostles were married.

Rudolf Bultmann, one of the most influential New Testament interpreters stated in his book *Jesus and the Word:*

> It is clear that Jesus actually lived as a Jewish rabbi and as such he disputed over questions of the Law with pupils and opponents. A Mishnaic injunction, Kiddushin 4:13, states categorically: "An unmarried man may not be a teacher."

In Leviticus 21:13-15, marriage was expected in every vocation, including the priesthood. The requirement for priests to marry is also commented on in *The Women's Bible Commentary:*

> Unlike religions that elevate celibacy above marriage, Israelite religion insisted that even its highest religious functionary take a wife and beget children. Sexuality was an

integral part of human life, and marriage and paternity were indispensable aspects of complete manhood.

Jewish theologian Schalom Ben-Chorin writes in *Bruder Jesus:*

> I am convinced that Jesus of Nazareth, like any rabbi in Israel, was married. His apostles and opponents would have mentioned it, if he had differed from the general custom. Ben-Chorin further points out: We know nothing about the wives of Hillel, Shammai, and many other notable men of that era and culture, but had they been unmarried, surely the adversaries would have pointed to their violation of sacred duty as a basis for criticism. The fact that Jesus' marital status is a non-issue in the Gospels suggests that he conformed to cultural expectations in regard to marriage.

In 2012, Karen L. King, Hollis professor of divinity from Harvard Divinity School – presented a fragment of a fourth century writing which included the words:

> Jesus said to them, my wife she will be able to be my disciple.

For scholars, Jesus' triumphant entry into Jerusalem at the first of the week with crucifixion by weeks end has serious chronology issues. Gospel of John states that Jesus came into the city during the Festival of Tabernacles and that pilgrims were carrying palm fronds and singing Hosannas as they greeted him. With this description of the festival being correct, Jesus entered the city of Jerusalem in October. And if he was arrested, tried and executed during Passover as reported, it means that he was crucified around April of the following year. In other words, Jesus did not spend four days in Jerusalem – he spent six months.

According to Roman historian Cassius Dio (164-235 CE) writing in *Roman History*, the political significance of this time frame rests in the fact that power in Rome was shifting. Emperor Tiberius had removed himself from Rome and was living in Capri. In his absence, he appointed his confidant Lucius Aelius Sejanus (20 BCE - 31 CE), Prefect of the Praetorian Guard, to run the government. As friend of Jesus and his mission, Sejanus planned to sponsoring Jesus' messiahship which meant that he could liberate the temple from the corrupt priesthood led by Caiaphas. With that outcome, political liberation of Judah would no longer be a military threat as the growing Jesus movement could then be peacefully relocated to the center of Judean religious life – the temple in Jerusalem. For Sejanus, by Jesus proclaiming that the "Kingdom of God" was not of this world, he was signaling that he was declaring war on the high priest and not Rome. A major problem arose during Jesus' extended stay in the city. Tiberius was informed by Antonia his wife, that their daughter Livilla and Sejanus, his appointed 'de facto' ruler in Rome, was about to have him assassinated thereby becoming emperor himself. Upon hearing this news, Tiberius returned to Rome and condemning Sejanus to death and having him summarily executed. This political upheaval put all supporters of Sejanus – like Herod Antipas and Pontius Pilate, on the defensive causing, Jesus to be handed over to the authorities for crucifixion.

30 CE

Jesus was crucified by the Romans for sedition.

What differentiated the teaching of Jesus from modern orthodoxy is the idea that knowledge of God and self alone, will save as opposed to faith. This means that the individual has it within himself to obtain salvation. How one interacts with his fellow man 'here and now' is what counts. The followers of Jesus stressed the fact that one can only be saved by what goes on within one's heart and soul. They believed that 'faith' was a poor cousin to 'knowledge' of God as faith effectively implied a distance between the believer and the divine.

James, brother of Jesus, was appointed leader of the Jerusalem church by Jesus himself. Scholars place the family of Jesus in the tradition of Jewish-Christianity which means they were observant of the Torah, adherence to traditions such as Sabbath observance, Jewish calendar, Jewish laws, customs, and synagogue attendance. They believed that the world was created good and had become evil only through man's sin. They believed that their God the Father was the same as the Hebrew Bible creator God; that Jesus was a holy man elevated to Messiah and that they wanted to see the elimination of Roman dominance over Israel by whatever means necessary. James believed that the human problem was not sin but ignorance of God as Jesus did not save people from sin but taught them about God so they could understand the moral responsibility required of each person in society. Hegesippus (110 -180 CE) describes James:

> Control of the church passed together with the Apostles, to the brother of the Lord, James, whom everyone from the Lord's time till our own has named James the 'Just', for there were many James, but this one was holy from birth; he drank no wine or intoxicating liquor and ate no animal food; no razor came near his head; he did not smear himself with oil, and he took no bath. He alone was permitted to enterthe holy of holies in the temple, for his garments were not of wool butof linen. He used to enter the sanctuary alone, and was often found onhis knees beseeching forgiveness for his people.

During the centuries of Persian, Greek, and Syrian occupation, Jews had yearned for a redeemer who would throw off the foreign yoke and restore Israel as a nation under God. This man was referred to as being the Messiah, a descendant from the Royal House of David who would rule over a unified nation. The idea of the restoration of a "Kingdom of God" had been circulating for some time. There was no agreement on what kind of savior, the Messiah figure would be. Some saw him as a descendant of King David; others as the archangel Michael; while Book of Daniel referred to him as "one like the son of man" (Daniel 7:13). John the Baptist described him in militant terms as a man whose "winnowing fork is in his hand, to clear his threshing floor" (Luke 3:17).

The *Talmud* is a collection of Jewish oral traditions that were put into writing between 70 CE and 200 CE. From the Babylonian Talmud, Sanhedrin 43a, the following is recorded about the trial and death of Jesus:

> On the eve of Passover they hanged Yeshu. And an announcer went out, in front of him, for forty days saying: 'He is going to be stoned (Jewish method of criminal justice) because he practiced sorcery and enticed and led Israel astray. Anyone who knows anything in his favor let him come and plead in his behalf.' But not having found anything in his favor, they hanged him (Roman form of criminal justice) on the eve of Passover.

No matter how Jesus understood his mission, he never referred to himself as being the Messiah. When it came to referring to himself, Jesus simply called himself "son of Man" which equates to being an offspring of Adam and Eve. When using that title, he was using the description found in Book of Daniel making a clear statement about how he viewed his identity and his mission. He was associating himself with the Davidic messiah, the king who will rule the earth on God's behalf, who will gather the twelve tribes together and restore the nation to its former glory.

Josephus describes the crucifixion of Jesus in *Antiquities of the Jews:*

> About this time there lived Jesus, a wise man, if indeed one ought to call him a man. For he was one who wrought surprising feats and was a teacher of such people as accepted the unusual gladly. He won over many Jews and many Greeks. He was the so-called Christ. When Pilate, upon hearing him accused by men of the highest standards amongst us, had condemned him to be crucified, those who had in the first place come to love him did not give up their affection for him. According to their report, he appeared to them restored to life, for the prophets of God had prophesied these and countless other marvelous things about him and the tribe called Christians, so called after him, have still to this day not disappeared.

Hyan Macoby, in his book *The Authentic Gospel of Jesus,* explains why Jesus was crucified:

> We must remind ourselves of what Jesus really was. He was not the founder of a church, but a claimant to a throne. When Peter hailed Jesus as messiah, he was using the word in its Jewish sense, not in the sense it requires in the later Christian church. In other words, Peter was hailing Jesus as being King of Israel. Jesus' response was to give Peter his title rock and to tell him that he would have "the keys of the kingdom of Heaven." The meaning of this phrase, in its Jewish context, is quite different from what later Christian mythology made of it, when it pictured Saint Peter standing at the gates of heaven, holding the keys, and deciding which souls might enter; the reference is not to some paradise in the great beyond, but to the

messianic kingdom on earth, of which Jesus had allowed himself to be proclaimed King, of which Davidic monarch constitutional ruler, while God was the only real King. By giving Peter the "keys of the Kingdom," Jesus was appointing Peter to be his chief minister.

In *Archko Volume*, high priest Caiphas discusses, in part, Jesus' ministry:

> Not-withstanding his youth and inexperience, Jesus started out asa public orator and teacher with the doctrines of John, and in that capacity referred exclusively to his authority, as every public teacherin these days has to be ordained by some acknowledged authority … The reprimands of Jesus were so severe against the rich and highly educated that they turned against him, and brought all the power theyhad, both of the wealth and talent, so that I saw a bloody insurrectionbrewing fast.

High priest Caiphas gives his defense to the Sanhedrim for the sentence given to Jesus:

> Jesus of Nazareth is a false teacher – Jesus completely ignores this temple; says the priests have made it a den of thieves and sets up a sneer, and even scoffs at its sacred ordinances, and with a sort of selfish triumph says it shall be destroyed; and from his manner of saying it, I have no doubt he would be glad to see it quickly done. But what would be the condition of our people if this temple was removed? What would be the use of our priesthood if the temple was destroyed? My argument is, if this temple is destroyed or even forsaken by the Jews, we as a nation are utterly ruined.

Scholars believe that Jesus was scourged but may not have died on the cross but later recovered from the effects of the sedative placed on the sponge given to him by Judas (aka Thaddeaus) while on the cross. He was revived by Mary Magdalene and others leaving the unguarded tomb assisted by his uncle Joseph of Arimathea and Nicodemus, an undeclared believer. He reached Rome where he was known to be living in seclusion as late as 64 CE with this view based upon a reading of non-biblical commentary written by first and second century historians such as *Gospel of Philip, Second Treatise of the Great Seth* and *Apocalypse of Peter* to name but a few. This scenario also reflects on first and second century tradition that says that Jesus did not die on the cross because he was not made of normal flesh and that a Messiah figure could not be vanquished. When Jesus appeared in a 'vision' to Peter and Paul, as recorded in Acts of the Apostles, it was the real flesh and blood Jesus holding audience with his ministers. For scholars, the narrative for the historical crucifixion of Jesus goes more like this:

> Pilate to placate the Zealots, who were calling for Jesus' arrest and execution, he condemned Jesus as being a political agitator, thus avoiding a Zealot threat of widespread disorder. For Pilate, this was the last thing he needed on his watch, especially since he had fallen out of favor with the authorities in Rome due to his mistreatment of the Jews in general. But while he condemned Jesus and had to go through with the required sentence of crucifixion, he could not dare to have it reported to Rome that Jesus had actually died. So Pilate took steps to ensure that Jesus would survive. He spoke with a member of the Sanhedrin and friend of Jesus, the wealthy Joseph of Arimathea, who recruited Nicodemus and others for the crucifixion plot.

Shortly after the crucifixion, a pregnant Mary Magdalene fled to Alexandria accompanied by Joseph of Arimathea, Martha and Lazarus with the small group settling in or near the temple of Onias remaining there until 38 CE. Some scholars believe that Jesus may have accompanied this group because the temple was a safe haven as it was under the jurisdiction of the Zadokite priests who accepted Jesus as Messiah. The Romans were after Jesus for sedition; Jews were after him for blaspheme, and Zealots were after him for refusing to lead an armed rebellion against Rome. Its location was in the district of Heliopolis 18 miles north of Cairo (Hegesippus: *Vita emeritica beatae Maria Magdale*).

In 1906, Egyptologist Sir William Flinders Petrie discovered the remains of the temple on a sandy mound attached to the city of Rameses III with this temple being discussed by both Flavius Josephus and the Talmud.

In 1941, archaeologists discovered the ossuary of Simon of Cyrene, the man who helped Jesus carry the cross in route to the crucifixion. The discovery was made in Simon's family burial plot in the Kidron Valley east of Jerusalem.

Hegesippus (110 -180 CE), affirms James's role as head of the Christian community in his manuscript *Memoranda:*

> Control of the church passed together with the Apostles, to the brother of the Lord, James, whom everyone from the Lord's time till our own has named James the 'Just', for there were many James', but this one was holy from birth; he drank no wine or intoxicating liquor and ate no animal food; no razor came near his head; he did not smear himself with oil, and he took no bath. He alone was permitted to enter the holy of holies in the temple, for his garments were not of wool but of linen. He used to enter the sanctuary alone, and was often found on his knees beseeching forgiveness for his people.

Jerusalem temple is described by Josephus in *Life of Flavius Josephus:*

> All who ever saw our temple are aware of the general design of the building and the inviolable barriers which preserved its sanctity. It had four surrounding courts, each with its special statutory restrictions. The outer court was open to all, foreigners included; women during their impurity were alone refused admission. To the second court all Jews were admitted and when uncontaminated by any defilement, their wives; to the third, male Jews, if clean and purified; to the fourth, the priests robed in their priestly vestments. The sanctuary was entered only by the high priests, clad in the raiment peculiar to themselves. So careful is the provision for all the details of the service, that the priests' entry is timed to certain hours. Their duty was to enter in the morning, when the temple as opened, and to offer the customary sacrifices, and again at mid-day, until the temple was closed. One further point: no vessel whatever might be carried into the temple, the only objects in which were an alter, a table, a censer (a vessel for burning incense), and a lamp stand, all mentioned in the law…nothing of the nature of food or drink is brought within the temple; objects of this kind may not even be offered on the alter, save those which are prepared for the sacrifices.

32 CE

Words of the Master was written shortly after the crucifixion by three followers of Jesus who were commissioned by James to record the original words of his brother that they could remember with these words being used to defined what it meant to belong to the "Kingdom of God" movement. Words of the Master were added to a much larger work titled *Gospel Sayings of Quelle* which was completed six years later. Some of the inspirational words were later expanded upon to become known as Sermon on the Mount, Golden Rule, Lord's Prayer and Beatitudes.

James, brother of Jesus, as leader of the Jerusalem church and Apostle Paul an evangelist representing Peter's assembly in Antioch, are the two most prominent figures of first-century Christianity with their two "brands" of spiritual belief being at opposite ends of a particular spectrum. Apostle Paul affirmed that he spoke with the authority granted by Peter when he spoke to Gentiles living in exile who expected to hear an "divine" teaching about Jesus which could compete with the likes of Zeus.

33 CE

Judas Iscariot committed suicide by hanging in Jerusalem.

34 CE

Peter, founder of the church in Antioch, remained there through at least 41 CE serving as its first bishop. As Gentiles began to convert from paganism to Christianity, a dispute arose between Peter and Apostle Paul as to whether or not Gentiles needed to observe the tenets of the Law of Moses as both were opposed in their beliefs concerning the 'being' of Jesus and purity laws being followed. From Antioch, Paul travelled north and west to Corinth remaining in the general area until such time as he made his way back to Jerusalem for the first Jerusalem church council meeting.

Stephen, who scholars believe was Jonathan Annas, a member of the Annas ben Seth family and student of Peter in Antioch, was first to preach that salvation brought through the person of Jesus was for all people with this view attaching Jewish conservatism. Stephen was seized and accused of blasphemy for disavowing the temple cult and its claim to be the sole authority in religious belief.

The priestly class believed that the Hebrew Bible and laws of God were for the Jews only whereas Stephen, a member of the Annas ben Seth family, insisted that the institution of Jewish law and temple were only temporary and that God intended the Jews to look beyond themselves to the coming Messiah who would provide righteousness for all mankind including the Gentiles and that the purpose of the Hebrew Bible was to foretell this event. Stephen believed that the death of Jesus' was done as a sacrifice for mankind and that the law of the Hebrew Bible did not apply to the followers of Jesus. For this belief, Stephen was stoned to death by the Jews. He is considered to be the first Christian martyr.

Mary Magdala gave birth to son Judah near Cairo with his schooling being done at Caesarea. By 46 CE , he underwent the ceremony of second birth in Aix en Provence, Gaul where he was symbolically born again from his mother's womb, his designated first year as an initiate into the Nazarite movement known as the "Way." In 53 CE, he was officially proclaimed crown prince at the synagogue in Corinth and duly received the Davidic Crown Prince title of 'Justus' formally succeeding his uncle James as the David. Some accounts hold that having reached the majority age of sixteen, Justus became the chief Nazarine, gaining entitlement to wear the priestly black robe of Isis. (Hegesippus: *Vita emeritica beatae Maria Magdale*)

35 CE

Saul, who we shall now call Apostle Paul was able to secure the necessary authority from high priest Caiaphas to travel to Damascus to search out and punish followers of Jesus that might be found there. As Saul approached Damascus, he experienced a blinding light and heard a loud voice from on high. Paul's conversion is referenced in one of his letters. He asserted that he received the gospel not from man, but directly by "the revelation of Jesus Christ." He claimed almost total independence from the Jerusalem community of James, brother of Jesus. He believed that everything was predetermined by God except for human obedience to the Torah with that being up to individual choice and that God would reward or punish accordingly. He placed emphasis on repentance and divine forgiveness which was a shared legacy with Jesus. He was against war with Rome and saw the source of human suffering in the failure of mankind to obey God's laws; he believed in afterlife and divine intervention. Like his father, Paul was a committed Pharisee. In *The Jewish Apostle Paul* by Dr. Eli Lizorkin-Eyzenberg, we learn that Paul did not abandon Judaism for Christianity, but converted from one form of Judaism to a Jesus-centered, apocalyptic Judaism. He joined the ranks of Jews that believed they were living in the latter days anticipated by the prophets. He came to realize that the time of the entire world's redemption was suddenly within reach of his generation. He was convinced that his God was no longer to be celebrated only as the God of Israel, but now, must be recognized as the God of the entire created order. In Romans 3:29-31 he said:

> " … is God the God of the Jews only? Is He not the God of the Nations also? Yes, of the Nations also, since indeed God who will justify the circumcised by faith and the uncircumcised through faith is one. Do we then nullify the Torah through faith? May it never be! On the contrary, we establish the Torah".

For scholars, the person who changed the narrative about Jesus of Nazareth was Apostle Paul. He is the filter through which orthodox Christianity eventually reached the modern world. More than anyone else, he is responsible for recasting Jesus' Jewish teaching in a light palatable to Gentiles, thoroughly redefining and revising Jesus's message. His many letters were intended to be read aloud at Christian services and answer questions of curious newcomers. Thirteen remain in the New Testament of which only eight can be directly traced to him. In first Corinthians Paul claims that he does whatever is necessary to win over converts which implies that if it is necessary to modify his mission statement about Jesus, so be it.

> Though I am free and belong to no one, I have made myself a slave to everyone, to win as many as possible. To the Jews, I became like a Jew, to win Jews. To those under the law, I became like one under the law so as to win those under the law. To those not having the law I became like one not having the law, so as to win those not having the law. To the weak, I became weak, to win the weak. I have become all things to all people so that by all possible means I might save some.

36 CE

Caiaphas was deposed for the crime of executing Stephen which was in violation of Roman law as he did not have the authority to do so in that era. In 1990, workers building a water park south of Jerusalem inadvertently broke through the ceiling of a hidden burial chamber dating to the first century. An ornately decorated ossuary was found containing the remains of a sixty-year-old man. The ossuary bore the inscription *Yehosef bar Qayafe* with this burial box belonging to the high priest of Jerusalem, Joseph Caiaphas who ordered the arrest of Jesus.

37 CE

In *Memoirs*, Hegesippus (110-180 CE) stated that Jesus visited the British Isles for a third time with his uncle Joseph of Arimathea.

Caligula became 3rd Emperor of Rome (37-41 CE). In the book *Gaius,* Suetonius describes the emperor:

> He was very tall and extremely pale, with an unshapely body, but very thick neck and legs. His eyes and temples were hollow, his forehead broad and grim, his hair thin and entirely gone on the top of his head, though his body was hairy. Because of this, to look upon him from a higher place as he passed by or for any reason whatever to mention a goat, was treated as a capital offence. While his face was naturally forbidding and ugly, he purposely made it even more savage, practicing all kinds of terrible and fearsome expressions before a mirror. He was sound neither of body nor mind.

38 CE

Mary Magdalene, daughter Tamar-Sarah, and son Judah left the Temple of Onias and travelled to Caesarea remaining there for nearly four years. (Hegesippus: *Vita emeritica beatae Maria Magdale*)

40 CE

In *Church Histories (III, 36),* Eusebius states that Peter, who founded the church of Antioch, was appointed first bishop of the Antioch assembly by James, himself, and that Peter serving as bishop and church patriarch through 52 CE. Peter, in turn, appointed Apostle Paul as one of his evangelists.

Gospel of the Holy Twelve proclaims that there is no forgiveness of sins against the laws of God except by repentance and amendment. Jesus received the Holy Spirit at the Jordan River and traveled the world in pursuit of knowledge.

The gospel is made up of 96 lections with the following being of particular interest to scholars when the wedding feast at Cana is discussed.

Lection 6.10:

"And in the eighteenth year of his age, Jesus was espoused unto Miriam."

The gospel points out that Jesus was engaged to and married Mary Magdalene so that he could have the "full experience of human life, and thus be a perfect example for all to follow." Based upon Greek Orthodox records, Miriam is the Greek name used when referring to Mary Magdalene.

Lection 12.1:

"And the next day there was a marriage in Cana of Galilee; and the mother of Jesus was there: and his brethren were there and both Jesus and Mary Magdalene were there, and his disciples came to the marriage."

When lection 12.1 is compared to John 2:1-2, the presence of Mary Magdalene and Jesus's siblings have been eliminated from the story thereby downplaying the fact that a family wedding had taken place.

Lection 12.4:

"When the ruler of the feast had tasted the water that was made into wine to them, and knew not what it was…"

When lection 12.4 is compared to John 2:9, the significance of the wine offering is threefold. First, based upon the Dead Sea Scrolls, the text indicates that Jesus was the bride-groom because only that person could be in charge of the wine offering per Essene custom. Secondly, by substituting holy water for wine, Jesus was declaring himself priest even though he was not of the Levite tribe. Third, he was substituting holy water for wine to signify that 'righteousness' comes from within oneself and not from the outside. The lection further notes that the ruler of the feast did not know 'what' it was that he was drinking because holy water had never been used as a substitute for wine before, which is quite a different statement than John's.

Lection 12.6:

"After this wedding feast in Cana Jesus went down to Capernaum, he, and his mother, with Mary Magdalene, and his brethren, and his disciples."

When lection 12.6 is compared to John 2:12, Mary Magdalene has been removed from the story to hide the fact that both Jesus and Mary Magdalene were traveling to Capernaum as a couple after their wedding.

41 CE

Tiberius Claudius Nero Germanicus became the 4th Emperor of Rome (41-54 CE) after Caligula (12 – 41 CE) was assassinated. From Suetonius's book titled *Claudius,* he describes the emperor:

He was eager for food and drink at all times and in all places... He hardly ever left the dining room until he was stuffed and soaked. Then he went to sleep at once, lying on his back with his mouth open, and a feather was put down his throat to release his stomach.

42 CE

Mary Magdalene, daughter Tamar-Sarah, son Jesus-Justus, Joseph of Arimathea, Martha and her maid Marcella, Philip, Mary-Jacob-Cleophas, and Mary- Salome-Helena set sail for Les Saints Maries de La Mar in southern France. This is the location where the 'grail legend' began which claims that the royal 'bloodline' of the French Merovingian Kings was brought ashore. For grail scholars, *sang-raal* in old French refers to blood-royal and not a chalice used by Jesus at the Last Supper meaning that the grail legend actually states that Mary Magdalene brought to the coast of France, in the form of her children, the legendary bloodline of the French Merovingian kings.

Matthais ben Ananus, became high Priest in Jerusalem (42- 43 CE); he is the one that is thought to be the sponsor of Gospel of Matthew; he was a follower of Jesus.

The term 'Christian' was first used in government circles to describe followers of Peter in Antioch.

43 CE

Apostle Paul began his first mission to the Gentiles traveling along the Mediterranean coast teaching in Antioch, Tarsus, Cyprus, Galatia, Lystra, Derbe and surrounding area with *Acts of Paul and Thecla* painting a portrait of him:

> Of a low stature, bald, crooked thighs, handsome legs, hollow eyed; had a crooked nose; full of grace; for sometimes he appeared as a man, sometimes he had the countenance of an angel (1:7).

Paul preached fearlessly and in doing so earning the anger of the Jews who held strict belief in the one transcendent God who was creator and ruler of the universe meaning that Jesus could not possibly be "son of God" as being proclaimed. Because
of the uproar he was creating among the Jews in Jerusalem, he fled to Caesarea where, by ship he headed to Tarsus remaining there until he met-up with Barnabus (Jesus' brother Judas) with both travelling on to Antioch. During the trip, Judas became alarmed about Paul's preaching because he had drifted away from the message being proclaimed by the mother church in Jerusalem that Jesus was the messiah in the image of King David and that some Torah law must be followed. For Apostle Paul the path to salvation was through Jesus and that salvation was only obtainable by him. The most unsettling aspect of Paul's gospel for members of the messianic movement was his view of the temporary nature of the Torah and redefinition of who constituted the people of Israel, because the Torah was revealed to Moses by God representing an eternal covenant made with the descendants of

Abraham, Isaac, and Jacob, the "chosen people." Through Paul's imaginative teaching, a whole new concept of Jesus arose. No longer was he simply the long-awaited "Anointed One" who would reinstate the Davidic line and free the Jews from oppression, he was now "Savior of the World" and that through acceptance of his death and resurrection, sinful humans could be reconciled to God and thereby offered salvation and the promise of eternal life. For Paul, outright worship of a "divine" Jesus was sufficient to ensure redemption and entry into the "Kingdom of God" with most of the social value professed by Jesus cast aside in his attempt to compete with the variety of pagan gods. For James and the Jerusalem church, this was nothing more than temple style pagan worship.

Secret Gospel of Mark was written. While looking for ancient documents at Mar Saba monastery in the Judean Desert, a letter from Clement, bishop of Alexandria (150 -215 CE) was discovered which contained verses which he said should have been inserted into the canonical Gospel of Mark published in 68 CE. In his letter, Clement commented that the missing passages sounded similar to the raising of Lazarus found in Gospel of John 11:1- 44.

And they come into Bethany. And a certain woman whose brother had died was there. And coming, *she prostrated herself* before Jesus and says to him, "*Son of David,* have mercy on me. " But *the disciples rebuked her.* And Jesus, being angered, went off into the garden where the tomb was, and straightway *a great cry was heard from the tomb.* And going near Jesus rolled away the stone from the door of the tomb. And straightway, going in where the youth was, he stretched forth his hand and raised him, seizing his hand….And going out of the tomb they came to the house of the youth, *for he was rich….*And after six days *Jesus told him what to do* and in the evening the youth comes to him, *wearing a line cloth over his naked body.* And he remained with him that night, for *Jesus taught him the mystery of the kingdom of God*

For scholars:

Statement – "And they come into Bethany" suggests the town where Mary Magdalene and her family lived.

Statement – "And a certain woman" suggests a person of nobility.

Statement – "She prostrated herself" suggests she was honoring a husband.

Statement – "Son of David" suggests the genealogy found in Matthew 1:1-17 were Abraham begot Isaac, Isaac begot Jacob, Jacob begot Judah …. and …. begot Joseph the husband of Mary, of whom was born Jesus who was called the Christ.

Statement – "The disciples rebuked her" suggests that the woman of nobility was espoused to Jesus per the Essene rule for matrimony as found in the Dead Sea Scrolls that explicitly state that a wife cannot greet her husband until she first received his permission to do so.

Statement – "A great cry was heard from the tomb" suggesting that the young man, per 1st century Essene custom, was serving his customary time of pentanes in the tomb.

Statement – "For he was rich" indicates that the woman's family was a member to nobility and had significant resources.

Statement – "Jesus told him what to do" suggests Jesus taught about the need for repentance and transformation from paganism to belief in the one God – Yahweh.

Statement – "Wearing linen cloth over a naked body" suggests baptismal attire.

Statement – "Jesus taught him the mystery of the kingdom of God" suggests the youth was baptized and converted.

Secret Gospel ends prior to a resurrection story being told. By the time the canonical gospel was published thirty years later, scholars believe a resurrection scene was needed for pious Jews who understood the messiah legacy, and for Gentiles who held the Greek view of the immortality of the soul with bodily resurrection theology being a religious idea that both Jews and Gentiles could build on.

44 CE

James the Greater, son of Zebedee, was beheaded by sword in the Armenian Quarter of Jerusalem.

48 CE

Mary Magdalene gave birth to second son Joseph in Ferries, France (Heggesipus: *Vita emeritica beatae Maria Magdale*).

Apostle Paul established a Gentile Christian congregations at Pergamum, Sardis, and Laodicea.

Mary, mother of Jesus, passed away at Aix en Province, Gaul. *Catholic Encyclopedia* presumes her death to have occurred between 36 and 48 CE.

Gospel of Thomas was written proclaiming that humanity should seek the kingdom of God from within ones' self and uncover the hidden wisdom of God found in nature and reject worldly pursuits that leads one away from God and into sin. Above all, it is Jesus' teaching that leads humanity to God, enlightenment and salvation. Two sayings are of particular interest to scholars with Saying 12 highlighting James leadership role in the church while Saying 77 expresses Jesus' concern that false doctrine might appear after he left the mortal realm.

Saying 12:

The disciples said to Jesus: "We know you will depart from us. Who then will rule over us?" Jesus said to them: "No matter where you come from, you should go to James the Just, for whose sake heaven and earth came into being".

Saying 77:

Jesus said to the disciples: "I am the light that shines over all things, I am everything. From me all came forth, and to me all returns. Split a piece of wood, and I am there. Lift a stone, and you will find me there. Do not lay down any rules beyond what I have given you, lest you be dominated by them".

49 CE

In *Adversus Haereses,* Irenaeus explains that Peter and Paul went to Rome sometime between 43 and 54 CE to organize a congregation there. Scholar James D.G. Dunn proposes that Peter was a "bridge-man" between the opposing spiritual views of Apostle Paul and James, brother of Jesus, when he said:

> "Peter was probably, in fact, and effect the bridge-man who did more than any other to hold together the diversity of first-century Christianity."

Apostle Paul began his second mission in Asia Minor. The more his view of Jesus separated from that of the Jerusalem church, the more Paul suggested that only he understood who Jesus really was. While maintaining several major assumptions of Judaism, Paul had changed the meaning of the Hebrew Bible and replacing it with his own theology. While visiting the mother church in Jerusalem, he was received by both James and Peter with some reluctance as they did not know exactly what the message was that he was proclaiming to his congregations in Asia Minor. After agreeing with church leadership about the guidelines for his mission, all went well until James learned that Paul was again saying that Jesus was "Son of God" rather than the messiah in the image of King David.
Apostle Paul established a Gentile Christian congregation in Thyatira.

Suetonius reported that Jesus was living in Rome.

A Jerusalem church Council Meeting was held with elders addressing a critical issue that threatened to split the Messianic Movement. Upon what basis should Gentiles be allowed into the Kingdom of God ? The conservative wing of the Nazarene party maintained that Gentiles should live like Jews, which would include circumcision and observance of Torah law with James, as leader of the church, ruling that Gentiles, in order to belong to the movement, need not be circumcised but must be observant of some Jewish law as prescribed by Jesus. The council delineated the parameters for the twin missions of the Jerusalem church to the Jews and Apostle Paul to the Gentiles. While the goal was the same for both missions, the missions were growing antagonistic of each other because Paul had expanded his understanding of Jesus going beyond the limits the mother church could tolerate, namely, that Jesus was "Son of God" and that Jews could live as Gentiles and totally forsake the Torah.

50 CE

The tradition of Jesus as 'Christ' began to surface when Apostle Paul began to preach his new version of the Jesus story which rejected the validity of Torah revelation and redefined Israel as "all those with faith in Jesus the Christ." Jewish distress over Paul's new interpretation of the Hebrew Bible was caused by their belief that if they turned away from God's commandments, their community would suffer as the commandments were the only language God had given them to express their love for him which meant that they would lose their share of the world to come.

51 CE

Apostle Paul established Gentile Christian congregations at Philadelphia and Corinth.

First Thessalonians was written by Apostle Paul in Corinth. As usual, he was met with two different responses to his gospel message, enthusiastic acceptance by the Gentiles and severe resistance from the Jews. He argued that salvation had been brought by Jesus, who died on the cross for the sins of the world and was then raised from the dead and that he would soon return in judgment of all.

53 CE

Apostle Paul began his final mission to the Gentiles throughout Asia Minor. Based on Acts of the Apostles, scholars believe that the mission lasted four years with representatives from the mother church in Jerusalem, visiting his congregations in Asia Minor to counter his teaching and they were beginning to win their support.

Apostle Paul established a Gentile Christian congregations at Ephesus.

Judah, first-born son of Mary Magdalene, was proclaimed Crown Prince at the synagogue in Corinth duly receiving the Davidic title 'Justus the

Righteous One' formally succeeding his father as the 'David'. By Essene tradition, the title of 'David' started with Jacob-Heli during the reign of Herod the Great, was passed down to his oldest son Joseph, to his oldest son Jesus, to his oldest son Judah.

54 CE

Apostle Paul established a Gentile Christian congregation at Smyrna.

Nero, at age eighteen, married Octavia the daughter of Emperor Claudius thereby becoming the fifth emperor of Rome (54 – 68 CE). In *The Twelve Caesars*, Suetonius describes Nero as being a gifted musician who had a deep love for music often giving concerts with attendance compelled for upper-class Roman citizens. Suetonius recounts how Nero, while watching Rome burn, exclaimed what a beautiful sight it was while singing and playing the lyre. Accused of having set the fire to make room for his new palace, which the Senate would not approve, he was condemned to die. When soldiers had been dispatched by the Senate to arrest him, he committed suicide at age thirty-one. In the book *Nero* by Suetonius, the emperor is described:

> He was for stature almost of complete height, his body full of specs and freckles and foul skin besides, the hair of his head somewhat yellow, his countenance and visage rather fair and lovely and well-favored, his eyes grey and somewhat with the dimmest, his neck full and fat, his belly and paunch bearing out, with a pair of passing slender spindle-shanks, but withal he was very healthful. About the trimming of his body and wearing of his cloths he was so nice as were shameful.

In 2009, archaeologists discovered Nero's Golden Palace in Rome with it extravagant banquet hall which rotated day and night to the earth's movement in order to impress his many VIP and government officials.

Letter to Philippians was written by Apostle Paul in Ephesus sending words of encouragement to his congregation during a time of persecution. He equated Jesus as "Lord" to passages in the Hebrew Bible which referred exclusively to the Lord God of Israel thus effectively making Jesus equal to God.

55 CE

Letter to Galatians was written by Apostle Paul in Ephesus to refute false teaching that had taken root in the region because of emissaries sent from the Jerusalem church who were preaching that followers of Jesus were not free from the law. Galatians is the first indication scholars have that followers of Paul were beginning to question the credibility of his gospel message. In Galatians, Paul makes a direct reference to the representatives of the Jerusalem church when he said:

> "I marvel that you are turning away so soon from him who called you in the Grace of Christ, to a different gospel, which is not another; but there are some who trouble you and want to pervert the gospel of Christ."

Letter to Philemon was written by Apostle Paul in Ephesus about a runaway slave named Onesimus, who belonged to a man named Philemon. After Onesimus had run away, Paul ran across him and urged him to return home encouraging Philemon to take him in and treat him as a brother rather than a slave.

56 CE

First Letter to the Corinthians was written by Apostle Paul in Ephesus. For scholars, Corinthians is the core of Paul's teaching in which he tells his followers that the Christ story is a tradition that he had received from past history. He presents Jesus as being a martyr because of the crucifixion which was done as a sacrifice for others.

For scholars, the Christ story that Paul presents is a combination of two popular themes of the day, the Greek story about "noble death" combined with the Jewish story of "persecuted sage." In the first century, the phrase *died for* comes from the Jewish story about the persecuted sage and refers to a martyr; *buried* underscores the Greek belief in the reality of death, while *sins* was a frequently used Jewish word meaning "behavior not in accordance with the Torah." *Raised* in Greek means "to awaken a person from sleep," but in Corinthians, Paul used the word raised to mean "bringing Christ back from the dead," while *appeared* underscores the Jewish belief that the messiah figure could not die but must be victorious.

Because Jesus had seen fit to suffer crucifixion for the sake of his belief, Paul said the following about the resurrection in 15: 3-4:

> ".... that Christ *died* for our sins according to the Scriptures and that He was *buried*, and that He *rose* again the third day according to the Scriptures...."

Later on in verses 44, 50 and 51 of chapter 15, Paul softened his view concerning bodily resurrection when he said:

> "There is a natural body, and there is a spiritual body. Flesh and blood cannot inherit the kingdom of God; neither doth corruption inherit incorruption. Behold, I show you a mystery."

Where Jesus' original message was designed to reinforce Jewish belief by eliminating Roman domination, Paul preached abrogation of the Torah. Where Jesus devoted himself to the welfare of the Jews by criticizing Roman policy, Paul absolved the Romans for crucifying Jesus, blaming the Jews instead. For scholars, these are thought to be authentic words of Jesus:

> Do not think that I have come to abolish the law; I have come not to abolish but to fulfill. For truly I tell you, until heaven and earth pass away, not one letter, not one stroke of the letter, will pass from the law. Therefore, whoever breaks one of the least of these commandments, and teaches others the same, will be called last in the Kingdom of Heaven. For I tell you, unless your righteousness exceeds that of the scribes and the Pharisees, you will never enter the Kingdom of Heaven (Matthew 5:17-20).

Where Paul preached that faith in Jesus is the sole criteria for salvation, Jesus proclaimed followers must act out their beliefs as directed by the commandments (James 1:22-24). Where Paul proclaimed Jesus to be 'Son of God'; Jesus claimed himself to be 'Son of Man.' When Paul attached Jewish belief as being obsolete, he shifted Jesus' mission statement in Matthew to emphasizing 'faith' in Jesus alone is all that matters:

> The blessing given to Abraham might come to the Gentiles through Christ Jesus, so that by faith we might receive the promise of the Spirit (1st Corinthians 9:19-22).

The reconciliation of God with humankind through Jesus Christ (atonement) is the centerpiece of Christianity, and it's what distinguishes it from all other religions with the name *Jesus* in Christology referring to the historical figure, a religious leader born in Galilee whereas the term *Christ* signifies "the anointed one" who was chosen for his divine role in history.

57 CE

By the time Apostle Paul wrote Romans 6:18, it was clear that the followers of Jesus needed to know why their Messiah, who was supposed to be militarily victorious over the enemy like Judas Maccabee in 167 BCE, could be vanquished. Apologists, who defended Christian beliefs from attacks by competing groups, needed to reconfigure their thinking about reconciliation with God around a new vision, the life, death, and resurrection of Christ.

Letter to Romans was written by Apostle Paul in Corinth dealing with the Jewish understanding of the 'earthly' Jesus as presented by the mother church of James in Jerusalem as compared to his 'divine' view presented to the Gentiles with Romans being the most complete statement of basic Christian truths. It is Paul's manifesto that faith in Christ, is the only grounds for man's acceptance by God.

Paul pulls no punches when he describes the state the world is in (1:18-32). Everyone stands condemned by God's standards even the Jews who have the privilege of knowing God's law but still cannot keep it (2:3-20). But God offers mankind a new life because Jesus, on the Cross, has served the sentence for our sins (Chapter 5). We are free to make a fresh start with all the power of God at our disposal (Chapter 6-8). God's forgiveness and love will spur us on to live up to our new calling; with the Good News meant to transform human relationships so as to treat all mankind as equals and with respect.
59 CE

Apostle Paul returned to Jerusalem in an effort to reach a compromise with the mother church of James on doctrinal issues. As a peace offering, he was bringing a sizeable collection of money to Jerusalem from his congregations in Asia Minor which he planned to lay at the feet of James and Peter because he and his Gentile assemblies owed their love and support to the mother church but not their obedience. By bringing the money offering, Paul believed that his 'vision' of Jesus *being* and abandonment of Torah law would be found acceptable to church elders thereby unifying the church.

For both James and Peter, Paul's view that Jesus should be worshipped as "son of God" coupled with his money offering appeared to them as being nothing more than pagan-style temple worship. As recorded by Pope Clement of Rome (88-99CE) in *Homilies and Recognitions,* a heated argument broke out between Apostle Paul and James, with Paul physically attacking James and throwing him down the temple steps causing James to be badly injury. Rescued by his elders, James was rushed to safety with Paul being arrested for causing a major riot in Jerusalem. With a body guard of several hundred Roman soldiers, Paul was whisked off to Caesarea to await trial which was to be held in Rome before emperor Nero as requested by Apostle Paul.

Because Paul's theology was soundly rejected by the Jerusalem church, all links of Apostle Paul to the Antioch assembly of Peter, which had given him the authority to preach the Good News, was severed with Paul being was ex-communicated from the Jerusalem church for proclaiming that Jesus was God on earth and abandonment of Torah law. Effort to remove Apostle Paul from the church was led by Jude, younger brother of Jesus.

60 CE

Matthew Annas, was martyred in Nadabah, Parthis.

Jesus traveled to Malta via the island of Crete accompanied by both Peter and Luke. They boarded a second ship and sailed to Rome, arriving on Easter Sunday with their group going to the communal center near the Appian Way. *(Protoevancelium of James; Bodmer Papyrus; Suetonius).*

61 CE

Lazarus, brother of Mary Magdalene, was martyred in Caistor, Lincolnshire, England.

According to Tertullian (160 – 225 CE), Apostle Paul was beheaded in Rome for the riots he caused in Jerusalem with details of the event given in letters written by Lactantius, Jerome, and Sulpicius Severus.

62 CE

James, brother of Jesus, was martyred in Jerusalem with his death causing a riot that lit the fuse of the Jewish-Roman War in 66 CE. By order of high priest Annas, James, was stoned to death thereby breaking Roman law as only Rome could sanction a death sentence. In *Memoranda,* Hegesippus describes the death of James:

> Control of the church passed together with the Apostles, to the brother of the Lord, James, whom everyone from the Lord's time till our own has named the Just, for there were many Jameses, but this one was holy from his birth; he drank no wine or intoxicating liquor and ate no animal food; no razor came near his head; he did not smear himself with oil, and he took no bath. He alone was permitted to enter the holy of holies in the temple, for his garments were not of wool but of linen. He used to enter the sanctuary alone, and was often found on his knees beseeching forgiveness for the people. Because of his unsurpassable righteousness he was called the Just fulfilling the declaration of the prophets regarding him.
>
> Representatives of the seven Jewish sects already described by me asked him what was meant by "the door to Jesus," and he replied that Jesus was the Savior. Some of them came to believe that Jesus was the Christ: the sects mentioned above did not believe either in a resurrection or in one who is coming to give every man what his deeds deserve, but those who did come to believe did so because of James. Since therefore many even of the ruling class believed, there was an uproar among the Jews and the scribes and Pharisees, who said there was a danger that the entire people would expect Jesus as the Christ. So they collected and said to James, "Be good enough to restrain the people, for they have gone astray after Jesus in the belief that he is the Christ. Be good enough to make the facts about Jesus

clear to all who come for the Passover day, so make it clear to the crowd that they must not go astray as regards Jesus: the whole people and all of us accept what you say. So take your stand on the temple parapet, so that from that height you may easily be seen, and your words audible to the whole people, for because of the Passover all the tribes have come together and the Gentiles too.

So the scribes and Pharisees made James stand on the sanctuary parapet and shouted to him, "Just one, whose word we all obliged to accept, the people are all going astray after Jesus who was crucified; so tell us what is meant by the 'door to Jesus.'" James replied as loud as he could, "Why do you question me about the Son of Man? I tell you he is sitting in heaven at the right hand of the great power, and he will come on the clouds of heaven." Many were convinced and gloried in James' testimony, crying, "Hosanna to the Son of David!"

Then again the scribes and Pharisees said to each other, "We made a bad mistake in affording such testimony to Jesus. We had better go up and throw him down, so that they will be frightened and not believe him." "Ho, ho!" they called out, "even the Just one has gone astray!" – fulfilling the prophecy of Isaiah. "Let us remove the Just one, for he is unprofitable to us." So they went up and threw down the Just one. Then they said to each other, "Let us stone James the Just," and they began to stone him as in spite of his fall he was still alive.

In *Ecclesiastical History of the Church*, Eusebius recorded a letter written by Peter to James warning him that Paul was revising the meaning of his teaching to suit his own needs. Peter wrote:

Peter to James, the lord and bishop of the holy Church, under the Father of all, through Jesus Christ, wishes peace always. For some from among the gentiles have rejected my legal preaching, attaching themselves to certain lawless and trifling preaching of the man who is my enemy. And these things some have attempted while I am still alive, to transform my words by certain various interpretations, in order to the dissolution of the law; as though I also were of such mind, but did not freely proclaim it, which God forbid! For such a thing were to act in opposition to the law of God which was spoken by Moses, and was borne witness to by our Lord in respect to the eternal continuance; for thus he spoke: 'The heavens and the earth shall pass away, but one jot or one tittle shall in no wise pass from the law' (Homilies; chapter 2).

The last years of James's life were spent sending emissaries from the mother church in Jerusalem to the congregations of Apostle Paul in Asia Minor to correct doctrine being taught about his brother. The anger that Paul felt toward these "false apostles," "deceitful workers" and "servants of Satan" seeps like poison through the pages of Paul's 2nd Corinthians and Galatians.

Simon, brother of Jesus, was appointed 2nd bishop of the Jerusalem church.

Hershel Shanks, editor of *Biblical Archaeological Review* (BAR), announced in 2002 that an ossuary had been found in a private collection of Oded Golan bearing the inscription *Ya'akov bar-Yosef akhui diYeshua*, or in English, "James, son of Joseph, brother of Jesus," with this discovery being the first physical evidence ever found by archaeologists relating directly to the family of Jesus. To verify that this find was authentic, renowned Jewish archaeologist Eleazer Levi Sukenik determined by carbon dating that the burial box dated to 63 CE, while Andre' Lemaire, one of the world's greatest epigraphers, confirmed that the inscription was authentic and dating from the same time period. What puzzled scholars most, where did the ossuary come from? The James ossuary story was not the first archaeological dig to generate worldwide headlines about ancient ossuaries and their possible relationship to Jesus and his family.

Letter to Colossians was written to proclaim that the resurrection of Jesus created a new world order into which people could be transformed by means of baptism because the Christian existence is to be understood as an imitation of the suffering and sacrificial death of Jesus. In Paul's letter, one more step was required in God's triumphant campaign into the human world of sin to take place – Believers were required to leed godly lives.

Apostle Paul viewed both the moment when the divine nature of Jesus united with his human nature in the womb of Virgin Mary (incarnation) and Jesus coming back to life after death (resurrection) as of extreme importance to the restoration of mankind friendly relations with God (reconciliation) and a new start for humanity. In order to do that, God changed himself into human form so that Christ, who was innocent of sin, could suffer crucifixion's undeserved agony, dedicating it to the Father on humanity's behalf.

In 1098, in *Why God Became Man*, Anselm, Archbishop of Canterbury, focused on Apostle Paul's lines in Timothy 2:6 calling Jesus's death a "ransom," positioning humanity owing God a ransom of "satisfaction" for the insult of sin caused by man's ways thereby turning Paul's dissertation concerning the cross, into the Western Christian Church icon of love. Anselm wrote that Jesus "paid for the sinners what he owed not for himself" with this doctrine referred to as ***substitution atonement.***

In the Eastern Orthodox Church atonement is commonly referred to as the ***Recapitulation Theory*** which dates back to 318 CE when Athanasius, bishop of Alexandria, wrote his book *On The Incarnation* which beautifully explains the theory. Recapitulation teaches that Christ became human to heal mankind by uniting human nature to the Divine Nature in His person. Through incarnation, Christ took on human nature, becoming the Second Adam, and entering into every stage of humanity, from infancy to adulthood, uniting it to God. He then suffered death in order to enter Hades and destroy it. After three days, he came back to life and completed his task by destroying death. Christ changed every aspect of human nature – what actions Adam had done with this enabling all those who say yes to God to be perfectly united with the Holy Trinity through Christ's person. By destroying death, Christ reversed the consequences of the fall so that now, all believers can be resurrected.

French theologian Perter Abelard (1079 – 1142) presented Jesus atonement less as a compact between God the Father and God the Son and more in the hearts of believers clinging to the message of Jesus's life and the love most dramatically expressed in his willingness to die rather than renounce his calling. Jesus death became less central, because it was no longer the price for lifting the burden of sin; instead exhorting the congregation to strive towards reconciliation with the Father by emulating the Son's behavior with this doctrine known as ***exemplary atonement***.

---

63 CE

Roman historian Cornelius Tactius (56–120 CE), reported in *Histories* that Jesus was living in Rome.

64 CE

Peter was crucified in Rome three months after the disastrous fire that destroyed half of Rome.

In 1947, archaeologists carrying out a dig below the alter of St. Peter Basilica on Vatican Hill, found the remains of a red-walled building incorporating 2nd century funerary monuments. On the wall of the building was etched in Greek letters, *Petros Eni*, meaning "Peter is within" which led archaeologists to bones from a man standing five-feet-five-inches, robust in build, between the age of 60 and 70. Clinging particles of a purple cloth with interwoven gold threads corresponded to cloth recorded as being wrapped around Peter's body for burial at the time of Constantine.

In 1997, archaeologists discovered a large complex of buildings near the theater at Caesarea, seat of first-century Roman administration. The site included a palace with luxurious bathhouse, and large ornamental courtyards. In one building was a mosaic floor bearing the Latin inscription *Adiviorbus office Custodiar* meaning, "I came to this office; I shall be secure." For scholars, this is most likely the room that held Apostle Paul prior to his trip to Rome for sentencing.

In 2002, archaeologists discovered an 8-foot long marble sarcophagus, inscribed with the words "PAULO APOSTOLO MART" during excavations near Basilica of Saint Paul Outside the Walls on the Via Ostiensis with Pope Benedict XVI announcing that the find had been verified for its authenticity. Inside the sarcophagus was found purple material lined in gold with bone fragments of Apostle Paul.

65 CE

Andrew, brother of Peter, was crucified in Patrae, Greece.

Thaddaeus (aka Judas, brother of Jesus) was crucified in Ardae, Syria.

Akiva ben Yosef (50 -135 CE), scholar, sage and contributor to the *Mishnah* and *Midrash halakha*, based his anthropology upon the principle that man was created, not in the image of God, but after an idea which Plato calls "the first heavenly man". A strict monotheist, he protested against any comparison of God with mankind declaring the interpretation of the Hebrew text as meaning "like one of us" to be arrant blasphemy.

He was first to declare that the canticle *Song of Songs* referred to the marriage of Jesus to Mary Magdalene.

Rabbi Aqiba (50-135 CE), leading theologian in Jerusalem, was first to notice that Moses could not have written the Torah because it referred to kings who did not live until well after his death.

66 CE

First Jewish-Roman War (66 -70 CE) was fueled by the death of James, brother of Jesus and messianic prophecies according to which the Messiah would come out of Zion, would be a descendant of the house of David and would give law to all nations.

At the first move toward war, a swath of violence swept Syria with twenty thousand Jews being killed in a single hour at Caesarea by pagans with Jewish militias seeking revenge. From *Antiquities of the Jews*, Josephus describes the upheaval in Syria:

> A terrible upheaval sized the whole of Syria. Every city was divided into two camps: the safety of one was the destruction of the other. They passed their days in blood, their nights, more awful still, in fear. For through each city thought it had rid itself of Jews, they still had under suspicion those who were drawn to Jewish ways. No one would undertake to destroy this ambiguous group among them out of hand; but everyone feared it, half native, half alien as it was, as much as they feared the unequivocally foreign.

Before warfare broke out in Jerusalem itself, leaders of the Jerusalem church were warned to leave the city and go to Pella across the Jordan River and from there form a church government in exile. Due to the breakdown of normal life in Judah and dislocation of the mother church to Pella, church authority was taken over by the churches of Apostle Paul in Asia Minor which were not involved with the uprising. With the mother church dispersed and original founders departed from the scene, the only Christian 'sect' of Judaism remaining was that led by the Gentile followers of Apostle Paul. Without the mother church to guide the "Kingdom of God" movement, Paul's theology became the sole vehicle through which a new generation of Christians would be introduced to Jesus the Christ.

In *Jewish War*, Josephus describes the strength of the defenders of Jerusalem:

> The strength of the insurgents within the city was as follows: Simon had an army of 10,000 men, John had an army of 6,000 men, buy now the Zealots having 2,400 led by Eleazar, their former chief, and Simon son of Arinus.

He describes the destruction of the Jerusalem temple:

> While the holy house was on fire, everything was plundered that came to hand, and ten thousand of those that were caught were slain ... the flame was also carried a long way, and made an echo, together with the groans of those that were slain; and because this hill was high, and the works at the temple were very great, one would have thought that the whole city had been on fire. Nor can one imagine anything either greater or more terrible than this noise, for there was at once a shout of the Roman legions, who were marching all together and a sad clamor of the seditious, who were now surrounded with fire and sword.

He describes a meeting between the rebels and Titus at wars end:

> The tyrants and their followers, beaten on all sides in the war and surrounded, now invited Titus to parley. Titus, after charging his troops to keep check on their rage and their missiles and stationing Josephus beside him, addressed them first. "Well, sirs, are you at length sated with your country's woes: you who, without bestowing a thought on our strength or your own weakness, have through inconsiderate fury and madness lost your people, your city, and

your temple, and are yourselves justly doomed to perish; you who from the first, ever since Pompey reduced you by force never ceased from revolution, and have now ended by declaring open war upon the Romans? Did you rely on your numbers? On the fidelity of allies? On physical strength? On the solidity of your walls? On the determination of spirit and astuteness of your generals?

In 2004, Pool of Siloam was discovered during excavation work on a new sewer line in the lower city of Jerusalem. The pool measured 225 ft long pool by 135 ft wide with massive steps located on three sides; it was used for a ritual purification.

68 CE

John Mark, was martyred in Alexandria, Egypt by pagans by placing a rope around his neck and dragging him through the city until dead; they resented his efforts to turn them away from worship of their traditional gods.

Gospel of Mark was written to followers of Jesus who had no knowledge of Judean culture or language in the period following the first Jewish Roman War. It is as a story about Jesus' adult life, public activity, and his journey to Jerusalem ending with his crucifixion and rising on Easter morning. The gospel portrays Jesus as being a man of action, an exorcist, a healer, and a miracle worker. He keeps his identity secret in keeping with prophecy which foretold the fate of the messiah as a suffering servant. From the onset, followers of Jesus depended heavily on Jewish literature to support their convictions with those beliefs involving a nucleus of key concepts such as messiah; son of man; son of God; suffering servant; day of the Lord, and "kingdom of God" with the uniting of these ideas being the common thread of apocalyptic expectations of the day. Both Jews and followers of Jesus believed that the end of history was at hand, that God would soon come to punish their enemies and establish his own rule, and that they were at the center of his plans. In Mark, the virgin birth is not mentioned because the gospel is about Jesus' adult life, public activity, and journey to Jerusalem, ending with his death and rising on Easter morning. For scholars, Mark's story about Jesus has remained the most original, the one in which the fewest after-elements have been added by theologians.

69 CE

Bartholomew was martyred in Kalyan, India.

In *The Twelve Caesars*, Gaius Suetonius Tranquillus (69-122 CE) makes the following observations about the four emperors who followed Nero with all being installed in office in 69 CE.

Galba, 6th emperor of Rome was assassinated by Otho loyalists after a few months in office.

Otho, 7th emperor of Rome stabbed himself to death when Aulus Vitellius was marching on Rome.

Aulus Vitellius, 8th emperor of Rome was killed by his subjects for incompetency in office ending the worst year the empire had ever had.

Vespasian, 9th emperor of Rome was modest and lenient drawing parallels   to the first emperor of Rome, Augustus who was extraordinarily just
preferring clemency over revenge.

In the book *Vespasian,* Suetonius describes the emperor:

From the very beginning of his reign until the end, he was unpretentious and un-despotic, never making any effort to conceal his former mean estate, but often glorying in it. Indeed, when some tried to trace back his origin of the Flavian family to the founders of Reate and the comrade of Hercules, whose memorial still stands on the Via Salaria, he just laughed at them.
So far was he from any desire for adventitious decorations that, on the day of his triumph, exhausted by the slowness and tediousness of the procession, he could not keep from observing, "It serves me right for being so silly in my old age as to hanker after a triumph, as if it were either due to my ancestors or had ever been among my own ambitions."

70 CE

Jude, brother of Jesus, was appointed 3rd bishop of the Jerusalem church.

In *Life of Apollonius of Tyana,* we learn that emperor Vespasian (69 - 78 CE) met with his friend Apollonius (15 - 100 CE) because he had heard of the coming "kingdom of God" and wanted to know what that meant. According to Hegesippus (110 CE - 180), Vespasian questioned Simon, brother of Jesus, who was bishop of the Jerusalem church. After learning that the kingdom was not of this world, Vespasian issuing an edict putting a stop to the persecution of the Christian church.

71 CE

Acts of Paul and Thecia is the story of a women's voice in church hierarchy which meant that salvation was something found within oneself through an independent life of teaching and healing in the Christ movement. It is a story about a 17-year old girl named Thecia who lived in a small village who heard Apostle Paul preach and was riveted. She was to be married against her will with the weight of her mother's expectations upon her because by law she had no right to follow her own dictates, until she heard a call from inside herself. She began to move in her own direction. She began to go against social expectations of a girl which was considered the inferior sex in her time. She began to do what her heart was telling her to do with this being an affront to those in power. She refused to validate any authority outside of her. At the end of the story, she baptized herself because she realized she could. She realized that all along it was within her, she had the power to save herself and she did.

72 CE

Didymus Thomas, also known as Crown Prince Philip, was martyred at the behest of Hindu priests in Muziris, India.

75 CE

Prayer of Apostle Paul seeks healing, gives deep praise, and wishes for unity with God and Jesus. The prayer weaves together the gestures of praise and request. The one who prays seeks a deep union with Jesus Christ as God's blessed, chosen, and firstborn.

76 CE

Epistle of James central theme is that followers of Jesus must act out their beliefs as directed by the commandments and to help one another through works and good deeds. The ethical content of the letter is directly parallel to the teaching of Jesus found in *Gospel Sayings of Quelle* when James declared:

> "Be doers of the word, and not hearers only, deceiving yourselves. For if anyone is a hearer of the word and not a doer, he is like a man observing his natural face in a mirror; for he observes himself, goes away, and immediately forgets what kind of man he was" (1:22-24).

Scholars believe that in this letter we have an actual reflection of the "kingdom of God" movement with its full political and social implications. It focusses on both social morals and the integrity of people.

77 CE

For scholars, fall of Jerusalem marked the end of the Apostolic Age because the original disciples of Jesus had departed from the scene with the churches that they founded passed on to new hands.

79 CE

Titus Flavius Vespasianus became 10th emperor of Rome (79 CE -81). Titus was the eldest son of Vespasian. In *The Twelve Caesars* Suetonius writes:

> Titus was extremely adept at the art of war and peace flourishing as a commander under his father in Judea when he took over the siegeof Jerusalem. As emperor, he tried to be magnanimous and always heard petitions with an open mind. And after going through a day having not granted any favors, he commented "I have wasted a day."

80 CE

Philip was crucified in the in Hierapolis, Egypt.

Letter to Ephesians is an exhortation for living in the church; that the death and resurrection of Jesus created a new human order but with a new twist:

"Even when we are dead through our trespasses, God made us alive together in Christ and raised us up with Him and seated us with Him in heavenly places in Christ Jesus."

Second Letter to Corinthians is a defense of Apostle Paul's ministry which had come under attack by emissaries sent by the Jerusalem church. Paul's vision of Jesus was of one who had changed the human condition which applied before by creating the concept of Old and New covenant with Adam representing the Old and Jesus representing the New to anchor his mission to the Gentiles in the epic tradition of Israel.

Second Letter to the Thessalonians was written because the congregation had grown concerned over those who had already died wondering if they would share in the glory of the Second Coming. The author argues that the end is not coming right away, that an uprising will first occur with an Antichrist-like figure appearing who will take his seat in the temple and declare himself God. Only then will Jesus come to "destroy him with the breath of his mouth" (2:3-8).

Gospel According to Hebrews presents the tradition of Jesus' pre-existence in the world, baptism, temptation, and resurrection appearance. It does not mention the 'virgin birth' because the first followers of Jesus believed that he was human, born to Joseph and Mary in a normal fashion and that he was adopted by God at the Jordan River; that he met with his brothers as part of the council of Twelve at the Last Supper; that James, as leader of the Jerusalem church arguing in favor of obedience to Jewish law. Hebrews
Is built on a two-tiered universe – an earthly sanctuary with its priesthood in Jerusalem compared to Jesus's heavenly priesthood due to the sacrifice he made on the cross. Having spiritually ascended with Jesus, his followers are now greater than Israel – they are now rivals to the emperor.

81 CE

Titus Flavius Domitianus became 11th Emperor of Rome (81 CE-96).

82 CE

Early church chronicler Heggesipus (69-122CE), in *Hypomnemata,* reported that Jesus had passed due to natural causes in southern France.

In 1996, a dramatic story broke in the *London Sun Times* that "Jesus' Family Tomb was Discovered" in 1980 during a construction project in East Talpiot but was never brought to public attention because of political implications. After the Israeli Antiquities Authority (IAA) removed and cataloged the ten ossuaries, the tomb was resealed and construction restarted. Of the ten boxes cataloged, seven were inscribed with the following names:

Jesus, son of Joseph
Judas, son of Jesus
Mariemne
James, brother of Jesus
Maria
Jose
Matya

The tomb, located halfway between the Old City of Jerusalem and Bethlehem was found when TNT was detonated by a construction crew putting up a new apartment complex. Upon discovery of the tomb, the construction site was shut down so that Israeli archaeologist Yosef Gath and Simon Gibson from IAA could verify the sight. For Gath, what made the tomb remarkable was not the grouping of the names found on the ossuary, but the fact that the ossuaries came from a documented and controlled archaeological context, with the bones still intact so that the tomb and its remains could be scientifically studied to determine if the various persons found were related to each other by birth. For this reason, Gath had the ossuaries moved from the tomb site to the Rockefeller Museum in Jerusalem for safekeeping, with the bones being reburied outside Jerusalem, as per Jewish custom. In 2004, Charles Pellegrino, who took part in the research, wrote to his friend Father Mervyn Fernando in Sri Lanka, asking if it would be possible to find and test the remains of Jesus, seeing that he was resurrected by God. From the book *The Jesus Family Tomb* by Jacobovici and Pellegrino, Father Mervyn responded to the inquiry on December 14:

Dear Charles,

Your query is very interesting, though hypothetical.

The Gospels which relate to the life of Jesus were probably composed between 75 CE and 110 CE. Among the earliest New Testament writings are some letters of St. Paul. The "classical locus" about the resurrection of the body in St. Paul's first letter to Corinthians, end of chapter 15, verse 33 onward. What he says there would apply to theresurrection of Christ, too That is, the risen body of Christ is a spiritual one, not the material/ physical one he had in his lifetime. That physicalbody would have perished, and if any parts of it are recovered/ identified, it would in no way effect the reality of his resurrection. Warm andheartfelt greetings for a joyful Christmas and a New Year full of divineblessings.

Mervyn

In 2007, Emmy award-winning journalist Simcha Jacobovici, along with film producer James Cameron of Titanic and Avatar fame, put together a team of scholars and forensic archaeologists and visited Jerusalem to produce a feature film to be viewed on Discovery Channel, titled *The Lost Tomb of Jesus,* with their research for the documentary starting three years earlier. After reopening the tomb and visiting Rockefeller Museum to study the ossuaries, they came to the following conclusion concerning the ossuaries:

Inscription "Jesus, son of Joseph" refers to the burial box of Jesus of Nazareth,

Inscription "Judah, son of Jesus" refers to Jesus and Mary Magdalene's oldest son;

Inscription "Mariamne" is for Mary Magdalene as she is described by the Greek Orthodox Church, meaning that she could only be housed in the Jesus' family tomb if she and Jesus were married as reported in several gospels. It also means that Mary Magdalene returned to the Jordan Valley from France after her missionary activity was finished as reported in Acts of Philip.

Inscription James, brother of Jesus, refers to Jesus brother James, 1st bishop of the Jerusalem church..

Inscription "Maria" refers to Mary, mother of Jesus, as found in the Gospel of Matthew;

Inscription "Jose" refers to Jesus' brother Joseph as found in the Gospel of Mark;

Inscription "Matya" refers to Matthew, brother of Maria mother of Jesus as mentioned in the Gospel of Matthew.

Statistician Andrey Feuerverger of the University of Toronto, who was brought into the research project, believes that the odds of the Talpiot Tomb being the true resting place of Jesus and his family are 99.9 percent probable as supported by modern scientific testing method.

84 CE

The Story of Joseph and his wife Aseneth is a compilation of ancient writings found by Zacharias Rhetor, bishop of Mytilene, on the Greek island of Lesbos. In the book titled *The Lost Gospel,* scholars Jacobovici and Wilson argue that the manuscript tells about the marriage of Jesus to Mary Magdalene. The symbolism associated with Joseph cannot be ignored. He is a savior-figure, a Jew who saves his people, is assumed to be dead but turns up alive being a king of sorts. The symbolism associated with Aseneth cannot be ignored. She comes from a wealthy family, partakes of a magical honeycomb with bees representing wisdom, immortality, fidelity, and industry. But how can it be that Artemis is not mentioned in the Bible? In the land of Canaan she was called Asherah. In the land of Phrygia, she was called Rhea. In the land of Egypt she was called Isis. In early Christianity, Mary Magdalene, a Phoenician priestess of Isis, was highly esteemed by Syriac Christians. Isis was first worshipped in Egypt with the worship later spreading throughout the Greco-Roman world. Isis was worshipped as being the mother of mankind and wife of Elyon.

On a purely historical level, this story should not surprise the modern reader as marriage and bearing children were expected of all Jewish men, then and now. If Jesus had not been married, the New Testament would have commented it if for no other reason than to explain and defend his unusual behavior. If Jesus had not married and had a male child he could not have assumed the messianic title of David because the bloodline must be maintained for future generations. Knowledge of Jesus' marriage went underground because the first centuries of Christianity were a gut-wrenching battle between various factions of Jesus followers who were trying to best understand who he was – the man, his mission, and his message.

Gospel of Matthew was written to Greek-speaking Jews living in Antioch, Syria. The community was facing pressure from the emerging pharisaic movement in the Galilee region, with the result being that Jews were now siding with the Pharisees and the followers Jesus were being marginalized. The divine nature of Jesus was a major issue within the Matthaeus community, the critical element separating them from their Jewish neighbors who held an earthly view of him. Where Mark begins with Jesus' baptism and temptation, Matthew goes back to Jesus' origins, showing him to be son of God from birth and the fulfillment of Hebrew Bible messianic prophecy. The author of Matthew composed his gospel by inter-weaving the teachings of Jesus found in *Gospel Sayings of Quelle, Gospel of Thomas*, and Mark's story and then adding sayings and stories of his own. Matthew tells how the promised messiah, is killed, and raised from the dead. It tells how he was born from the long line of Abraham and David with an unbroken genealogy that continued through the exile and restoration of Israel to end with Joseph and Mary and the miraculous birth of Jesus, who was God's Messiah. Matthew's story, was directed to a Jewish audience citing the "virgin birth" as being the fulfillment of the prophecy with Isaiah claiming that the story refers to a specific child being born from the bloodline of King David to be sent by God to save his people with Jesus' genealogy making the point that he was a direct descendant of Abraham going directly to God as being his father. In Matthew, the title "Son of David" identifies Jesus as the Messiah sent to Israel alone. As "son of Man" he will return to judge the world. As "son of God," Jesus is God revealing himself through his son. The gospel reflects on the conflicts taking place between the author's community and other Jewish believers. The author of Matthew wanted Jesus to be viewed as being "Jew of the Jews" whereas Luke's gospel, which was directed to a Gentile audience, emphasized his relationship with the whole human race. Luke traces Jesus lineage from Adam all the way through Joseph. The two distinctively different birth stories make scholars believe that the gospel message of Jesus' birth was intended for two distinctly different audiences – the Jews of the Jerusalem church and the Gentiles of the church of Apostle Paul in diaspora. In Matthew it says the following about the virgin birth:

> Now the birth of Jesus Christ was as follows: after his mother Mary was betrothed to Joseph, *before they came together, she was*

found with child of the Holy Spirit. Then Joseph her husband, being a just man, and not wanting to make her a public example, was minded to put her away secretly. But while he thought about these things, behold, an angel of the Lord appeared to him in a dream, saying, "Joseph, son of David, do not be afraid to take to you Mary your wife, for that which is conceived in her is of *the Holy Spirit* (1:18-20).

In ancient Hebrew, the word for a "young woman of child bearing age" was *almah* which scribes incorrectly translated to mean "virgin" in a modern sense of the word which has nothing to do with virginity. The Nazarene rule for marriage dictated a celibate lifestyle until such time as to guarantee that the Messiah would be born in the month of September – the month of Atonement (Jesus was born March 2). If it happened that during the betrothal period, but before the first wedding took place, passions ran too high and a child was conceived, it would be said that "a virgin had conceived." In the case of Joseph and Mary, before the first wedding took place *(before they came together),* Mary conceived with Joseph committing a breach of Essene wedding rules. Joseph taking advice from the Holy Spirit stayed with Mary. In ancient Mediterranean cultural, an individual's identity was determined by some aspect of their role played in society. When John the Baptist identified Jesus as being the Messiah, the combination of priest and messiah equated to the title of "Holy Spirit." For scholars, because Jesus could be referred to "Holy Spirit", based upon his credentials, so too, could Joseph, at the time of Jesus' birth be referred to as the "Holy Spirit". There were strong reasons in the first century why a story of non-virginal conception of Jesus should be promoted in the Hellenistic world. Pagan worship included the cult of a virgin. The name varied in different places but the myth expressed the Greek desire to separate the spiritual from the material world with Jesus having to compete with the likes of Zeus.

In Gospel of Matthew is found the 'Great Commandment' which is the center piece of Jesus' teaching. For scholars, Matthew is considered the most accurate gospel defining the Jewish teachings of Jesus.

And one of them, a lawyer, asked Jesus a question to test him. "Teacher, which are the great commandments in the Law?" And Jesus said to him, "You shall love the Lord your God with all your heart and with all your soul and with all your mind. This is the great and first commandment. And a second is like it: "You shall love your neighboras yourself. On these two commandments depend all the Law and the Prophets" (2:35-40).

86 CE

Luke, the evangelist, died in Boeotia, Greece with his tomb located in Thebes. For scholars, Luke wrote to proclaim, persuade, and to interpret; he did not write to preserve historical records for posterity.

90 CE

Clement, bishop of Rome (88-99 CE), in *Letter to the Corinthians*, wrote about the jealousy that was surrounding the missions of Apostle Paul and Peter as they argued over the 'being' of Jesus as each faction was trying to steal converts from the other due to new lessons being taught.

Gospel of Luke is the only non-Jewish text in the New Testament and, as such, emphasizes the Gentile version of Christianity as espoused by Apostle Paul. The gospel was written to a Gentile congregation, with the text reflecting on the history of the Jesus movement and how far it had come since the days when the Jesus community was founded. For scholars, Luke used Mark as his primary source for the narrative of Jesus' public life with 90 percent of Mark appearing in Matthew and two-thirds of Mark in Luke. This is the reason the gospels known as Mark, Matthew, and Luke are called the synoptic gospels with both Mathew and Luke being significantly expanded over Mark making additional theological points. Luke built his story around a different savior. By his time, Jerusalem and its temple had been razed to the ground. The revolution that Luke's savior brings is compassion to all those who acknowledge the place of Jesus and his church as being God's plan. Luke's historical value is much weaker than either Mark or Matthew.

The gospel is a story about the origin, ministry, death, resurrection, and ascension of Jesus. For Luke, the life of Jesus was a significant moment in history because it marked the point in time when God's spirit became available to all people, not just the Jews, and that the life of Jesus was important because the Spirit was upon him. Because the Gentile author of Luke was not familiar with Jewish custom and scripture, his description of the virgin birth, contradicts the description given by the author of Matthew who was a Jew. Luke writes:

> Now in the sixth month *(of Mary's pregnancy)* the angel was sent by God to a City of Galilee named Nazareth (1:26). To a virgin *(young girl)* betrothed to a man whose name was Joseph, of the house of David. The virgin's name was Mary (1:27). Then the angel *(Levite priest)* said to her, "Do not be afraid, Mary, for you have found favor with God (1:30). "And behold, you will conceive in your womb and bring forth a Son, and shall call His name Jesus (1:31) …. Now Jesus Himself began His ministry at about thirty years of age, being the son of Joseph, the son of Heli (3:23).

The author of Luke needed to define the position of Christians in relation to two social and political entities, the Roman Empire and Judaism. The author makes it clear that the rulers of this world had obtained their power from Satin. Because Christian loyalty is only to God, the world will be transformed into the "kingdom of God" which will be ruled by Christ the king. The author also makes it clear that the earliest followers of Jesus were Jews and that they had rejected him. By the time the gospel was written, a majority of Christ-followers were Gentiles living in exile with the Christian mission now being placed in the hands of the followers of Apostle Paul. Gospel of Matthew and Luke were both designed to convey understandings of Jesus. Yet while many details differ between the two stories, both accounts have some important points in common:

- The human parents of Jesus are Mary and Joseph (Matthew 1:18; Luke 1:27).

- Mary and Joseph are in the engagement stage of marriage and are not yet living together (Matthew 1:18; Luke 1:26).

- Joseph is a descendent of King David (Matthew 1:16; Luke 1:27).

- Levite priest (Angel) announces the forthcoming birth of Jesus (Matthew 1:20-23; Luke 1:30-35).

- Conception of Mary's child is not through intercourse (Matthew 1:24-25; Luke 1:34) but through the Holy Spirit (Mathew 1:18, 20; Luke 1:35).

- Angel (Levite priest) declared that the child is to be named Jesus (Matthew 1:21; Luke 1:31).

- Angel (Levite priest) asserts that Jesus is to be a savior (Matthew 1:21-23; Luke 2:11).

- Birth takes place after Mary and Joseph became engaged (came together) (Matthew 1:24-25; Luke 2:5-6).

- Jesus' birth takes place in Bethlehem (Matthew 2:1; Luke 2:2-6).

- Birth is related to the reign of Herod the Great 37 – 4 BC (Matthew 2:1; Luke 1:5).

- Jesus is reared in Nazareth (Matthew 2:23; Luke 2:39).

92 CE

Bishop Clement of Rome said the following about Apostle Paul in *First Epistle of Clement to the Corinthians*, 5:5-6:

> By reason of jealousy and strife Paul by his example pointed out the prize of patient endurance. After he had been seven times in bonds, he had been driven into exile, had been stoned, had preached in the East and in the West, he won the noble renown which was the reward for his faith, having taught righteousness unto the world and having reached the farthest bonds of the West; and when he had borne his testimony before the rulers, so he departed from the world and went unto the holy place, having been found a notable pattern of patient endurance.

93 CE

Roman historian Suentonius (69 – 122 CE) reported that Jesus was living in Rome having survived the crucifixion.

94 CE

John of Zebedee was exiled to the island of Patmos by Emperor Domitian (51 -96 CE). While in exile, John wrote *Revelation of Jesus Christ.* He returned home to Ephesus two years later under the rein of Emperor Nerva Pertinax. He died of natural causes in 96 CE.

95 CE

Emperor Domitian (81 - 96 CE) believed that Christians were "atheists" meaning that they refused to worship the gods of the empire with this new sect of Judaism being radically incompatible with paganism.

First Letter of Peter presents the concept that the Christian church is a network of sister congregations and that Christ is the cornerstone of the church so that all members of the community must behave properly.

Revelation of Jesus Christ was written by John, son of Zebedee, while in exile on the Island of Patmos off the coast of Turkey. In her book titled *Revelations,* Elaine Pagel, professor of religion at Princeton University, makes the following observation:

> Revelation is not only the strangest book in the Bible it is the most controversial. Instead of stories and moral teaching of Jesus, it offers only visions, dreams and nightmares.

In *Revelation: Four Views, Revised and Updated,* Dr. Robert G. Clouse, Professor of Religion Emeritus at Indiana State University comments:

> Revelation is a unique book, in that a person seems either to make everything of it or else to make nothing of it.

For scholars, the first step toward gaining an understanding of *Revelation of Jesus Christ* is to recognize that it is an epistle written to a particular group of Christians, bearing a message relevant to them at the time it was written. Revelation's message is written in the style of apocalyptic literature which was popular between 200 BCE and 100 CE. The book was written during a time of great persecution by emperor Nero (54-68 CE) in the city of Rome and emperor Domitian (81-96 CE) throughout the empire to encourage believers that, even if they should be called upon to suffer, or even die for their faith, vindication was sure to follow in the not too distant future.

The book opens as John, tells how he was "in the Spirit" when he suddenly heard the loud voice of Jesus speaking to him announcing that God is about to make war on the evil powers that have taken over the world and that ultimately God will prevail, throwing evildoers into a lake of eternal fire, while at the same time welcoming the righteous into his kingdom. The book is considered wartime literature as John witnessed the first Jewish-Roman War when militant Jews, fired with religious fervor, attached Roman soldiers in the name of God as a result of Rome's occupation of Judah. Followers of Jesus, who viewed him as being the Messiah, expected him, like Judas Maccabee to militarily lead Israel to victory over the hated Romans and reestablish God's kingdom in a New Jerusalem and eventually over the whole world. When Jesus was crucified they were in shock. How could the Messiah be vanquished? John was one of those who insisted that Jesus would reappear and vanquish his enemies as God's chosen ruler. Taking heart, John saw the conquering messiah, standing before God's throne appearing as "a lamb who had been slaughtered having seven horns and seven eyes, which are the seven spirits of God." John began to see heavenly secrets unfold to show the coming end time. Believers, who had lived through great persecution in Christ' name were now standing before God's throne, waiting to enter Paradise where Jesus would guide them to the water of life.

The following translation of Revelation of Jesus Christ is based on most recent research combined with the teaching of *Preterist School of Thought* which believes that John's visions are of contemporary events of his time combined with *Idealist School of Thought* which believes that the great themes of "good over evil" are played out repeatedly throughout John's visions without reference to a single historical event being made.

CHAPTER 1:

The Revelation of Jesus Christ, which God gave Him to show His servants *(followers)* – things which must shortly take place. And He sent it by His angle to his servant John who bore witness to the word of God, and to the testimony of Jesus Christ, to all things that he saw. Blessed is he who reads and those who hear the words of this prophecy, and keep those things which are written in it; for the time is near *(judgment day)*. John, to the 'seven' churches which are in Asia: Grace to you and peace from Him *(God)* who is *(ruler of the world)* and who was *(creator of the world)* and who is to come and from the seven Spirits *(spirit of the Lord - of wisdom - of understanding - of council - of might - of knowledge - of fear of the Lord: Isaiah 11:2)* who are before His throne, and from Jesus Christ, the faithful witness, the firstborn from the dead *(first resurrected)* and the ruler over the kings of the earth. To Him who loved us and washed us from our sins in His own blood *(Jesus's death on the cross represents a second Exodus as Israel was first delivered by God from bondage in Egypt whereas Christ delivers 'believers' from the bondage to sin)*, and has made us kings and priests *(redeemed humanity)* to His God and Father, to Him be glory and domination forever and ever. Amen. Behold, He *(Jesus)* is coming with cloud, and every eye will see Him, even they who pierced Him *(Romans)*. And all tribes of the earth will mourn *(judgment is coming)* because of Him. Even so, Amen. I am the Alpha and the Omega, the Beginning and the End says the Lord, "who is and who was and who is to come, the Almighty." I, John, both your brother and companion in the tribulation and the kingdom *(Christian belief)* and patience of Jesus Christ *(rejection of physical violence)*, was on the island that is called Patmos for the word of God and for the testimony of Jesus Christ. I was in the Spirit on the Lord's Day *(Sunday)*, and I heard behind me a loud voice *(Jesus)*, as of a trumpet, saying, "I am the Alpha and the Omega, the First and the Last and, "What you see, write in a book *(Revelation)* and send it to the seven churches which are in Asia: to Ephesus, to Smyrna, to Pergamos, to Thyatira, to Sardis, to Philadelphia, and to Laodicea." Then I turned to see the voice that spoke with me. And having turned, I saw seven golden lampstands *(Jerusalem temple)*, and in the midst of the seven lampstands One like the Son of Man *(Jesus)* clothed with a garment down to the feet *(standard peasant attire)* and girded about the chest with gold bands *(high rank)*. His head and hair were white like wool, as white as snow *(honor, age and purity)*, and His eyes like a flame of fire *(piercing vision)*; His feet were like fine brass refined in a furnace *(irresistibility of his judgment)*, and His voice as the sound of many waters *(wisdom throughout antiquity)*; He had in His right hand seven stars *(clergy of the seven churches)*, out of His mouth went a sharp two edged sword *(truth and wisdom)*, and His countenance was like the sun shining *(power, glory, and might)* in its full strength .... And when I saw Him, I fell at His feet as dead. But He laid His right hand on me, saying to me, "Do not be afraid; I am the First and the Last. "I am He who lives, and was dead *(Jesus)*, and behold, I am alive forevermore *(church lives on)*. Amen. And I have the keys of Hades and of Death *(Jesus brings eternal life to believers who are faithful unto death)*. Write the things which you have seen *(war)*, and the things which are *(persecution)*, and the things which will take place after this *(God's judgment)*. "The mystery of the seven stars which you saw in My right hand, and the seven golden lampstands: The seven stars *(clergy)* are the angels of the seven churches, and the seven lampstands which you saw are the seven churches."

CHAPTER 2:

"To the angel of the church of Ephesus write, 'These things says He who holds the seven stars in His right hand *(Jesus)*, who walks in the midst of the seven golden lampstands *(churches)*"I know your works *(reputation)*, your labor, your patience *(resistance to violence)*, and that you cannot bear those who are evil. And have tested those who say they are apostles *(apostate Jews)* and are not, and have found them liars *(they believe that they are not totally fee from the commandments brought down by Moses)*; and you have persevered and have patience, and have labored for My name's sake and have not become weary. Nevertheless I have this against you, that you have left your first love *(God is not pre-eminent in the congregation's life)*. Remember therefore from where you have fallen repent and do the first works *(love God and neighbor before yourself)* or else I will come quickly and remove your lampstand *(God will not protect them from the coming wrath)* from its place unless you repent. But this you have, that you hate the deeds of the Nicolaitans *(early Christian* sect who were followers of Nicolas the Deacon who was one of the seven first ordained deacons by Peter. Nicolaitans were considered heretical by the mainstream early Christian Church and were known in the cities of Ephesus and Pergamum. They lead lives of unrestrained indulgence, were indifference to the practice of adultery and eating things sacrificed to idols) which I also hate. He who has an ear, let him hear what the Spirit says to the churches. To him who overcomes, I will give to eat from the tree of life *(eternal life for the faithful)*, which is in the midst of the Paradise of God. And to the angel of the church in Smyrna write: 'These things say the First and the Last *(Jesus)*, who was dead, and came to life: I know your works, tribulation, and poverty and I know the blasphemy of those who say they are Jews and are not, but are a synagogue of Satin *(apostate Jews)*. Do not fear any of those things which you are about to suffer. Indeed, the devil *(Rome)* is about to throw some of you in prison, that you may be tested, and you will have tribulation ten days *(a short time)*. Be faithful until death, and I will give you the crown of life *(immortality)*. He who has an ear, let him hear what the Spirit says to the churches. He who overcomes shall not be hurt by the second death" *(eternal life exempts one from a second death)*. And to the angel of the church in Pergamos write, 'These things says He who has the sharp two-edged sword *(truth and wisdom)*: "I know your works, and where you dwell, where Satan's throne is *(Pergamos is the first city in Palestine to erect temples to Caesar Augustus, to Zeus, and to the serpent-god Asclepius)*. And you hold fast to My name, and did not deny My faith even in the days in which Antipas *(Bishop of Pergamm)* was My faithful martyr, who was killed among you *(92 CE during the reign of Emperor Domitian)*, where Satan dwells. But I have a few things against you, because you have those who hold to the doctrine of Balaam, *(son of Beor, a biblical character, a non-Israelite prophet who advocated idolatrous practices and sexual immorality)* who taught Balak *(son of Zippor, King of Moab)* to put a stumbling block before the children of Israel, to eat things sacrificed to idols *(un-kosher food)*, and to commit sexual immorality. Thus you have those who hold the doctrine of the Nicolaitans, which thing I hate. Repent or else I will come to you quickly and will fight against them with the sword of My mouth *(truth and wisdom)*. He who has an ear, let him hear what the Spirit says to the churches. To him who overcomes, I will give some hidden manna to eat *(Ancient Jewish tradition which states that when Jeremiah returns to Jerusalem, he will bring the Ark of the Covenant back with him and hold a great feast for all believers using the manna that is hidden in the ark).* And I will give him a white stone *(Token of vindication)* and on the stone a new name written *(repentant sinner)* which no one knows except him who receives it." "And to the angel *(clergy)*of the church of Thyatira write, 'These things says the Son of God, who has eyes like a flame of fire, and His feet like fine brass *(impending judgment).* I know your works, love, service, faith, and your patience; and as for your works, the last are more than the first. "Nevertheless I have a few things against you, because you allow that woman Jezebel *(woman of ill repute who worships pagan gods),* who calls herself a prophetess, to teach and seduce My servants to commit sexual immorality *(Jews marrying Gentiles thereby diluting the Hebrew race)* and eat things sacrificed to idols *(un-kosher food).* And I gave her time to repent of her sexual immorality *(paganism)*, and she did not repent *(convert to Christianity).* Indeed I will cast her into her sick bed *(bed of fornication)*, and those who commit adultery *(pagan belief)* with her into great tribulation, unless they repent their deeds. I will kill her children with death *(spiritual death)*, and all the churches shall know that I am He who searches the minds and hearts. And I will give to each one of you according to your works. Now to you I say, and to the rest of Thyatira, as many as do not have this doctrine *(pagan belief)*, who have not known the depths of Satan, as they say, I will put on you no other burden. But hold fast what you have *(little faith)* till I come. And he who overcomes, and keeps My works until the end, to him I will give power over nations. He shall rule them with a rod of iron; they shall be dashed to pieces like the potter's vessels' – as I also have received from my Father; and I will give him the morning star *(Jesus is the "hidden manna" promised to those who overcome sin).* Who has an ear, let him hear what the Spirit says to the Churches."

CHAPTER 3:

"And to the angel *(clergy)* of Sardis write: 'These things says He who has the seven Spirits of God and the seven stars *(churches):* "I know your works, that you have a name *(Christian)* that you are alive *(physical church)*, but you are dead *(spiritually).* Be watchful, and strengthen the things which remain, that are ready to die, for I have not found your works perfect before God. Remember therefore how you have received and heard the word; hold fast and repent *(church had gotten lazy).* Therefore if you will not watch, I will come upon you as a thief, and you will not know what hour I will come upon you. You have a few names even in Sardis who have not denied their garments *(a few are doing good works);* and they shall walk with Me in white, for they are worthy, He who overcomes *(laziness and arrogant)* shall be clothed in white garments, and I will not blot out his name from the Book of Life; but I will confess his name before My Father and before his angels. "He who has an ear, let him hear what the Spirit says to the churches." And to the angel *(clergy)* of Philadelphia write: 'These things says He who is holy, He who is true, He who has the key of David *(Jesus),* He who opens and no one shuts, and shuts and no one opens *(Jesus has the power to either admit or deny a person's entry into the king's house):* I know your works. See, I have set before you an open door *(opportunity to enter Paradise),* and no one can shut it; for you have a little strength, have kept My word, and have not denied My name. Indeed I will make those of the synagogue of Satan *(apostate Jews),* who say they are Jews and are not, but lie – indeed I will make them come and worship before your feet, and to know that I have loved you. Because you have kept My command to persevere, I also will keep you from the hour of trial which shall come upon the whole world, to test those who dwell on the earth. Behold, I am coming quickly! Hold fast what you have *(faith),* that no one may take your crown *(church will weather the storm).* He who overcomes, I will make him a pillar in the temple of My God, and he shall go out no more *(believers will no longer be persecute).* I will write on him the name of My God and the name of the city of My God, the New Jerusalem *(citizenship in a perfect world),* which comes down from heaven from My God. And I will write on him My new name *(Christian).* "He who has an ear, let him hear what the Spirit says to the churches." And to the angel *(clergy)* of the church of Laodiceans write: 'These things says the Amen, the Faithful and True Witness, the Beginning of the creation of God: I know your works, that you are neither cold or hot *(lack of zeal).* I wish you were cold or hot. So then, because you are lukewarm, and neither cold nor hot, I will vomit you out of My mouth *(this behavior will not be tolerated long).* Because you say, I am rich, have become wealthy, and have need of nothing – and do not know that you are wretched, miserable, poor, blind and naked *(wealth has a way of imparting a false sense of self- sufficiency)* – I counsel you to buy from Me gold refined in the fire *(character that has been refined by affliction),* that you may be rich; and white garments, that you may be clothed, that the shame of your nakedness may not be revealed; and anoint your eyes with eye salve *(church has a vision problem by worshipping money),* that you may see. As many as I loved, I rebuke and chasten. Therefore be zealous and repent. Behold, I stand at the door and knock. If anyone hears My voice and opens the door, I will come in to him and dine with him, and he with Me. To him who overcomes *(transformation)* I will grant to sit with Me on My throne, as I also overcame *(worldly needs)* and sat down with My Father on His throne. He who has an ear, let him hear what the Spirit says to the churches."

CHAPTER 4:

After these things I looked, and behold, a door standing open in heaven. And the first voice which I heard *(Jesus)* was like a trumpet speaking with me, saying, "Come up here, and I will show you things which must take place after this." Immediately I was in the Spirit and behold, a throne set in heaven, and One sat on the throne *(God).* And He who sat there was like a jasper *(crystal, pure like a diamond)* and a sardius stone *(red which calls to mind God's avenging wrath)* in appearance; and there was a rainbow *(mercy)* around the throne, in appearance like an emerald *(principle color of the rainbow).* Around the throne were twenty-four thrones, and on the thrones I saw twenty-four elders *(representatives the redeemed, glorified, and enthroned)* sitting clothed in white robes *(redemption);* and they had crowns of gold *(victory and joy)* on their heads. And from the throne proceeded lightening, thunder, and voices *(power and wisdom).* Seven lamps of fire *(holiness of the church)* were burning before the throne, which are the seven Spirits of God. Before the throne there was a sea of glass, like crystal. And in the midst of the throne, and around the throne, were four living creatures *(wild beasts, domesticated animals, human beings, and flying creatures)* full of eyes in front and in back. The first living creature was like a lion *(king of beasts),* the second creature like a calf *(king of domesticated animals),* the third had a face like a man *(intellectual creature)*, and the fourth was like a flying eagle *(king of birds)*. The four living creatures, each having six wings, were full of eyes around and within *(signifying the cherubim described in Ezekiel 1 and seraphim described in Isaiah 6)*. And they do not rest day or night, saying: "Holy, holy, holy, Lord God Almighty. Who was and is and is to come!" *(God created the world - God rules the world - God will judge the world)* Whenever the living creatures give glory and honor and thanks to Him who sits on the throne, who lives forever and ever, the twenty-four elders fall down before Him who sits on the throne and worships Him who lives forever and ever, and cast their crowns *(Victory and Joy)* before the throne saying: "You are worthy, O Lord, to receive glory and honor and power; for You created all things, and by Your will they exist and were created."

CHAPTER 5:

And I saw in the right hand *(power and glory)* of Him who sat on the throne, a scroll written *(redemptive plan for mankind)* and on the back sealed with seven seals *(plaques which were about to befall mankind)*. Then I saw a strong angel proclaiming with a loud voice *(Michael)*, "Who is worthy to open the scroll and to loose its seals?" And no one in heaven or on the earth or under the earth was able to open the scroll, or to look at it. So I wept much, because no one was found worthy to open and read the scroll, or to look at it. But one of the elders said to me, "Do not weep, Behold, the Lion of the tribe of Judah *(Jesus)*, the Root of David *(royalty)*, has prevailed to open the scroll and to loose its seven seals" *(God's dealings with sinful Roman Empire can now begin)*. And I looked and behold, in the midst of the throne and of the four living creatures, and in the midst of the elders, stood a Lamb *(Jesus)* as thought it had been slain, having seven horns *(omniscience)* and seven eyes, *(sign for omniscience)* which are the seven Spirits of God *(Spirit of wisdom - of understanding - of council- of might- of knowledge – of fear of the Lord)* sent out into all the earth. Then He came and took the scroll out of the right hand of Him who sat on the throne *(God)*. Now when He had taken the scroll, the four living creatures and the twenty-four elders fell down before the Lamb *(Jesus is acknowledged king)* each having a harp, and golden bowls full of incense, which are the prayers of the saints.

And they sang a new song *(New Covenant)* saying, "You are worthy to take the scroll, and open its seals; for You were slain, and have redeemed us to God by Your blood *(crucifixion)* out of every tribe and tongue and people and nation, and have made us kings and priests to our God and we shall reign on earth...

CHAPTER 6:

Now I saw when the Lamb opened one of the seals *(retribution begins)*; and I heard one of the four living creatures saying with a voice like thunder, "Come and see." And I looked and behold a white horse *(signifying war)*. He who sat on it *(death)* had a bow; and a crown *(conquest)* was given to him, and he went out conquering and to conquer. When He opened the second seal, I heard the second living creature saying, "Come and see." Another horse, fiery red *(bloodshed and death)* went out. And it was granted to the one who sat on it *(death)* to take peace from the earth, and the people should kill one another; and there was given to him a great sword *(truth and wisdom)*. When He opened the third seal, I heard the third living creature say, "Come and see." So I looked, and behold, a black horse *(famine and disease),* and he who sat on it *(Death)* had a pair of scales in his hand *(prices will skyrocket due to food and fuel shortages)*. And I heard a voice in the midst of the four living creatures saying, "A quart of wheat for a denarius, and three quarts of barley for a denarius; and do not harm the oil and the wine." *(luxury goods will not be in short supply for those who can afford them)*. When I opened the fourth seal, I heard the voice of the fourth living creature saying, "Come and see." So I looked, and behold, a pale horse *(pestilence, and disease)*. And the name of him who sat on it was Death and Hades followed with him. And power was given to them over a fourth of the earth *(Roman Empire only covered a portion of the world),* to kill with sword, with hunger, with death, and the beasts of the earth. When He opened the fifth seal, I saw under the alter *(animals had more value than those humans who were being persecuted)* the souls of those who had been slain for the word of God and for the testimony which they held. And they cried with a loud voice saying, "How long, O Lord, holy and true, until you judge and avenge our blood on those who dwell on earth?" Then a white robe *(redemption)* was given to each of them and it was said to them that they *(martyred)* should rest a little longer, until both the number of their fellow servants and their brethren, who would be killed as they were, was completed. I looked when He opened the sixth seal, and behold, there was a great earthquake, and the sun became black as sackcloth of hair, and the moon became like blood. And the stars of heaven fell to the earth, as a fig tree drops its late figs when it is shaken by a mighty wind. Then the sky receded as a scroll when it is rolled up, and every mountain and island was moved from its place *(this scene describes political chaos taking place in Rome as Christians were being slaughtered in mass by Emperor Nero)*. And the kings of the earth, the great men, the rich men, the commanders, the mighty men, every slave and every free man, hid themselves *(unrepentant sinners)* in the caves and in the rocks in the mountains, and said to the mountains and rocks, "Fall on us and hide us from the face of Him who sits on the throne and from the wrath of the Lamb! For the great day of His wrath has come, and who is able to stand?"

CHAPTER 7:

After these things I saw four angels standing at the four corners of the earth, holding the four winds of the earth *(God is in control of everything and can prevent things from happening until such time as the faithful can be accounted for)*, that each wind should not blow on the earth, on the sea, or on any tree. Then I saw another angel ascend from the east, having the seal of the living God *(power and glory)*. And He cried with a loud voice to the four angels – "Do not harm the earth, the sea, or the trees till we have sealed the servants of our God *(Passover story)* on their foreheads. And I heard the number of those who were sealed. One hundred and forty-four-thousand of all the tribes of the children of Israel were sealed. After these things I looked, and behold, a great multitude which no one could number, of all nations, tribes, and tongues, standing before the throne and before the Lamb, clothed with white robes *(redemption)*, with palm branches in their hands, and crying out with a loud voice, saying, "Salvation belongs to our God who sits on the throne, and to the Lamb!" .... Then one of the elders answered, saying to me, "Who are these arrayed in white robes, and where did they come from?" And I said to him, "Sir, you know." So he said to me, "These are the ones *(martyrs)* who come out of the great tribulation and washed their robes and made them white in the blood of the Lamb *(atoning death of Jesus Christ on the cross)*. Therefore they are before the throne of God, and serve Him day and night in His temple *(wherever believers meet to worship)*. And He who sits on the throne will dwell among them for the Lamb who is in the midst of the throne will shepherd them and lead them to living fountains of waters *(salvation)*. And God will wipe away every tear from their eyes."

CHAPTER 8:

When He *(Jesus)* opened the seventh seal, there was silence in heaven for about half an hour *(time needed to count the righteous)*. And I saw seven angels *(clergy of the seven churches)* who stand before God and to them were given seven trumpets *(church would announce the calamities that were about to befall unrepentant sinners)*. Then another angel, having a golden censer *(bowl used for vindication)*, came and stood at the alter. He was given much incense *(offering that would please God)* that he should offer it with the prayers of all the saints *(believers who had passed away)* upon the golden alter which was before the throne. And the smoke of the incense, with the prayers of the saints, ascended before God from the angel's hand. Then the angel took the censer, filled it with fire from the alter *(God had heard the prayers of the church)* and threw it to the earth. And there were noises, thunderings, lightenings, and an earthquake. So the seven angles who had the seven trumpets prepared themselves to sound. The first angel sounded: And hail and fire followed *(God's wrath)*, mingled with blood, and they were thrown to earth. And a third of the trees were burned up *(Roman Empire covered a portion of the earth)*, and all green grass as burned up. Then the second angel sounded and a great mountain *(city of Rome)* burning with fire was thrown into the sea, and a third of the sea became blood; And a third of the living creatures in the sea died, and a third of the ships were destroyed. Then a third angel sounded: and a great star fell from heaven like a burning torch, and it fell on a third of the rivers and on the springs of water. The name of the star was Wormwood *(affliction resulting from divine wrath)*. A third of the waters became wormwood, and many men died from the water, because it was made bitter. Then the fourth angel sounded: And a third of the sun was struck, a third of the moon, and a third of the stars, so that a third of them were darkened. A third of the day did not shine, and likewise the night. And I looked, and I heard an angel flying through the midst of heaven, saying with a loud voice, "Woe, woe, woe to the inhabitants of the earth because of the remaining blasts of the trumpets of the three angels who were about to sound!"

(First "woe" signifies sedition against Rome by the Jews; the second "woe" signifies the besieging of Jerusalem by the Roman army; third "woe" signifies the destruction of Jerusalem and the burning of the Temple during the first Jewish-Roman War in 66-70 CE)

CHAPTER 9:

Then a fifth angel sounded: And I saw a star fallen *(Angel who has been degraded and deprived of his rank - Satan)* from heaven to the earth. To him was given the key to the bottomless pit *(hell)*. And he opened the bottomless pit and smoke arose out of the pit like the smoke of a great furnace. So the sun and the air were darkened because of the smoke of the pit *(evil cloud men's minds and darken their understanding)*. Then out of the smoke locusts came *(moral and spiritual errors)* upon the earth. And to them was given power, as the scorpions of the earth have power. They were commanded not to harm the grass of the earth, or any green thing, or any tree *(God is in control of all things)*, but only the men who do not have the seal of God on their foreheads *(Christians)*. And they were not given authority to kill them, but to torment them for five months *(lifecycle of the locust)*. Their torment was like the torment of a scorpion when it strikes a man *(burns but it does not kill)*. In those days men will not seek death and will not find it; they will desire to die, and death will flee from them. The shape of the locusts were like horses *(Roman army)* prepared for battle. On their heads were crowns of something like gold *(false authority as the army did not represent God but only the emperor)*, and their faces were like the faces of men. They had hair like women's hair, and their teeth were like a lion's teeth. And they had breast-plates like breast-plates of iron *(invincibility)*, and the sound of their wings was like the sound of chariots with many horses running into battle. They had tails like scorpions and there were stingers in their tails *(Rome possessed powerful weapons)*. Their power was to hurt men five months *(a short period of time)*. And they had as king over them the angel of the bottomless pit *(Satan)*, whose name in Hebrew is Abaddon, but in Greek he has the name Apollyon *(destruction & death)*. One woe is past. Behold, still two more woes are coming after these things. Then the sixth angel sounded: and I heard a voice from the four horns of the golden alter which is before God *(prayers of the saints)*, saying to the sixth angel who had the trumpet, "Release the four angels bound at the great river Euphrates" *(Roman 10th legion from the east, led by Titus, who destroyed Jerusalem)* So the four angels, who had been prepared for the hour and day and month and year, were released to kill a third of mankind *(God was in control using the Roman army as a tool to perform his vindictive act)*. Now the number of the army of the horsemen was two hundred million; I heard the number of them. And thus I saw the horses in the vision: those who sat on them had breastplates of fiery red, hyacinth blue, and sulfur yellow; *(highly organized military force with military rank)* and the heads of the horses were like the heads of lions; and out of their mouths came fire, smoke, and brimstone *(death)*. By these three plagues a third of mankind was killed – by the fire and the smoke and the brimstone which came out of their mouths. For their power is in the mouth *(false doctrine)* and in their tails *(military power)*; for their tails are like serpents, having heads; and with them do harm. But the rest of mankind *(those who had not yet received the Word of God)*, who were not killed by these plagues, did not repent of the works of their hands *(pagans)*, that they should not worship demons, and idols of gold, silver, brass, stone, and wood which can neither see nor hear nor walk. And they did not repent of their murders or the sexual immorality or the thefts *(sinners come in all shapes, sizes, and degree of ungodliness)*.

CHAPTER 10:

I saw still another mighty angel *(Jesus)* coming down from heaven, clothed in a cloud *(divinity)*. And a rainbow was on his head and his face was like the sun, and his feet like pillars of fire *(judgment)*. He had a little book open in his hand *(God's redemptive plan)*. And he set his right foot on the sea and his left foot on the land *(God's message was for the entire world to hear),* and cried with a loud voice, as when a lion roars. When he *(Jesus)* cried out, seven thunders *(God's impending judgement)* uttered their voices. Now when the seven thunders uttered their voices I *(Jesus)* was about to write; but I heard a voice from heaven *(God)* saying to me, "Seal up the things which the seven thunders uttered, and do not write them"*(mankind will never fully understand the factors that determine the future).* The angel whom I saw standing on the sea and on the land *(Jesus)* raised up his hand to heaven and swore to Him who lives forever and ever, who created heaven and the things that are in it, the earth and the things that are in it, and the sea and the things that are in it, that there should be delay no longer *(God's retribution should begin),* but in the days of the sounding of the seventh angel, when he is about to sound, the mystery of God *(union of Jews and Gentiles into one body in Christ)* would be finished as He declared to His servants the prophets. Then the voice which I heard from heaven *(God)* spoke to me again and said, "Go, take the little book which is open in the hand of the angel who stands on the sea and on the earth. So I went to the angel *(Jesus)* and said to him, "Give me the little book." And he said to me, "Take and eat It; and it will make your stomach bitter, but it will be as sweet as honey in your mouth" *(while the gospel is glorious and sweet, its proclamation can be followed by persecution)* Then I took the little book out of the angel's hand and ate it, and it was sweet as honey in my mouth. But when I had eaten it, my stomach became bitter. And he *(Jesus)* said to me, "You must prophesy again about many peoples, nations, tongues, and kings" *(John must spread the Good News)*

.

CHAPTER 11:

Then I was given a reed like a measuring rod. And the angel stood, saying, "Rise and measure the temple of God, the Alter, and those who worship there. But leave out the court which is outside the temple, and do not measure it, for it has been given to the Gentiles." And they will tread the holy city underfoot *(not respect Jewish heritage)* for forty-two months *(length of Jesus's ministry).* And I will give power to my two witnesses *(Prophets Enoch & Elijah),* and they will prophesy one thousand two hundred and sixty days *(length of the first Jewish-Roman War in 66 CE),* clothed in sackcloth *(humility and penance).* These are the two olive trees *(Holy oil used by the Church in prayer)* and the two lampstands *(evangelists who traveled in pairs to spread the 'Light' of Jesus Christ)* standing before the God of the earth. And if anyone wants to harm them, fire proceeds from their mouth *(power of the gospel message)* and devours their enemies. And if anyone wants to harm them, he must be killed in this manner. These have power to shut heaven, so that no rain falls in the days of their prophecy; and they have power over waters to turn them into blood, and to strike the earth with all plagues, as often as they desire. When they finish their testimony, the beast *(Rome)* that ascends out of the bottomless pit will make war against them *(Jesus Christ and his Church),* overcome them, and kill them. And their dead bodies will lie in the street of the great city *(Jerusalem)* which spiritually is called Sodom and Egypt *(a city that abandoned its covenant made with God)* where also our Lord was crucified. Then those from the peoples, tribes, tongues and nations will see their dead bodies three and a half days, *(sign of incompleteness and imperfection)* and not allow their dead bodies to be put into graves. And those who dwell on earth *(politicians, wealthy, and the corrupt temple priests)* will rejoice over them, make merry and send gifts to one another, because these two prophets tormented those who dwell on the earth. Now after three and a half days the breath of life from God entered them and they stood on their feet, and great fear fell on those who saw them. And they heard a loud voice from heaven *(God)* saying to them "Come here." And they ascended to heaven in a cloud, and their enemies saw them. In the same hour there was a great earthquake *(destruction of Jerusalem by the Roman army)* and a tenth of the city fell. In the earthquake *(attack on Jerusalem)* seven thousand people were killed, and the rest were afraid and gave glory to the God of heaven. The second woe is past. Behold, the third woe is coming quickly *(destruction of the Temple).* Then the seventh angel sounded: And there were loud voices in heaven, saying, "The kingdoms of this world have become the kingdoms of our Lord and of His Christ, and He shall reign forever and ever!" *(Christianity became a stand-alone religion due to the destruction of the Jerusalem temple)* .... The nations were angry *(those being judged),* and Your wrath has come, and the time of the dead, that they should be judged and that You should reward Your servants the prophets and the saints, and those who fear Your name, small and great *(those who were made alive in the blood of Jesus Christ)*, and should destroy those who destroy the earth" *(Rome)*. Then the temple of God was opened in heaven, and the ark of His covenant was seen in His temple *(God's faithfulness to His covenant people)*. And there were lightenings, noises, thunderings, an earthquake, and great hail.

CHAPTER 12:

Now a great sign appeared in heaven: a woman *(Israel)* clothed with the sun, with the moon under her feet, and on her head a garland of twelve stars *(Tribes of Israel)*. Then being with child she cried out in labor and in pain to give birth. And another sign appeared in heaven, behold, a great, fiery red dragon *(Rome)* having seven heads *(universal authority]* and ten horns *(military strength)*, and seven diadems *(political authority)* on his heads. His tail drew a third of the stars of heaven and threw them to the earth *(Satan and his agents)*. And the dragon *(emperor)* stood before the woman *(Israel)* who was ready to give birth, to devour her Child *(Christianity)* as soon as it was born. She bore a male Child *(Jesus the Nazarine)* who was to rule all nations with a rod of iron *(truth and wisdom)*. And her Child was caught up to God and His throne *(baptism at the Jordan River)*. Then the woman *(Jerusalem church)* fled into the wilderness *(Pella across the Jordan River)* where she had a place prepared for God that they should feed her there one thousand two hundred and six days *(length of the first Jewish-Roman War)*. And war broke out in heaven: Michael and his angels *(Christians)* fought with the dragon *(Rome)* ; and the dragon and his angels fought back, but they did not prevail, nor was a place found for them *(Romans)* in heaven any longer. So the great dragon was cast out that serpent of old, called the Devil and Satan, who deceives the whole world: was cast to the earth and his agents were cast out with him. Then I heard a loud voice saying in heaven, "Now salvation, and strength, and the kingdom of our God, and the power of His Christ have come, for the accuser *(emperor Nero)* of our brethren, who accused them *(Christians)* before our God day and night, has been cast down *(Nero committed suicide)*. And they *(Christians)* overcame him by the blood of the Lamb and by the word of their testimony, and they did not live their lives to the death *(victory over sin is not always measured in faithful martyrdom)*. Therefore rejoice, O heaven, and you will dwell in them! Woe to the inhabitants of the earth and the sea *(Satan will continue to do his malicious work)!* For the devil has come down to you, having great wrath, because he knows that he has a short time." Now when the dragon saw that he had been cast down to the earth, he persecuted the women *(Israel)* who gave birth to the male Child *(Jesus)*. But the woman *(Jerusalem church)* was given two wings of a great eagle that she might fly into the wilderness *(Pella prior to the destruction of Jerusalem by Titus in AD 70)* to her place, where she is nourished for a time and times and half a time *(Three and a half years)*, from the presence of the serpent *(Roman)*. So the serpent spewed water out of his mouth *(a stream of lies, delusions, political utopias, philosophical falsehoods, etc.)* like a flood after the woman *(church)*, that he might cause her to be carried away by the flood *(believers would accept pagan doctrine)*. But the earth *(nations)* helped the woman *(church)* and the earth opened its mouth and swallowed up the flood *(lies)* which the dragon *(Rome)* had spewed out of his mouth. And the dragon *(Rome)* was enraged with the woman *(church)* and went to make war with the rest of her offspring *(Christians)* who keep the commandments of God and have the testimony of Jesus Christ.

CHAPTER 13:

Then I stood on the sand of the sea *(nations of Gentiles)*. And I saw a beast rising up out of the sea *(Rome)*, having seven heads *(city of Rome was built on seven hills)* and ten horns *(Rome's ten subordinate kingdoms)*, and on his horns ten crowns *(first ten emperors of Rome)*, and on his heads a blasphemous name *(pagan belief)*. Now the beast *(Rome)* which I saw was like a leopard *(full of stealth)*, his feet were like the feet of a bear *(big imprint)*, and his mouth like the mouth of a lion *(deadly)*. The dragon *(emperor)* gave his power, his throne, and great authority. And I saw one of his heads as if it had been mortally wounded, and his deadly wound was healed *(upon the death of Nero, the empire was thrown into violent civil war but then, it was saved by the appointment of Vespasian as emperor)*. And all the world marveled *(it survived civil war)* and followed the beast. *(The empire been made more powerful under Emperor Vespasian and his son Titus)*. So they *(nations)* worshiped the dragon *(emperor)* who gave authority to the beast *(Rome)*; and they worshipped the beast saying, "Who is like the beast? *(No power on earth is equal to Rome)* Who is able to make war with him?" *(No power dares to confront Rome)* And he *(Rome)* was given a mouth speaking great things and blasphemies, and he was given authority to continue for forty-two months *(reign of Emperor Nero)* .... It was granted to him *(Nero)* to make war with the saints *(church)* and to overcome them. And authority was given him *(emperor)* over every tribe, tongue, and nation. All who dwell on earth will worship him *(emperor)*, whose names have not been written in the Book of Life of the Lamb slain from the foundation of the world. If anyone has an ear, let him hear. He who leads into captivity *(Rome)* shall go into captivity; he who kills with the sword must be killed with a sword. Here is the patience *(Christians who endured imprisonment and martyrdom never resorted to violence)* and faith of the saints. Then I saw another beast coming up out of the earth and he had two horns *(Satan)* like a lamb and spoke like a dragon *(emperor)*. And he *(Satan)* exercises all the authority of the first beast *(Rome)* in his presence and causes the earth and those who dwell in it to worship the first beast, whose deadly wound *(civil war)* was healed. He *(Rome)* performs great signs, so that he even makes fire come down from heaven on the earth *(flaming projectiles shot from Roman catapults)* in the sight of them *(church)*. And he *(Rome)* deceives those who dwell on earth by those signs *(force and persecution)* which he *(emperor)* was granted to do in the sight of the beast *(Rome)*, telling those who dwell on the earth to make an image to the beast *(gold and silver idols with the emperors likeness affixed)* who was wounded by the sword and lived. He *(emperor)* was granted power to give breath to the image of the beast, that the image of the beast *(emperor)* should both speak and cause as many as would not worship the image of the beast *(emperor)* to be killed. He *(emperor)* causes all, both small and great, rich and poor, free and slave, to receive a mark on their right hand or on their foreheads *(servitude to Rome was often branded onto a conspicuous part of the body to show ownership)*, and that no one may buy or sell except one who has the mark *(Raman citizenship)* or the name of the beast *(one of the 10 subordinate kingdoms)*, or the number of his name. Here is wisdom. Let him who has understanding calculate the number of the beast for it is the number of a man – his number is 666 *(Based on the ancient numerological system called Gematria – emperor Nero's name appears)*.

CHAPTER 14:

Then I looked, and behold, a Lamb *(Jesus)* standing on Mount Zion and with Him one hundred and forty-four thousand, having His Father's name *(Christian)* written on their forehead. And I heard a voice from heaven, like the voice of many waters, and like the voice of loud thunder. And I heard the sound of harpists playing their harps *(joy and happiness)*. They sung as it were a new song before the throne *(redemption from the bondage to sin through the blood of Jesus Christ compared to the old message of redemption from bondage in Egypt found in the Old Testament)* and before the four living creatures, and the elders, and no one could learn that song except the hundred and forty-four thousand who were redeemed from earth. These are the ones who were not defiled with women *(Rome who was a prostitute due to her pagan practices)*, for they were virgins *(worshipped the most high God)*. These are the ones who follow the Lamb wherever he goes. These were redeemed from among men, being the first fruits of God and the Lamb. And in their mouth was found no deceit *(They did not worship the emperor)*, for they are without fault before the throne of God. Then I saw another angel flying in the midst of heaven, having the everlasting gospel to preach to those who dwell on earth - to every nation, tribe, tongue, and people - saying with a loud voice, "Fear God and give glory to Him, for the hour of His judgment has come; and worship Him who made heaven and earth, the sea and springs of water." And another angel followed, saying, "Babylon is fallen, is fallen, that great city *(Jerusalem that city of idolatry, the occult, immorality, and rebellion against God)* because she has made all nations drink the wine of wrath of her fornication ". Then a third angel followed them, saying with a loud voice, "If anyone worships the beast *(Rome)* and his image and receives his mark on his forehead or on his hand *(enslaved to Roman ideology)*, he himself shall drink of the wine of the wrath of God, which is poured out full strength into the cup of His indignation". He shall be tormented with fire and brimstone in the presence of holy angels and in the presence of the Lamb. And the smoke of their torment ascends forever and ever; and they have no rest day or night, who worship the beast *(Rome)* and his image *(emperor)*, and whoever receives the mark of his name. Here is the patience of the saints; here are those who keep the commandments of God and the faith of Jesus. Then I heard a voice from heaven saying to me, "Write: Blessed are the dead who die in the Lord from now on" ...."that they may rest from their labors, *(enter Paradise)* and their works follow them*" (character will be made known)*. Then I looked, and behold, a white cloud, and on the cloud sat One like the Son of Man, having on His head a golden crown *(Lordship)* and in his hand a sharp sickle *(judgment has come)*. Another angel came out of the temple crying with a loud voice to Him who sat on the cloud *(Jesus)* , "Thrust in your sickle and reap, for the time has come for You to reap, for the harvest of the earth is ripe" *(the first harvest is for the gathering of the righteous = 144,000 = Church = Saints)*. So He who sat on the cloud thrust in His sickle on the earth, and the earth was reaped. Then another angel came out of the temple which is in heaven, he also having a sharp sickle. And another angel came out from the alter who had power over fire, and he cried with a loud cry to him who had the sharp sickle, saying, "Thrust in your sharp sickle and gather the clusters of the vine of the earth, for her grapes are fully ripe." So the angel thrust his sickle into the earth and gathered the vine of the earth and threw it into the great winepress of the wrath of God. And the winepress was trampled *(wicked were judged)* outside the city and blood came out of the winepress, up to the horses' bridles *(so many were killed during the siege of Jerusalem by the Roman army that blood ran deep)* for one thousand six hundred furlongs *(a distance so great that it made it impossible for sinners to escape God's judgment)*

CHAPTER 15:

Then I saw another sign in heaven, great and marvelous: seven angels having the seven last plagues, for in them the wrath of God is complete. And I saw something like a sea of glass mingled with fire, *(God's transparent righteousness revealed in judgment upon the wicked)* and those who have victory over the beast *(church)*, over his image and over his mark and over the number of his name *(Emperor Nero)*, standing on the sea of glass, having harps of Gold *(glories of God)*. They sing a song of Moses, the servant of God, and the song of the Lamb *(Overthrow of the Old Covenant and establishment of* the New), saying, "Great and marvelous are Your works, Lord God Almighty! Just and true are Your ways, O King of the saints! Who shall not fear You, O Lord, and glorify Your name? For You alone are holy. For all nations shall come and worship before You, for Your judgments have been manifested. After these things I looked, and behold, the temple of the tabernacle of the testimony in heaven was opened *(God's righteousness)*. And out of the temple came the seven angels having the plagues, clothed in pure bright linen, and having their chests girded with golden bands *(God's Glories)*. Then one of the four creatures gave to the seven angels seven golden bowls full of wrath of God who lives forever and ever. The temple was filled with smoke *(God cannot be approached at the moment He is revealing Himself)* from the glory of God and from His power, and no one was able to enter the temple till the seven plagues of the seven angels were completed.

CHAPTER 16:

Then I heard a loud voice *(God)* from the temple saying to the seven angels, "Go and pour out your bowls of wrath upon the earth. So the first went and poured out his bowl upon earth, and a foul and loathsome sore came upon the men who had the mark of the beast *(Rome)* and those who worshiped his image. Then a second angel poured out his bowl on the sea and it became blood as of dead man *(Rome arose from the sea as a spiritually dead society)*; and every living creature in the sea died. Then the third angel poured out his bowl on the rivers and springs of water *(God poisoned them with Wormwood)* and they became blood. And I heard the angel of the waters saying, "You are righteous, O Lord, the One who is and who was and who is to be, because You have judged these things. For they *(Rome)* have shed the blood of the saints and prophets, and You have given them blood *(death)* to drink for it is their due." And I heard another angel *(who oversees the prayers of the saints)*from the alter saying, "Even so, Lord God Almighty, true and righteous are Your judgments." Then the fourth angel poured his bowl on the sun *(source of all physical and natural life)* and power was given to him to scorch men with fire *(war)*. And men were scorched with great heat, and they blasphemed the name of God who has power over these plagues; and they did not repent and give Him glory. Then the fifth angel poured out his bowl on the throne of the beast *(emperor)*, and his kingdom *(Rome)* became full of darkness *(confusion— disorder—distress—calamity)*; and they *(unrepentant sinners)* gnawed their tongues because of the pain. They blasphemed the God of heaven because of their pains and their sores, and did not repent of their deeds. Then the sixth angel poured his bowl on the great river Euphrates, and its water was dried up so that the way of the kings from the east might be prepared *(God gave assistance to the Roman army led by General Titus which approached from the east so that he could destroy sinful Jerusalem)*. And I saw three unclean spirits *(spirit of infidelity - of popery, and priest-craft)* like frogs coming out of the mouth of the dragon *(Satan)* out of the mouth of the beast *(Rome)*, and out of the mouth of the false prophet *(emperor Nero)*. For they are spirits of demons performing signs which go out to the kings of the earth and of the whole world to gather them to the battle of that great day of God Almighty. Behold, I *(Jesus)* am coming as a thief *(little time exists between the battle of Armageddon and second coming of Christ)*. Blessed is he who watches and keeps his garments *(steadfast belief in God almighty and His Son Jesus Christ)*, lest he walk naked and they see his shame. And they gathered them together to the place called in Hebrew, Armageddon *(a plain located at the foot of Mount Carmel in present day Israel where Jews fought historical battles against invading armies from the north: Assyrians, Babylonians, Persians, Greeks, and Romans)*. Then the seventh angel poured out his bowl into the air *(earth)*, and a loud voice came out of the temple of heaven saying, "It is done!" *(judgment is now upon God's enemies)*. And there were noises and thundering and lightning and there was a great earthquake, such a mighty and great earthquake as not occurred since men were on earth.

(Old Testament covenant at Mount Sinai was accompanied by the shaking of the earth, so also is the dissolution of the Old covenant is accompanied by an even greater shaking of both the earth and heaven (Hebrews 12:26-28). The Old covenant vanished (Hebrews 8:13) amid great tumult when Roman troops destroyed the Temple in Jerusalem, the dwelling place of God in the Holy of holies).

Now the great city was divided into three parts *(three Jewish factions defended Jerusalem – Sadducees, Pharisees, and Zealots)* and the cities of the Nations fell. And great Babylon *(Jerusalem)* was remembered *(place where Jesus and his brother James the Less were martyred)* before God, to give her the cup of the wine of the fierceness of His wrath. Then every island fled away, and the mountains were not found *(no part of the Roman Empire escaped God's judgment)*. And great hail from heaven fell upon men, every hailstone about the weight of a talent *(stones hurled over Jerusalem's walls by Roman catapults each weighed about 100 pounds)*. Men blasphemed God because of the plague of the hail, since that plague was exceedingly great.

CHAPTER 17:

Then one of the seven angels who had the seven bowls came and talked with me, saying to me, "Come, I will show you the judgment of the great harlot who sits on many waters, with whom the kings of the earth committed fornication and the inhabitants of the earth were made drunk with the wine of her fornication". So he carried me away in the Spirit into the wilderness. And I saw a woman *(city of Rome)* sitting on a scarlet beast *(roman empire)* which was full of names of blasphemy, having seven heads *(empires which had invaded Israel over the centuries: Assyrians, Babylonians, Persians, Greeks, Egyptians, and Rome (2 times)* and ten horns *(Rome's subordinate kingdoms)*. The woman *(city of Rome)* was arrayed in purple and scarlet, and adorned with gold and precious stones and pearls, having in her hand a golden cup full of abominations and the filthiness of her fornication *(paganism, emperor worship, and worship of material wealth)*. And on her forehead a name was written : MYSTERY, BABYLON THE GREAT, THE MOTHER OF HARLOTS AND OF THE ABOMINATIONS OF THE EARTH. I saw a woman *(city of Rome)*, drunk with the blood of the saints and with the blood of the martyrs of Jesus. And when I saw her, I marveled with great amazement. But the angel said to me, "Why did you marvel? I will tell you the mystery of the woman and of the beast *(Roman Empire)* that carries her, which has seven heads and ten horns. The beast that you saw was, and is not, and will ascend out of the bottomless pit and go to perdition. And those who dwell on the earth will marvel whose names are not written in the Book of Life *(emperors)* from the foundation of the world, when they see the beast that was *(Roman Republic)*, and is not yet *(Roman Empire)*, and yet is. Here is the mind which has wisdom: The seven heads are the seven mountains on which the woman sits *(city of Rome)*. There are also seven kings. Five have fallen *(Octavius, Tiberius, Caligula, Claudius, Nero)*, one is *(Galba)*, and the other has not yet come *(Ortho)*. And when he comes, he must continue a short time *(he too, will be overthrown)*. The beast that was *(Galba)*, and is not, is himself also the eighth and is of the seven, and is going to perdition. The ten horns which you saw are the ten kings *(rulers of territories that forcible came under Roman rule)* who have received no kingdom yet *(Christian belief has not yet reached them)*, but they have received authority for one hour *(a short time)* as kings with the beast. These are of one mind *(pagan)*, and they will give their power and authority to the beast *(Rome)*. These will make war with the Lamb, and the Lamb will overcome them, for He is Lord of Lords and King of kings; and those who are with Him are called, chosen, and faithful." And he said to me, "The waters which you saw, where the harlot sits, are peoples, multitudes, nations, and tongues. And the ten horns which you saw on the beast *(ten subordinate kingdoms)*, these will hate the harlot *(turn against Rome)*, make her desolate and naked, eat her flesh and burn her with fire. For God has put it into their hearts to fulfill His purpose, to be of one mind, and to give their kingdom to the beast *(subordinate kings will play along with the emperor for a short while)*, until the words of God are fulfilled. And the woman whom you saw is that great city *(city of Rome)* which reigns over kings of the earth."

CHAPTER 18:

After these things I saw another angel coming down from heaven *(Jesus Christ)*, having great authority, and the earth was illuminated with his glory. And he cried mightily with a loud voice, saying, "Babylon the great is fallen *(Jerusalem had accepted the culture of Rome)*, and has become a dwelling place of demons, a prison for every foul soul, and a cage for every unclear and hated bird! For all the nations *(those who have visited Jerusalem)* have drunk of the wine of wrath of her fornication the kings of the earth have committed fornication with her, and the merchants of the earth have become rich through the abundance of her luxury. And I heard another voice from heaven saying, "Come out of her, my people, lest you share in her sins, and lest you receive of her plagues. For her sins have reached to heaven, and God has remembered her iniquities. Render to her just as she rendered to you, and repay her double according to her works; in the cup which she has mixed, mixed double for her. In the measure that she glorified herself and lived luxuriously, in the same measure give her torment and sorrow; for she says in her heart, 'I sit as queen *(arrogant),* and am no widow *(God will never leave Jerusalem),* and will not see sorrow *(God's grace will never end).* Therefore her plagues will come in one day—death and morning and famine. And she will be utterly burned with fire, for strong is the Lord God who judges her. The kings of the earth who committed fornication *(politicians, merchants, temple priests)* and lived luxuriously with her will weep and lament for her, when they see the smoke and the burning, standing at a distance for fear of her torment, saying, 'Alas, alas, the great city of Babylon *(Jerusalem),* that mighty city! For in one hour your judgment has come. And the merchants of the earth will weep and mourn over her, for no one buys their merchandise anymore: merchandise of gold and silver, precious stones and pearls, fine linen and purple silk and scarlet, every kind of citron wood, every kind of object of ivory, every kind of object of most precious wood, bronze, iron, and marble; and cinnamon and incense, fragrant oil and frankincense, wine and oil, fine flour and wheat, cattle and sheep, horses and chariots, and bodies and souls of men *(human life is placed at the end of a list of material objects)* The fruit that your soul longed for **(***God's Grace***)** has gone from you, and all the things which are rich and splendid have gone from you, and you shall find them no more at all. The merchants of these things, who became rich by her, will stand at a distance *(Jerusalem is under bombardment from the Roman army)* for fear of her torment, weeping and wailing, and saying, 'Alas, alas, that great city that was clothed in fine linen, purple, and scarlet *(controlled by Rome through the temple priests),* and adorned with gold and precious stones and pearls! For in one hour great riches came to nothing.' Every shipmaster, all who travel by ship, sailors, and as many as trade on the sea, stood at a distance and cried out when they saw the smoke of her burning saying, 'What is like this great city? They threw dust on their heads *(mourned her destruction),* and cried, weeping and wailing, and saying, 'Alas, alas, that great city, in which all who had ships on the sea became rich by her wealth! For in one hour she is made desolate.' Rejoice over her, O heaven, and you holy apostles and prophets, for God has avenged on her. Then a mighty angel *(Gabriel)* took up a stone like a great millstone and threw it into the sea, saying "Thus with violence the great city of Babylon shall be thrown down, and shall not be found anymore". The sound of harpists, musicians, flutists, and trumpeters shall not be heard in you anymore *(joy and happiness)*. No craftsman of any craft shall be found in you anymore, and the sound of a millstone *(commerce has ceased to exist)* shall not be heard in you anymore. And the light of the lamp shall not shine in you anymore *(Jerusalem temple was destroyed)*, and the voice of bridegroom and bride *(marriage of God to the people of Israel in the form of the Mount Sinai covenant)* shall not be heard anymore *(Old Testament period has ended)*. For your merchants were the great men of the earth *(They knew know how to make money but lost their spiritual compass)* for by your sorcery all the nations are deceived *(Holy city committed all types of fornication)*. And in her was found the blood of prophets and saints, and all who were slain on earth.

CHAPTER 19:

After these things I heard a loud voice of a great multitude in heaven *(choir of angels)*, saying, "Alleluia! Salvation and glory and honor and power belong to the Lord our God! For true righteous are His judgments, because He has
judged the great harlot *(Roman Empire)* who corrupted the earth with her fornication *(pagan religion)*; and He has avenged on her the blood of His servants *(martyrs)* shed by her." And they said, "Alleluia! Her smoke rises up forever and ever!" *(Roman Empire is hell on earth)*. And the twenty-four elders and the four living creatures fell down and worshipped God who sat on the throne, saying, "Amen! Alleluia!" Then a voice *(Jesus)* came from the throne, saying, "Praise our God, all you servants and those who fear Him, both small and great!" And I heard, as it were, the voice of a great multitude *(faithful)*, as the sound of many waters and as the sound of mighty thundering, saying, "Alleluia! For the Lord God Omnipotent reigns! Let us be glad and rejoice and give Him glory, for the marriage of the Lamb *(Jesus)* has come, and His wife *(Church)* has made herself ready." And to her it was granted to be arrayed in fine linen, clean and bright, for the fine linen is the righteous acts of saints. Then he

(Gabriel) said to me, "Write: Blessed are those who are called to the marriage supper of the Lamb!" And he said to me, "These are the sayings of God." And I fell at his feet to worship him. But he said to me, "See that you do not do that! I am your fellow servant, and of your brethren who have the testimony of Jesus. Worship God! For the testimony of Jesus is the spirit of prophecy." Now I saw heaven opened, and behold, a white horse *(retribution)*. And He who sat on him was called Faithful and True *(Jesus)* and in righteousness He judges and makes war. His eyes were like a flame of fire *(intense),* and on His head were many crowns *(kingship over all Nations)*. He had a name written that no one knew except Himself *(Savior)*. He was clothed with a robe dripped in blood *(passion)* and His name is called The Word of God. And the armies in heaven, clothed in fine linen, white and clean, followed Him on white horses. Now out of His mouth goes a sharp sword *(word of God),* that with it He should strike all nations. And He Himself will rule them with a rod of iron *(truth and wisdom)*. He himself treads the winepress of the fierceness and wrath of Almighty God. And He has on His robe and on His thigh a name written: KING OF KINGS, AND LORD OF LORDS. Then I saw an angel standing in the sun *(of great brilliance)* and he cried with a loud voice, saying to all the birds that fly in the midst of heaven, "Come and gather together for the supper of the great God, that you may eat the flesh of kings, the flesh of captains, the flesh of mighty men, the flesh of horses and those who sit on them, and the flesh of all people, both free and slave, both small and great *(Roman Empire had become a corpse given to scavengers which no power can stop)*. And I saw the beast *(Rome)*, the kings of the earth *(sub-ordinate kingdoms)*, and their armies, gathering together to make war against Him who sat on the white horse *(Jesus)* and His army. Then the beast *(Satan)* was captured, and with him the false prophet *(Devil)* who worked signs in his presence *(fornication of all types),* by which he deceived those who received the mark *(pagan)* of the beast and those who worshipped his image. These two were cast alive into the lake of fire burning with brimstone. And the rest *(non-repentant sinners)* were killed with the sword which proceeded from the mouth of Him *(Jesus)* who sat on the horse. And all the birds were filled with their flesh.

CHAPTER 20:

Then I saw an angel *(Jesus)* coming down from heaven, having the key to the bottomless pit and a great chain in his hand. He laid hold of the dragon *(emperor)*, that serpent of old, who is the Devil and Satan, and bound him for a thousand years; and he cast him into the bottomless pit, and set a seal upon him, so that he should deceive the nations no more till the thousand years had finished.

(Millennium Revelation is the most hotly contested part of the Book of Revelation when it comes to meaning. Apostolic fathers; Papias, Justin Martyr, Irenaeus, Tertullian, and Lactantius all believed that Millennium Revelation speaks about the future glorious age in which the influence of the Christian gospel will have universal sway).

But after these things he must be released for a little while. And I saw thrones, and they sat on them, and judgment was committed to them. Then I saw the souls of those who had been beheaded for their witness to Jesus and for the word of God, who had not worshipped the beast *(Rome)* or his culture, and had not received his mark on their foreheads *(slave to material wealth and other forms of fornication)* or on their hands. And they lived and reigned with Christ for a thousand years. But the rest of the dead did not live again until the thousand years were finished *(those who had not received the Word of God and been redeemed)*. This is the first resurrection. Blessed and holy is he who has part in the first resurrection. Over such the second death has no power *(the redeemed, who received eternal life due to their belief in the sacrifice made by Jesus Christ on the cross, are safe in heaven)* but they shall be priests of God and of Christ, and shall reign with Him a thousand years. Now when the thousand years have expired, Satan will be released from his prison and will go out to deceive the nations which are in four corners of the earth *(those which were located so far from the center of Christ's ministry that they had never received the Word of God and would therefore still believe Satan's message)*, Gog and Magog, to gather them together to battle, whose number is as the sand of the sea.

(Evil powers are assembling to launch a final assault on the church of Jesus Christ. In Ezekiel 38 & 39, Gog is the name of a ruler; Magog is the name of his kingdom which invaded Israel from the north).

They went up on the breadth of the earth *(Satan and his army arose out of the bottomless pit)* and surrounded the camp of the saints *(Church)* and the beloved city *(Jerusalem)*. And fire came down from God out of heaven *(missiles fired by Roman catapults)* and devoured them. The devil *(emperor)*, who deceived them, was cast into the lake of fire and brimstone where the beast *(Rome)* and the false profit *(Satan)* are. And they will be tormented day and night forever and ever. Then I saw a great white throne and Him who sat on it *(God)*, for whose face the earth and the heaven fled away. And there was found no place for them *(sinners)*. And I saw the dead, small and great, standing before God, and the books were opened *(there are more than one category of person waiting for judgment)*. And another book was opened, which is the Book of Life *(names of the righteous)*. And the dead were judged according to their works, by the things which were written in the books. The sea gave up the dead who were in it *(those martyred)*, and Death and Hades delivered up the dead who were in them *(sinners of various types)*. And they were judged, each one according to his works. Then Death and Hades were cast into the lake of fire. This is the second death. And anyone not found written in the Book of Life was cast into the lake of fire.

CHAPTER 21:

Now I saw a new heaven and a new earth, for the first heaven and the first earth had passed away *(Old Covenant system)*. Also there was no more sea *(nations of the Gentiles had discovered the glories of God)*. Then I, John, saw the holy city, New Jerusalem *(Christian church)*, coming down out of heaven from God prepared as a bride adorned for her husband *(Jesus)*. And I heard a loud voice from heaven saying, "Behold, the tabernacle of God is with men *(Jesus Christ is with the faithful wherever they gather together in brotherhood)*, and He will dwell with them, and they shall be His people. God Himself will be with them and be their God. And God will wipe away every tear in their eyes; there shall be no death, nor sorrow, nor crying. There shall be no pain *(persecution)*, for the former things have passed away.' Then He who sat on the throne *(God)* said, "Behold, I make all things new." And He *(Jesus)* said to me, "Write, for these words are true and faithful." And He said to me, "It is done! I am the

Alpha and the Omega, the Beginning and the End. I will give of the fountain of the water of life *(salvation and eternal life)* freely to him who thirsts *(believes)*. He who overcomes *(sinfulness)* shall inherit all things, and I will be his God and he shall be My son. But the cowardly *(those who do not commit to the will of God)*, unbelieving, abominable, murderers, sexually immoral, sorcerers, idolaters, and all liars shall have their part in the lake which burns with the fire and brimstone, which is the second death". Then one of the seven angels who had the seven bowls filled with the seven last plagues came to me and talked with me saying, "Come, I will show you the bride *(Christian Church)*, the Lamb's wife". And he carried me away in the Spirit to a great and high mountain, and showed me the great city, the holy Jerusalem, descending out of heaven from God, having the glory of God. Her light was like a most precious stone, like a jasper stone, clear as crystal. Also she had a great and high wall *(Church is a spiritual city)* with twelve gates, and twelve angels at the gates, and names written on them, which are the names of the twelve tribes of the children of Israel: three gates on the east, three gates on the north, three gates on the south, and three gates on the west *(universal access)*. Now the wall of the city had twelve foundations, and on them were the names of the twelve apostles of the Lamb. And he who talked with me had a gold reed to measure the city, its gates, and its wall. The city is laid out as a square *(Shape of the Holy of holies in Jerusalem which God dwelt before the destruction of the temple by the Romans)* its length is as great as its breadth. And he measured the city with the reed: twelve thousand furlongs *(15 miles)*. Its length, breadth, and height are equal. Then he measured its wall: one hundred and forty-cubits *(216 feet)*, according to the measure of a man, that is, of an angel. The construction of its walls was of jasper; and the city was pure gold, like clear glass. The foundations of the wall of the city were adorned with all kinds of precious stones *(used to adorning a bride during a wedding ceremony)*: the first foundation was jasper, the second sapphire, the third chalcedony, the fourth emerald, the fifth sardonyx, the sixth sardis, the seventh chrysolite, the eight beryl, the ninth topaz, the tenth chrysoprase, the eleventh jacinth, and the twelfth amethyst. The twelve gates were twelve pearls: each individual gate was one pearl.

As a pearl is created from a rough grain of sand irritating the tissue of the oyster, a secretion (Word of God) transforms the source of irritation (a sinful state) into a pearl (salvation).

And the street of the city *(way of life)* was pure gold, like transparent glass. But I saw no temple in it for the Lord God Almighty and the Lamb are the temple.

In antiquity, Jews believed that God only dwelled in the Holy of holies which was housed in the midst of the Jerusalem Temple. When the temple was destroyed by the Romans in 70 CE, it marked the end of God's covenant with the Jews as He could no longer be worshipped there. For the more liberal minded Hellenized Jews who were exiled to Babylonia who had no temple in which to worship, they worshipped God wherever believers met; usually in personal homes. Because many Hellenized Jews returned to Israel after their exile in support of Jesus Christ, early Christians also came to believed that they too could find both God and Jesus wherever they met.

The city had no need of the sun or the moon to shine in it, for the glory of God illuminated it. The Lamb *(Jesus)* is its light. And the nations of those who are saved shall walk in its light, and the kings of the earth bring their glory and honor into it. Its gates shall not be shut at all by day there shall be no night *(Father and the Son are always present)*. And they shall by no means enter it with anything that defiles *(lies and untruth; idols)*, or causes an abomination or a lie, but only those who are written in the Lamb's Book of Life.

CHAPTER 22:

And he showed me a pure river of water of life, clear as crystal, proceeding from the throne of God and of the Lamb *(blessings flowing from God's throne into the heart of the believer)*. In the middle of the street *(way of life)*, and on either side of the river, was the tree of life *(spiritual food which is needed to nourish and sustain the believer)*, which bore twelve fruits *(Apostolic message)*, each tree yielding its fruit every month *(continual announcement of the gospel message)*. The leaves of the tree were for the healing of nations *(converted Gentiles)*. And there shall be no more curse *(God brought upon Israel due to her covenant unfaithfulness),* but the throne of God and the Lamb shall be in it, and His servants shall serve Him. They shall see His face and His name shall be on their foreheads *(Christian).* There shall be no night there *(sadness):* They need no lamp nor light of the sun, for the Lord God gives them light. And they shall reign forever and ever. Then he said to me, "These words are faithful and true." And the Lord God of the holy prophets sent His angel to show His servants the things which must shortly take place. Behold I *(Jesus)* am coming quickly! Blessed is he who keeps the words of the prophecy of the book." Now I, John, saw and heard these things. And when I heard and saw, I fell down to worship before the feet of the angel *(Jesus)* who showed me these things. Then he said to me, "See that you do not do that. For I am your fellow servant, and of your brethren the prophets, and of those who keep the words of this book. Worship God." And he said to me, "Do not seal the words of the prophecy of this book, for the time is at hand" *(Time for believers to read and discuss the meaning of the Book of Revelation).* "He who is unjust, let him be unjust still; he who is filthy, let him be filthy still; he who is righteous, let him be righteous still; he who is holy, let him be holy still". And behold, I *(Jesus)* am coming quickly, and My reward *(life or death)* is with Me to give to every one according to his work. I am the Alpha and the Omega, the Beginning and the End, the First and the Last."

(Alpha and Omega are the first and the last letters in the Greek alphabet. In Christianity, Alpha and Omega represent the nature of God and Christ, who encompass all that can be.)

Blessed are those who do His commandments, that they may have the right tree of life, and may enter through the gates into the city *(find salvation).* But outside are dogs and sorcerers and sexually immoral and murderers and idolaters, and whoever loves and practices a lie. "I, Jesus, have sent My angel to testify to you these things in the churches. I am the Root and the offspring of David *(Messiah),* the Bright and Morning Star". And the Spirit and the bride say, "Come!" And let him who hears say, "Come!" And let him who thirsts come. Whoever desires let him take the water of life freely. For I testify to everyone who hears the words of prophesy of this book. If anyone adds to these things, God will add to him the plagues that are written in this book; and if anyone takes away from the words of the book of this prophecy, God shall take away his part from the Book of Life. He who testifies to these things says, "Surely I am coming quickly." Amen. Even so, come, Lord Jesus! The grace of our Lord Jesus Christ be with you all. Amen.

96 CE

Emperor Nerva (96 – 98 CE) decided not to take action against Christians. He recalled those who had been banished and forbade the government from bringing action against the practice of Jewish customs.

97 CE

Timothy was martyred in Ephesus by pagans when he tried to block a procession at the pagan Feast of Catagogion.

Hillel Codex contains over six hundred letters written by Hillel the Elder and other famous Jewish scholars from the first century. He taught a personal and ethical renewal, which was expressed through baptism in water with those who had been so purified, becoming Jews. His concept of new covenant went beyond the Old, whereby being a son of Abraham was not good enough to assure salvation. His New covenant would not only require linage, it would also be based upon one's freedom of personal choice to join. There would be a new Israel with his ideas being used to bring Jews into the new covenant by baptism. He was not only associated with the development of the *Mishnah* and *Talmud*, he was renowned within Judaism as being a sage and scholar. He was founder of the House of Hillel School for the Sages which stood at the head of the Jews living in the land of Israel until roughly the fifth century CE. He was recognized as being the highest authority among the Pharisees doing most of his work between 30 BCE and 10 CE. During the reign of Herod the Great, he was president of the Sanhedrin, an assembly of seventy-one sages who operated as highest court in the nation. The Sanhedrin never met at night or on religious holidays.

Hillel is credited with creating the Golden Rule. According to the Talmud, a Gentile asked Rabbi Shammai of the House of Shammai School for Sages to teach him the Torah while he, the Gentile, stood on one foot. Shammai angrily refused so the Gentile went to Hillel with the same request with

Hillel nicely telling the Gentile: "That which is hateful to you, do not do to your fellow man. That is the entire Torah, and the rest is commentary. Now go and study."

Archko Volume contains a group of letters written by Hillel the Elder who lived at the time of Jesus. In these letters he discusses the history of the Jewish Nation, Jesus, and John the Baptist. In greatly abbreviated form he said:

> Behold our desolate condition as we must know there is a good reason somewhere. From our former history, and the dealings of God with our forefathers, it is evident that it is not because he is neglectful of the interests of His children. It must be on our own account ......
>
> Now, I wish my brethren to understand that I am not a follower of this Nazarene that has created so much strife among the people, neither do I endorse his new doctrines; yet I think it would be well for us not to be too hasty in forming our conclusion on this ...... This is the peculiar power of Jesus of Nazareth; and because he did not work according to Jewish rule they condemned him to die. It was not because his works were not good works, but because he did not do them according to Jewish custom ..... The universal expectation seems to have been that Jesus was to be a prophet like Moses, but greater. A much larger class gave the Messianic prophecies a more worldly meaning. The great personage whose coming they shortly expected was to be king, but greater than any who had sat upon the Jewish throne. It was this expectation evidently that his disciples followed him through his whole ministry ....The baptism of John and that of Jesus were essentially the same, one into a profession of belief in the Messiah yet to come, and the other into a possession of belief in the Messiah already come.

98 CE

Under Emperor Trajan (98-117 CE), prosperity and peace reigned. Urban life was in full expansion with its vitality an essential element in the life of the whole empire. Never before had philosophy and reason been given so much honor as when the emperor himself was pleased to accept the title of philosopher. The worship of the emperor was officially discouraged with the ruling class prepared to take part in religious exercises which had been previously considered incompatible with Stoicism, a philosophy of personal ethics. According to Stoic teaching, the path to happiness for humans is found in accepting the moment as it presents itself, by not allowing oneself to be controlled by the desire for pleasure or fear of pain, but by using one's mind to understand the world and do one's part by working together and treating others fairly and justly. Pliny, a provincial governor and friend of Tarjan, wrote him saying that as far as he was concerned, Christianity did not constitute a political threat to the state and concluded:

"I have found nothing more than a malignant and immoderate superstition underlining the Christian commitment to a morally and legally blameless life."

In reply, Tarjan made it clear that he was not interested in correcting Christians.

99 CE

Odes of Solomon is a collection of "songs" from different communities of early Christianity. They are "psalms" which never use the name Jesus, and rarely the title "Christ" or "Anointed One." Overall, the odes ring with enthusiasm and happiness in the merging relationship of God, Christ, and humans.

100 CE

John, son of Zebedee, died of natural causes in Edessa, Turkey.

Gospel of Ebonite proclaims that Jesus was interpreter of the law; that he commissioned the twelve disciples to witness to the nations; that he was chosen to be God's son at the Jordan River; that he abolished many Jewish sacrifices. The baptismal scene is one in which the Holy Spirit is said to descend on Jesus in the form of a dove and enter into him. His adoption by God is characterized by the belief that Jesus was a mere man, who, by virtue of his perfect righteousness, was imbued with the divinity of the eternal through in order to carry out the prophetic task for which he had been chosen. Other distinctive features include the absence of the virgin birth, resurrection and the genealogy of Jesus.

Ebonite's insisted on following Jewish law and rites rejecting the epistles of Apostle Paul whom they regarded as an apostate from the Law.

1st Epistle of Paul the Apostle to Timothy is a manual of instruction for church life with emphasis placed on the role and conduct of elders and deacons. The epistle is concerned with limiting the role of women. In addition to the ban on women being elders and teachers, women's dress was strictly prescribed with modesty being the norm; no braided hair or jewelry allowed; women could only be saved by bearing children and behave modesty (2:15).

2nd Epistle of Paul the Apostle to Timothy defends Paul's life while he was on death row in Rome. It seamlessly mixes the dangers of outside persecution and self-serving teachers from within the Christ movement. The presence of false teachers around Christ assemblies is associated with the coming of the last days.

101 CE

Mary Magdalene passed away at the place now called Saint Baume in Southern France. She was laid to rest in an alabaster sepulcher at the Chapel of St. Maximus. In her youth she was reported to have had red hair, brown eyes, olive skinned complexion and standing about five feet six inches, which was considered tall in the first century. By the time of her death, her youngest son Joseph had become bishop of Saraz with his son Joseu becoming the "seed" of the Fisher Kings of Gaul, which eventually extended on to the Merovingian kings of France. Her oldest son Judah married the daughter of Nicodemus with their son Jesus dying of natural causes at a young age.

102 CE

Epistle of Jude reminds followers to remain faithful to the teaching of Jesus as compared to that being taught by Apostle Paul. The most unsettling aspect of Paul's teaching was his view of the temporary nature of the Torah and his redefinition of who constituted the people of Israel.

106 CE

Simon, brother of Jesus, died of natural causes.

110 CE

Gospel of John was written to a Samarian community that had become fully separated from the temple in Jerusalem. The community was facing challenges from the Jerusalem church which was preaching an earthly view of Jesus with Samarian's believing that Jesus was not merely God's messenger on earth but God himself revealed in human form.

The gospel focus is theological with Jesus now identified as God on earth. In the synoptic gospels the chief theme is the earthly "Kingdom of God" whereas in John, the theme is now Jesus as the source of "Eternal Life". The portrayal of Jesus' death is unique among the four gospels in that it presents the death of Jesus as being his glorification and return to the Father.

For scholars, John 1:10-13 is one of the most important passage to be used for understanding the meaning of the gospel because it is the way one understands the prologue that will affect how one reads the rest of what John has to say.

> He was in the world, and the world was made through Him, yet the world did not know Him. He came to His own, and His own people did not receive Him. But to all who did receive Him, who believed in His name, He gave the right to become children of God, who were born, not of blood, nor of the will of the flesh, nor of the will of man, but of God.

The original Greek wording for John 1:16-17 declares that two blessings are given to mankind by God. First, the law was given through Moses and secondly, truth and justice were given through Jesus with the original Greek wording being:

> For from His fullness we all have received, grace upon grace. For the

law was given through Moses and grace **and** truth came through Jesus
Christ.

When the King James Bible was published in 1611, the word **but** was inserted into the text in place of the word **and** changing the complexion of the gospel story so that the modern reader is led to believe that the law was which was brought down by Moses was counter to the grace and truth that was brought by Jesus. Another widely quoted passage of Christian faith is John 3:16:

> For God so loved the world, that he gave his only **begotten** Son, that whosoever believeth in him should not perish, but have everlasting life.

The second century Greek word for **begotten** was translated to mean that God had a child, when in reality the ancient word begotten means that Jesus "had no peer" with the idea of Jesus being "Son of God," first appears in John 1:14-15 when he said:

> And the Word became flesh and dwelt among us, and we have seen His glory, glory as of the only Son from the Father, full of grace and truth.."

In John, the verb 'lifted-up' reflects a double meaning at work in John's theology of the cross. When Jesus was physically 'lifted up' and placed on the cross, he was glorified, with "raised to life" being the theological meaning of the word "resurrection." When mankind witnessed the glorification of Jesus on the cross, they in turn, strived to eliminate their own deficiencies which is the theological meaning of "general resurrection" of mankind. John saw Jesus as being divine, pre-existent, and son of the one true God.

Another text in John that remains an enigma is the post resurrection story where Jesus cautioned Mary Magdalene to not touch him shortly after the resurrection but invites Thomas to do just that (John 20:26-27). In order to understand the different instructions to Mary Magdalene and Thomas, one must understand the purity requirements for a Jewish high priest on the Day of Atonement. For seven days, a high priest was forbidden to come into contact with anything that could be considered ceremonially unclean (a Samaritan woman) in order to avoid being disqualified from entering God's presence in the heavenly tabernacle (Hebrews 9:11). It is significant that Jesus appeared to the disciples after eight days and told Thomas he could touch him because he had already been ordain priest (Ex. 29:35).

Jesus' role as prophet was carried out during his earthly life, while his role as King was yet to be realized at the time of the crucifixion whereas after the ascension he was ordained to carry out his heavenly duties. For theologians, spiritual ascension refers to the process of elevating ones consciousness and connecting to a higher power; it involves the shedding of old patterns, beliefs, and behaviors that no longer serve the individual, and embrace new perspectives and experiences. As you ascend, you move towards spiritual awakening, gaining a higher level of awareness and growth.

Thomas, who was a member of the **eastern Hebrew party**, did not believe that Jesus was rightful heir to the thrown of David but later changed his mind accepting Jesus as the Messiah causing theologians to brand him "doubting Thomas" suggesting Thomas did not believe in the bodily resurrection story. Marcus J. Borg in *Jesus, Uncovering the Life, Teaching, and Relevance of a Religious Revolutionary*, discusses the meaning of gospel stories:

> Exploring the meaning of the gospel stories involves asking the question, what kind of stories are they? Are they intended as historical reports, as history remembered, and thus to be believed or disbelieved? Or do they use language of parable and metaphor to express "truths" that are much more than factual? Are they history or parable? The obvious point is that parabolic narratives can be true. To worry or argue about the factual truth of a parable misses the point. Its point is its meaning.

Gospel of John presents a divine view of Jesus as it was known to the Alexandria School of Scriptural Interpretation. For scholars, Gospel of John is a theological thesis without historical value because it presents a story of Jesus life which differs considerably from that of Mark, Matthew, and Luke..

Second Epistle of Peter concentrates on the need for believers to respect apostolic authority and the coming punishment for many. The readers of the letter are exhorted to exhibit model behavior, self-control, endurance, and mutual affection.

111 CE

First Epistle of John is a position paper on the subject of spirituality. This is the only text that contains the idea that "God is love." Love is used for both the love between God and humans and love among humans, with this connection being made explicitly in the command to "love one another, because love comes from God".

112 CE

Second Epistle of John is addressed to "the lady" and her children with the central theme of the letter being to love one another. The letter shows concern about antichrists – those who do not believe that Jesus, as Christ, is coming in the flesh.

113 CE

Third Epistle of John was written because the confidence of Christian congregations had been shattered because leaders of the church had totally disregarded contradictions in the Christ story. Church leaders had dismissed the differing views and practices of various Christion groups with the church call to unity being based upon loyalty to a divine Jesus with a threat of final judgement being the ultimate hurdle of mankind on their way to eternal life. While the vague sense of Jesus' divine nature worked for some parishioners, it did not for others. It was now time for Christian thinkers to define a new religion that Greeks, Romans, Jews and others might be able to understand.

117 CE

Apologists for Christianity asked emperor Hadrian (117-138 CE) to decide if the Jewish sect was a penal offence or a mental aberration. Hadrian, in-turn, ruled that Christians could only be charged with "false doctrine" through normal legal channels and that the one making the charge must produce evidence. The problem – Hadrian never defined what type 'evidence' was required.

118 CE

Gospel of Truth portrays Jesus as being a spiritual guide who has come to reveal the mysteries of the hidden Father, ignorance of whom can only lead to sin and improper behavior. It is knowledge of God which leads to salvation, not adhering to the letter of the law. The crucifixion was not meant to be interpreted as being a sacrifice for sins but a means of public disclosure of the will of the Father and the incorruptibility of the Son with the Son's teaching bringing about the return of the Father, eliminating error and showing the way like a shepherd. While the gospel acknowledges that Jesus suffered on the cross, it interprets the crucifixion as being a publication of his teaching. The revelation that Jesus brings is restoration of unity with the Father by eliminating the deficiencies of a sinful state. The Spirit reveals the Son, and the Son's teaching brings the return of the Father, eliminating error and showing the way like a shepherd.

120 CE

Didache is a manual of instruction for Christian congregations. It begins with ethical instruction about two ways, one of life and the other of death. The way to life is summed up by the commandments; the way to death is described in a catalog of vices and wicked practices. The most remarkable thing about the Didachi – there is no mention of the divinity of Jesus – no atonement through the body and blood of Christ, and no mention of the resurrection. Jesus is the one who brings knowledge of God, life and faith. The sacred meal of bread and wine is described as follows:

> With respect to the Eucharist you shall give thanks as follows: First with respect to the cup: "We give thanks our Father for the holy vine of David, your child which you made known to us through Jesus your child. To you be glory forever." And with respect to the bread: "We give you thanks our Father for the life and knowledge that you made known to us through Jesus your child. To you be glory forever."

125 CE

Gospel of Mary Magdalene presents Jesus teaching as a path to inner spirituality. It shows Jesus as a healer and protector of the poor. The path that we follow to liberate the soul is here in this lifetime. Ascension is more accurately described as being a descent into the heart; so farther up is actually further in. Sin is forgetting the truth and reality of the soul and acting in a forgetful manner. The soul is the eternal aspect of our being that allows us to feel loved and to experience that we are love. The human body is the soul's chance to be here. The soul lives in silence. Words are how the ego breaths and fuels the flames of thought. Sin is something we produce within ourselves when we misunderstand the truth of who we are; when we forget that we are not just human, the soul inhabits us while we are alive. We are capable of integrating the self and the soul. We realize this aspect of who we are, our divinity, our angelic self, by allowing the soul to ascend with this ascension being about going inward, more fully into our own emotions to purity of heart. The soul ascends because it does not seek to judge, does not attempt to dominate anything or anyone. Salvation is not earned, salvation is waking up, becoming more alive, more present.

Upon the crucifixion, Mary assumed Jesus' role as mediator of divine wisdom; she exercised the authority of spiritual guide and instructor. She proclaimed that Jesus was a teacher of wisdom and that his teaching holds the keys to eternal life with the goal of salvation being the ascent of the soul by following his teaching as only the soul is immortal and lives on forever. The resurrection is misunderstood as it is not a bodily event but a spiritual event. Only the soul infused with the Spirit knows the truth of what it means to be a human being. Salvation is achieved only by discovering within oneself the spiritual nature of humanity and overcoming temptation. By turning to the good, the soul comes to follow its true spiritual nature and is no longer disturbed by the confusion of the body.

130 CE

Gospel of Judas Iscariot proclaims that Jesus is called Savior because his teaching reveals the divine spark which dwells within every human being. Death was not a tragedy nor was it done to bring about the forgiveness of sins as for Jesus, death was the means to liberate his soul from its earthly body so that it could raise-up to a higher plain. For the followers of Judas, his act of turning Jesus into authorities exemplified the true meaning of discipleship as he was serving his master.

132 CE

Second Jewish-Roman War (132 CE - 135)

When emperor Hadrian announced plans to rename Jerusalem, Aelia Capitolina in honor of the Roman god Jupiter Capitolinus and build a temple in Jupiter's honor where the Jewish temple had once stood, a major rebellion broke out in Jerusalem against Rome. Rebels under the leadership of Simon Bar-Kokhba captured 50 fortified towns and over 985 villages including Jerusalem. To the followers of Simon, he was the messiah figure that they had been waiting for not Jesus who had died on the cross years earlier.

The final battle of the war took place at Bethar, located seven miles southwest of Jerusalem with the emperor's army destroying the city with its walls falling and every person in the city being slaughtered. With the war over, Hadrian changed the country name from Israel to Palestine. By decree, he ordered that Jews could no longer live in Jerusalem as only Romans now had the right to do so. In the years that followed the war, only two Jewish sects survived – Pharisees in the land of Israel and followers of Apostle Paul in surrounding countries with the followers of Christ becoming a 'stand-alone' religion.

133 CE

Resurrection stories begin to circulate widely based on letters written by Apostle Paul.

From *Antithesis of Jesus's Preaching and Judaism*, theologian Johann Franz Wilhelim Bousset gives his view concerning the divinity of Jesus:

> Jesus is best understood by contrasting him with the Baptist. John was a preacher of repentance whose eyes were fixed upon the future. Jesus preaching of repentance was not gloomy and forbidding, it was the proclamation of a new righteousness. He desired to communicate this personal piety by personal influence. His work was accomplished mainly among little groups and individuals with the work carrying the Gospel far and wide as a legacy to the community of his followers. This genuine joy of life was not left

unnoticed by the contemporaries of Jesus. He live not in anxious expectation but in cheerful gladness, because by the native strength of his piety he had brought the present and future into one.

134 CE

Acts of the Apostles attest to the fact that all that was said in church canon really happened because the apostles were the eyewitness to the Christ story from the beginning to the end. For scholars, Acts is a theological attempt to hold together the position of Apostle Paul's Gentile missionary work with the position of the Jerusalem church and to bring together the conservative Jewish practices of Jesus which were the position of the Jerusalem church to the position of Paul's ministry which was rooted in the liberal practices of Jesus that, at times, broke the boundary of the Jewish purity laws.

135 CE

Hebrew Bible was finalized.

138 CE

Justin Martyr (100 -165 CE) proclaimed that the gospel stories written by Mark, Matthew, Luke, and John should be considered nothing more than memoirs of the apostles and that these works were never intended to be considered to be Holy Scripture.

In *First Apology* Justin Martyr defended the divinity of Jesus by saying:

> In saying that the *Logos*, who is the first offspring of God, was born for us without sexual union, as Jesus Christ our teacher, and that he was crucified and died and after rising again ascending into heaven, we introduce nothing new beyond what you say of those whom you call sons of Zeus … but the Son of God who is called Jesus, even if only an ordinary human, is worthy to be called Son of God because of his wisdom (1.21-22).

140 CE

Epistle of Paul the Apostle to Titus outlines strategies for Christian communities that are facing persecution and criticism; it requires all community members to be moderate and to act within their expected family roles.

142 CE

The next generation of Christian intellectual converged in Rome to sort out different opinions concerning Jesus *being*. At this meeting, Marcion of Sinope (85-160 CE), Valentinus of Alexandria (108 -160 CE), and Justin Martyr of Samaria (100 -165 CE) decided that the apostolic story of Jesus could only survive scrutiny by being part of a much larger understanding of world history. They would need to include the epic history of Israel so that the Christian story could end with Jesus and his miraculous birth.

These leaders, who taught Christianity as a philosophy, began to develop a theological system built around the teaching of Apostle Paul with his triumph being a literary one in that his letters influenced the teaching embedded in the New Testament. By default, the first followers of Jesus, who used the Hebrew Bible and held an earthly view of him, lost out on sharing his story which stressed the importance of women in his life and ministry.

Second and third century orthodoxy centered it's theology on God the Father's only begotten' Son with his family – save the Virgin Mother – either placed in a peripheral position or eliminated altogether. A denial of the significance of Jesus's family members is discernible as the Gentile church pulled itself away from its Galilean and Judean roots.

145 CE

Sophia of Jesus Christ is a discussion between the risen Jesus and twelve disciples, seven of which were woman. Mary Magdalene and her male counterparts posed questions to the Lord as all were perplexed about the underlying reality of the universe and God's plan for it. The discussion is composed of thirteen questions with brief discourse from Jesus. Topics include: the futility of searching for God; how to find truth; how things began; how the spirit connects to the material; where mankind came from and what purpose it should have. Sophia represents the divine feminine wisdom, the balance between male and female energies. In Sophia, Jesus describes the 'Father of the Universe':

> He has a semblance of his own – not like what you have seen or received. He is imperishable and has no likeness to anything. He is unchanging good. He is faultless. He is eternal. He is blessed. He isimmeasurable. He is untraceable. He is perfect, having no defect. He is imperishability blessed.

150 CE

Gospel of Peter is the earliest non-canonical account of Jesus trial, death, and resurrection. In the story, twenty-nine variations of fact are found when compared to the canonical gospels. Noteworthy variations:

- Herod gave the order to execute Jesus.

- Joseph of Arimathea was a friend of Pilate.

- Jesus hands were nailed to the cross.

- Jesus legs were not broken nor feet nailed but tied to the cross.

- Jesus side was not pierced by a spear.

- Jesus was given the sour wine by his brother Judas and Nicodemus a non-declared follower.

- Jesus did not suffer while on the cross or die.

- It was standard practice to Medicate the person being crucified to ease the pain.

- Major sand storm came up.

- In darkness, confusion seized the people with some holding lamps and falling down.

- Resurrection and Ascension are a single event.

- Disciples went into hiding because they were hunted as criminals.

- Time went by before guards were placed at the tomb.

- Petronius, a Centurion, kept watch at the tomb.

- When the stone was moved away, two men entered with three men walking out.

- Mary Magdalene played a prominence role.

151 CE

Gospel of Philip defines the significance of the virgin birth; Jesus receiving the Holy Spirit; the resurrection; his relationship with Mary Magdalene, as their partnership had special meaning.

> Some said, "Mary was conceived by the Holy Spirit." They were in error. They do not know what they are saying. Mary is the virgin whom no power defiled. She is a great anathema to the Hebrews, who are the apostles and the apostolic men; the Lord would not have said, "My Father who is in Heaven" (Matthew 16:17) unless he had had another father, but he would have said simply, "My father."

Virgin birth refers to the significance of those who have received the Holy Spirit. Thus, as Jesus was born to Joseph and Mary he was later born spiritually when the Holy Spirit descended upon him at baptism. At baptism those who receive the Holy Spirit are not only born again, they are raised from the spiritual dead. Resurrection, like the virgin birth, is a paradigm for what happens to each person who undergoes spiritual transformation.

The physical act of love between man and woman harbors a secret that had serious implications, as the nuptial act must be based upon trust and consciousness, because the embrace of man and woman creates new life that is the icon of that union and the future of mankind. The kiss that unites man and woman is exemplified by the kiss that Jesus gave Mary Magdalene:

> There were three who always walked with the Lord: Mary, his mother, and his sister (Mary-Salome), and Magdalene, the one who was called his companion. His sister and his mother and his companion were each a Mary. And the companion of the Savior is Mary Magdalene. But *Christ loved her more than all the disciples* and used to kiss her often on the mouth. The rest of the disciples were offended by it and expressed disapproval. They said to him, "Why do you love her more than all of us?" The Savior answered and said to them, "Why do I not love you like her?" When a blind man and one who sees are both together in darkness, they are no different from one another. When the light comes, then he who sees will see the light, and he who is blind will remain in darkness" (Philip 63:30-64:10).

152 CE

Secret Book of John highlights Jesus as a teacher of wisdom; it is about the unfolding of the divine mind and implications for mankind. Jesus describes God:

> The One is not corporal and it is not incorporeal. The One is not large and it is not small. It is impossible to say, how much it is. What kind is it? For no one can understand it. The One is a realm that gives a realm, life that gives life, a blessed One that gives blessedness, knowledge that gives knowledge, a good One that gives goodness, mercy that gives mercy and redemption, grace that gives grace.

154 CE

Secret Revelation of John reveals the nature of the universe as being the invisible spirit and Father. From the Father came first the mother and then the Son, followed by a multitude of other luminous powers. Earth originated when the youngest of the luminous powers Wisdom-Sophia, boldly gave birth without the consent of God the Father, with her child being the creator God of earth. The God of the lower world then created Adam according to the divine image but also in his own flawed likeness. The Savior, created in the image of God and filled with the Spirit of Wisdom-Sophia, revealed the differences between the world above with the world below. He told John that injustice and cruel domination are overcome by the power of the Spirit, by knowledge, and by goodness without violence and destruction.

155 CE

Marcion (85 -160 CE), a wealth Greek ship owner from the city of Sinope, was especially attracted to Apostle Paul's idea that a person is made right with God by having faith in Jesus' death and resurrection. In his opinion, since no one can keep the law of God as delivered by Moses, everyone is condemned. He believed that the loving God of Jesus never had anything to do with the material world because God had sent Jesus into the world as an act of love to redeem people who were subject to the wrath of the Jewish Creator God. Marcion came to believe that Jesus only seemed to be part of the material world and that his coming was to depose the Jewish God and usher in the worship of the true God of grace. He was first to insist that there should be an official canon of faith and as such selected gospel to bolster his claim. He selected ten of Paul's letters and Gospel of Luke with all being 'edited' to eliminate portions that seemed too Jewish. In addition, Marcion had other books written in the name of Paul to support his theology: Colossians, 3rd Corinthians, Ephesians, 2nd Thessalonians, 1st and 2nd Timothy and Titus.

161 CE

As the Roman Empire expanded in size, the custom of the empire having two emperors began – one ruling over the Latin speaking western Empire headquartered in Rome and one ruling over the Greek speaking eastern Empire located at Constantinople.

165 CE

Infancy Gospel of Thomas reveals events in the life of Jesus when he was a child between ages of two and twelve years. It fills the gaps in the New

Testament between the stories of Jesus' birth and conversation with scholars in the Temple in Jerusalem. The text presents Jesus as being a precocious child who starts his education early. The story covers how the young Incarnation of God matures and learns to use his powers for good and how those around him first respond in fear and later in admiration. One episode involve Jesus making clay birds and bringing them to life. In another, when a child disperses water that Jesus has collected, he kills him. In another, he reprimands a boy for his actions causing him to wither and die. When Joseph and Mary's neighbors complain about Jesus' actions, he strikes them blind.

Jesus then starts receiving lessons in school, his teacher suspects that he has supernatural powers. Jesus confirms the teachers suspicions and revokes all cruelty he had done. Subsequently, he resurrects a friend who was killed when he fell from a roof and heals another who cut his foot with an axe. Although the miracles seem randomly inserted in the story, three come before he receives his education with three coming after Jesus receives life lessons about the power of good vs evil.

170 CE

School of Scriptural Interpretation in Antioch, Syria emphasized a literal interpretation of scripture and tended toward a Christology that made a distinction between an earthly man named Jesus the Nazarite and God the Father. The school tended to be an adoptionist Christology whereby God temporarily adopted Jesus as his son at the Jordan River when baptized. Theophilus, bishop of Antioch, founded the school with his theology being rooted in Jewish ideas and the Hebrew scripture.

Hegesippus (110 – 180 CE), early church historian, gave his view concerning the original Word of God as taught by Jesus and how it was being distorted in meaning. In addition to the message being distorted, the very essence of Jesus was being distorted as well. In *Memoirs,* he wrote:

> The brothers of Jesus came, then, and took the presidency
> of every church, as witness for Christ, and as being of the
> kindred of the Lord. Up to that period the Church had
> remained like a pure virgin, pure and uncorrupted: for, if
> there were any persons who were disposed to tamper with

the wholesome rule of the preaching of salvation, they still lurked in some dark place of concealment or other. But, when the sacred band of apostles had in various ways closed their lives, and that generation of men to whom it had been vouchsafed to listen to Godlike Wisdom with their own ears had passed away, then did the confederacy of godless error take its rise through the treachery of false teachers.

171 CE

Irenaeus, bishop of Lyon, France (130 - 200 CE) originated the belief that the founder of the Church in Rome was Peter. In *Ecclesiastical History of the Church,* Eusebius stated that Rome was first evangelized by Christian soldiers between 43 - 49 CE with Peter not arriving in Rome until 61 CE at which time he and Paul, selecting Linus as first bishop of Rome.

172 CE

Muratorian Canon is the oldest known manuscript that contains the books of the New Testament. Unlike todays canon of Truth, scripture not accepted by the Church of Rome were: Hebrews, James, 1 & 2 Peter, 2 & 3 John with Apocalypse of Peter accepted.

175 CE

Irenaeus (120 – 202 CE), bishop of Lyon in Gaul, assembled the first Christian Bible. He chose four gospels because the number corresponded to the four corners of the world, the four winds, the four areas of heaven, and the four beasts of the Apocalypse. He adopted the term "Orthodox" which means "straight thinking" in Greek – with those who didn't agree with his ideas called "Heretics." In Gaul, as many as 70 martyrs were tortured and executed for their faith, with Irenaeus becoming frustrated because he was aware of theological fragmentation. He campaigned heavily for a united belief about the *being* of Jesus because there were many gospel stories giving alternative views about him. In *Adverus Haereses* he attempted to discredit competing ideas not to his liking.

Irenaeus is of importance to Christian thinking because he was the first exponent of Catholic orthodoxy. He was the first to treat New Testament scripture on par with the Hebrew Bible with the Hebrew Bible being a prophetic record of the coming of the "Son of God".

176 CE

Marcus Aurelius Antoninus was emperor from 161 to 180 CE. He had a logical mind with his notes representative of Stoic philosophy which holds that by becoming a clear and unbiased thinker, one understands the universal reason *(logos)*. His book *Meditations* is still revered today as a literary monument to a government of service and duty. He acquired the reputation of "philosopher king" within his lifetime given the title by Christians such as Athenagoras (133-190 CE) and Eusebius (260-340 CE). He thanked his grandfather Marcus Annius Verus II for teaching him 'good character and avoidance of bad temper.'

180 CE

Proof of the Apostolic Preaching is the oldest known writing to include the doctrine of apostolic succession. Apostolic succession states that the ministry of the Christian Church is derived from the Apostles by continuous succession.

182 CE

Old Roman Creed is considered the forerunner of *Apostles Creed* which is the summary of Christian belief.

183 CE

Stomateis was written by Clement, bishop of Alexandria (150-217 CE). It states that Peter traveled with his wife and children as did the other disciples including the brothers of Jesus. The memory of Peter being married, as well as the other disciples, persisted in the church until the end of the second century at which time women were excluded from the Christian story by the all-male church leadership.

193 CE

Alexandrian School of Scriptural Interpretation located in Alexandria, Egypt was founded by Clement, bishop of Alexandria (153-217 CE). The school emphasized an allegorical interpretation of scripture that focused on the union of an earthly man named Jesus of Nazareth with God the Father. The school drew on the methods devised by Philo of Alexandria which allowed the literal interpretation of scripture to be supplemented with allegory as he argued that it was necessary to look beneath the surface of the meaning of the scriptures to discern what hidden information lay beneath. He taught a fusion of Greek philosophy, notably the power of reason, with Jesus becoming the *Word*, the knowledge of God. The school believed that Jesus was the hidden content found in Hebrew Bible prophecy and that he was God-like and, as such, divine.

Gregory Thaumaturgus (205-265 CE), head of the Alexandrian School, considered the following views as being worthy of excommunication from the Church:

- If anyone refuses to acknowledge that Jesus is first created and eternal and the wisdom of God.

- If anyone says that Jesus is just a prophet and perfect man.

- If anyone says that Jesus was saved by his virtue but refuses to acknowledge that he is the Savior.

- If anyone says Jesus is just a perfect man but not the Word of God.

- If anyone says Jesus is not God.

195 CE

New Testament was placed along-side the Hebrew Bible with the New fulfilling prophesy given in the Old.

197 CE

The Thunder: Perfect Mind is a feminine voice that points out important aspects of women in Christian belief because they perform important roles in the life of the church; they are glamourous, powerful and associated with the Divine. They are extremely importance relative to life's challenges and promises.

198 CE

Authorship of Mark, Matthew, Luke, and John was assigned as they were written anonymously.

199 CE

Origen (185 -251 CE), head of the school of Christian Theology in Alexandria, believed that there are three levels of meaning to the Bible: literal, moral, and spiritual. In the field of Christology, he was the first person to establish the tradition of distinguishing between the full divinity of the Father and lesser divinity of the Son. He was first to present the intellectual framework of Christian faith as he realized that if Christianity was to succeed in shaping civilization, it must justify itself to the intellect of man as well as the heart. His Christology was the doctrine of titles for Jesus as they corresponded to his different activities relating to humanity. The two most important titles for Jesus were *Wisdom* and *Word*. As Wisdom, Jesus is the intelligible world containing principles of all beings. As Word, he is the revealer of all mysteries with the Hebrew Bible being the only revelation because it is a prophecy of Christ with the New Testament allowing mankind to apply what is said about Christ to the Christian.

200 CE

The word *Trinitas* was first coined by Tertullian (160 – 225 CE) because he envisioned Jesus as being generated from the Father as the *Word* in the course of creation, revelation, and redemption making Jesus a later creation and lesser being than God. He envisioned the Holy Spirit as being a creation of the Father and lesser being than Jesus, similar to an angel.

202 CE

Eusebius (260-339 CE), Orosius (375-420 CE) and Jerome (342-420 CE) all speak of the persecution of the churches under Emperor Septimius Serverus (193 – 211 CE) with historians agreeing that persecution was essentially aimed at putting a stop to Christian teaching first by preventing new conversions and then by attacking new converts. Historians agree that on a whole, a period of religious tolerance between the Christian religion and the Roman state existed in direct proportion to the extent to which Christians were prepared to participate in the public life of the empire without allowing their prejudices to interfere.

205 CE

Hippolytus (170 - 235 CE), presbyter of the Church of Rome, is considered the most important theologian of the Roman Church in the pre-Constantine era. In *Commentary on Canticle of Canticles,* he states the following about Mary Magdalene in the development of Christianity:

> The initiative of Mary Magdalene was central to the development of Christianity. Because the woman was troublesome in a Jewish environment where only the testimony of men counted in the first centuries; troublesome also to a Church attempting to establish a masculine ministry hostile to prophetism often incarnated in women and troublesome to the type of Christianity which depended upon Peter and Paul, Mary Magdalene is historicallydepicted in Gospel of Mark as being a speechless witness; in Gospel of Matthew as being a fearful messenger; in Gospel of Luke as a former sinner; and in Gospel of John as the intimate of Jesus with Mary Magdalene's role minimized and her experience and authority relegated to the background by the primitive community in its process of spiritual organization. (8.2)

Mary Magdalene is not only mentioned more than any other individual in the New Testament, she is the central figure in early non-canonical Christian writings, including the *Dialogue of the Savior, Pristis Sophia, Gospel of Thomas, Gospel of Philip* and *Gospel of Mary* but to name a few. The inaccurate portrayal of Mary Magdalene being a woman of ill repute and prostitute began in 591 CE when Pope Gregory I (540-604 CE) confused her with Mary of Bethany in his Easter sermon. In 1969, the identification of Mary Magdalene as being "sinful woman" was removed by Pope Paul VI (1963-1978) with Mary Magdalene now considered a Saint by the Roman Catholic, Eastern Orthodox, Anglican and Lutheran churches.

210 CE

Tertullian (160 – 225 CE) was first to use the term *Trinity* to describe the Godhead. He used the term in *Against Praxeus* to defend his teaching against Monarchianism which was a theology that emphasized God as one, in direct contrast to Trinitarianism which defines God as three persons coexisting consubstantially as one being.

218 CE

Origen (185 - 254 CE) was the most important theologian of the third century due to his intense study of the Holy Scriptures. He developed a symbolic method of reading the Bible. He studied the Hebrew language and original works written in Hebrew and in the hands of the Jews. He investigated the editions of others, who, besides the seventy, had published their translations of the scriptures, some different from the well-known translations done by Aquila (22-97 0CE), and Theodotion (110-190CE). Having collected all the versions, Origen arranged them opposite one another into parallel columns in the *Hexapla*. He concluded that the 'virgin birth' of Christ should not to be understood as a literal event but as the birth of the divine wisdom in the soul. He did not believe that mankind had been saved by the death of Jesus. He believed that man had ascended to God under their own power through Jesus teaching of wisdom. He believed that the resurrection of Jesus represented a public disclosure of his commitment to God the Father with all who believing in him should elevate their love for their fellow man. He equated Mary Magdalene as being the bride of Jesus as mentioned in the Jewish canticle Song of Songs.

225 CE

Letter of Peter to Philip emphasizes the need of announcing Christ's message and healing despite any threat from Rome. The story opens with Peter and Philip going to Mount of Olivet to seek out Jesus because they are being threatened with death and needed to know why this was happening and what they should do. Jesus's answer to the first question is that there has been a cosmic mistake in the relationship between the Mother and Father God with this divine mistake resulting in arrogant powers taking over humanity. Jesus then told them to go out and proclaim salvation with this salvation announcing the divine goodness and power of God and the falseness of the arrogant and violent powers.

241 CE

The first modern large-room church was built in Syria. Until that time, church services had been held in secret in private home settings.

244 CE

Seeing the enthusiasm with which Emperor Phillip the Arab viewed Christianity, pagan elements of society began to fear that Christians were becoming all too active in the life of the empire. As *Historia Augusta* relates, the fear was that everyone including the emperor and the state itself would become converted to Christianity and that the old pagan religion would be abandoned.

250s CE

Christians were the most dynamic religious group in the Roman world, still not as large numerically as the Jewish community but far surpassing them in the rate of expansion with the thought being that this growth was caused by the decline in Roman fortunes. The period saw a campaign of persecution by emperors Decius and Valerian who blamed the Christians for the empires many misfortunes.

251 CE

Pistis Sophia highlights the teaching of Jesus after his resurrection as he remained with the disciples eleven years revealing knowledge necessary for the soul to reach the highest divine. The first two books outline the fall and restoration of a figure known as Pistis Sophia, a major female divinity who dwells outside of the divine realm with Mary Magdalene the featured disciple who asks questions of Jesus. The third book is concerned with ethical lifestyle. It outlines what is needed for right thinking and action. The fourth book is about the destiny of various types of souls and punishment of sinners. Jesus serves as teacher to give his disciples information about the divine world they will need in order to progress to a higher state of being. He teaches them about baptismal rites and instructs them to give these to all who show themselves to be worthy.

254 CE

Pope Stephen I (254-257 CE) was first bishop to claim Rome's primacy over all other bishops due to Rome's succession from Apostle Peter.

257 CE

Emperor Valerian's persecution of the Christian religion (253-260 CE) opened a new era which culminated in the *Edict of Milan*. He penalized Christianity as a church and as an organized structure. His persecutions were a reaction to Philip the Arab and the fear of the Christianization of the empire through the ruling class. He attacked Christians of the ruling class because he did not want them integrated into the political life of the empire.

260s CE

A wave of Christian conversions in the Roman Empire swelled to tidal proportions in the largest, most prosperous and culturally advanced cities of the East. Christianity, by contrast to paganism, expressed a new sense of inner space in which an individual could struggle with the devil, communicate with God, and discover his or her own spirituality with the Christian message having a profound appeal to an increasing number of Romans dissatisfied with their frozen, public rituals. They were seeking "a God with whom they could be alone."

262 CE

Emperor Gallienus (260-268 CE) edict of tolerance gave Christianity the legal right to exist. His change in policy towards the Senate went hand in hand with the official recognition of the Christian religion which the Senate had forbidden for the previous two centuries. He broke completely with the pro-senate policy of the preceding emperors. He forbade the senators military command and cut them off from all the sources of real power. It was this break with the Senate that made it possible for him to grant to Christians the recognition which was necessary for the well-being of the empire, but which the senate had always feared so much.

272 CE

Helena (248-328 CE), wife of emperor Constantius Chlorus (305-306 CE), gave birth to Constantine I. By the time he was 31 (303 CE), he was in line to become emperor of the Western Roman Empire.

284 CE

Emperor Diocletian (284-305 CE) took control over both the Eastern and Western Empire. He reinstated pagan gods and traditional forms of worship as the foundation upon which the empire would be built, meaning that tolerance of Christianity would collapse and that Christians would once again find themselves victims of pagan persecution. From *Ecclesiastical History of the Church*:

> It was the nineteenth year of the reign of Diocletian (293 CE) and the the month of March, in which the festival of our Savior's passion was at hand, when the imperial edicts were everywhere published to tear down the churches to their foundations and to destroy the sacred scriptures by fire. They commanded, also, that those who were in honorable stations should be degraded and those who were freedmen should be deprived of their liberty if they persevered in their adherence to Christianity.
>
> The first edict against Christians was of this nature; but it was not long before other edicts were also issued, in which it was ordered that all the prelates in every place should first be committee to prison, and then, by every artifice, constrained to offer sacrifice to the gods. Such was the state of things throughout the whole period of the persecution. This, by the goodness of God, had entirely ceased in the tenth year, although it had already begun to relax in the eighth. When Maximus was removed, who had proved the worst of all the surviving enemies of religion, the renovation of the churches was begun from the very foundations by the goodness of God, theomnipotent Ruler.

Thus, then, the impious being cleared away, the government was deservedly reserved secure and without rival for the only two, Constantine and Licinius.

307 CE

Constantius Chlorus, father of Constantine I, died in the imperial palace. Upon his death, Constantine I, at age thirty-two, who favored paganism, was elevated to emperor of the Western Empire while Licinus, his brother-in-law, was elevated to emperor of the Eastern Empire.

312 CE

Ecclesiastic History of the Church describes Constantine's battle for sole power against Emperor Maxentius (306-312 CE) of the Western Empire:

> In the spring of the year, with 40,000 soldiers behind him, Constantine rode toward Rome to confront an enemy whose numbers were four times his own. Maxentius, vying for supremacy in the West, waited in Rome with his Italian troops confident no one could successfully invade the city. With Constantine still miles away from the city, Maxentius bolstered by prophecy, left the city to confront his foe. Meanwhile, Constantine, in a dream, saw a vision in the afternoon sky; a bright cross with the words *In Hoc Signe Vinces* emblazoned meaning "in this sign you will conquer." As the story goes, Christ himself told Constantine to take the cross into battle as his standard. When Constantine awoke the next morning, he ordered his soldiers to mark their shields with the now famous Chi-Rho. When Maxentius's troops saw the cross they fled in disarray toward the surging Tiber River. The would-be emperor, attempting to escape over a narrow wooden bridge erected to span the river, was forced into the river, where he drowned by weight of his own armor.
>
> Constantine entered Rome the undisputed ruler of the West, the first Roman emperor with a cross in his diadem. Once supreme in the West, Constantine met Licinus, the ruler of the Balkan provinces, and issued the famous *Edict of Milan* that gave Christians freedom to worship. The edict directed the governors to restore all property seized during the severe Diocletian persecution.

313 CE

Ecclesiastical History of the Church was written by Eusebius, bishop of Caesarea (313-339 CE). He was a pioneer who worked on giving a chronological account of the early development of Christianity from the 1ˢᵗ to 4ᵗʰ century. He had access to the Theological Library of Caesarea and made use of ecclesiastical documents, acts of martyrs, letters, extracts from earlier Christian writings, lists of bishops, and similar sources, often quoting the originals at great length so that his work contains materials not found elsewhere preserved. He attempted to present history of the Church from the apostles to his own time. Ramsay Mac Mullen in *Christianizing the Roman Empire: AD 100-400* regarded Eusebius' work as being representative of early Christian historical accounts in which:

> "Hostile writings and discarded views were not recopied or passed on, or they were actively suppressed … matters discreditable to the faith were to be consigned to silence with several of Hegesippus' writing found to be in that category."

What Flavius Josephus (36 - 100 CE) was to exposing Old Testament history, Eusebius (260-339 CE) was to exposing New Testament history.

314 CE

Civil war broke out between Constantine I and Licinius because Licinius refused to honor the humane regulations mandated by the Edict of Milan. After ten years of warfare, Licinius was defeated at the battles of Hadrianople and Chrysopolis with Constantine the Great becoming sole emperor of Rome.

315 CE

When emperor Constantine I made Christianity a lawful religion of the Roman Empire, it stopped being a Jewish sect and became its own religion. With this acceptance came the construction of large churches, to serve the worship needs of Christians with the remains of these churches now turning up in archaeological findings around the world. The findings help to answer the question of how Christianity which started in places like Turkey and Egypt spread beyond Israel throughout the Roman Empire.

In 2011, a large Christian church was found in the city of Laodicea, Turkey even though the city has been uninhabited since 1968. In 363 CE, clergy from all over Asia Minor convened there for *Council of Laodicea*.
321 CE

Battles raged between competing Christian groups of the Roman Empire as to the *being* of Jesus and his relationship to God with spiritual preference of the reigning emperor dictating the outcome. *Arians* viewed Jesus as being an "earthly man" following the Antioch School of Scriptural Interpretation whereas *anti-Arian* viewed Jesus as being "divine" followed the Alexandrian School of Scriptural Interpretation. Bishop Alexander, of Alexandria, an *anti-Arian* delivered a series of sermons maintaining strongly that Jesus was eternal God on earth in the form of a man and that any belief contrary to that was heretical. In reply to this sermon, Arius, a parish priest of a section of Alexandria known as Baucalis, published an open letter challenging the prelate's views. In a fit of rage, Alexander ordered Arius to appear before him to defend his position with the controversy escalating sharply from there.

Was Arius denying Christ's divinity? No – because the Son's divinity was perfected by either his will or by his nature. Whether he was God's subordinate or his equal, God raised him up to rule by his side in heaven and there was no other like him – Jesus was truly unique but he was not the son of God!

Alexander would have none of that theology ordering Arius to preach correct doctrine as he saw it – that Jesus was no less than God on earth, the Creator had become human in order to redeem our sins.

More than 100 Egyptian bishops attended the Council of Alexandria with the proceedings being stormy. Half the bishops supported Arius in his views that Jesus was an extraordinary human being with the other half accepting Alexander's position that Jesus was God in the flesh. Anti-Arian bishops who attended the meeting drew up a creed – *Confession of Orthodoxy* which they laid before Arius and his supporters with a demand that they sign it. When they refused, the council excommunicated Arius and his followers and banished them from Alexandria with street fighting ensuing immediately between competing Christian Groups.

After the groups expulsion, Eusebius, bishop of Nicomedia, not only welcomed Arius and his followers into his church, he wrote to other bishops on Arius's behalf, with the result being that bishop Alexander was soon receiving scores of letters from other bishops asking him to readmit Arius and his followers to communion in Alexandria and restore him to his pulpit.

324 CE

Constantine I triumphed over Licinus with *Ecclesiastical History of the Church* explaining the reason for the war:

> For Constantine, as most gracious emperor, exhibiting the evidence of true benevolence, had not refused affinity with Licinus, had not denied him the illustrious marriage with his sister, and had honored him as a sharer in the eminent nobility of the imperial family, which he derived from his fathers. He had shared with him the government of the whole empire as his kinsman and partner, granting him the power to rule and govern no less a part of the empire than himself. But he, on the contrary, pursued a course directly opposite to this by plotting every kind of mischief against his superior .... He drove away all Christians, he devised illegal laws to extraction money from the people subject to him, he banished nobles and illustrious men, he attacked bishops, and razed some churches to the ground while closing others.

325 CE

Two letters led up to Council of Nicaea being called by Constantine I. The first was written by Alexander, bishop of Alexandria, to Constantine I stating that the "nature" and "being" of Jesus was under an attach led by Arius, presbyter of his church. The second was written by Constantine I to both Alexander and Arius acknowledging their difference of opinion stating that there needed to be harmony in the church.

As sole ruler of the empire, Constantine summoned 220 bishops to Council of Nicaea over which he would preside. He ordered the bishops to work out a standard formulation for Jesus *being* as debate was raging within the church about his relationship to God, his substance, and the personality of God. What did it mean that Christ was both human and divine? Constantine realized it was now time for his intervention.

Arius, pastor of Baucalius church, argued that Jesus was an earthly man even though he was totally extraordinary. Pelegius, a monk from Rome, argued that salvation was located within humanity itself because individuals had the capacity to save themselves by following the law and moral example set by Jesus during his life-time. Alexander, bishop of Alexandria, argued that Jesus was God on earth.

From this meeting emerged the *Nicene Creed* that clarified the correct canon of belief; twenty-seven writings known as the New Testament and twenty-two writings known as the Old Testament with scripture dealing with women in church leadership being removed by the all-male bishops.

Eusebius gives a description of Constantine I as he entered the hall at Council of Nicaea to discusses the meaning of Trinity:

At the signal which announced the entrance of the emperor, all rose and he appeared in the midst of them, his purple robe, resplendent with gold and precious stones, dazzling the eyes of the beholders. Thus his mind was impressed with religious awe was evident in his downcast eyes and his modest step and movement. He was taller than any of those by whom he was surrounded. Nor was he in stature only but also in elegance of form and robustness of frame, superior to the others. When he reached the upper end of the hall, he remained standing in the middle between the highest places before a small chair burnished with gold, which was prepared for his accommodations, until he was requested to be seated by the bishops, who then resumed their places....

The emperor remarked that the power of the enemy being destroyed and no one remaining to make resistance to the church, it would be deplorable indeed, if they, the bishops, now molest one another and give occasion to those who regarded them with no friendly aspect to turn their quarrels into ridicule. Their business, he said, was with matters of theology, the decision of which depended on the instruction which the Holy Spirit had left them.....

The emperor then gave those who presided in the council an opportunity of speaking and permitted the members to examine matters of doctrine and religious differences. The opinions of Arius were first examined in the presence of the emperor. The other bishops, beyond comparison the greater number, mildly required them to give an account of their doctrine and to support it by suitable proofs. But no sooner had they began to speak than they seemed to be at variance with themselves; they remained confounded, and seeing the absurdity of their heresy,
confessed their shame by their silence....

The emperor patiently listened to the disputes, which were agitated at first with considerable warmth. Constantine spoke kindly to everyone in the Greek language, gaining over the bishops to his opinion by the strength of his arguments and softening others by his entreaties. He commended those who spoke judiciously, persuaded them all to concord, and reduce them at last to an agreement on the contested points....

Emperor Constantine wrote two letters in order to promulgate the ordinances of the council. The first was particularly addressed to the church in Alexandria, and informed them that the faith had been examined and placed in so clear a light that no difficulty remained. Copies of this letter were dispatched to all provinces. The second was directed to the churches in general. He published also an edict, directed to the bishops and people condemning Arius and his writings....

At the conclusion of this splendid festival, the emperor courteously saluted every individual of the company and presented his guests with rich and valuable gifts, according to their respective ranks and merits. When they were about to separate, he took a friendly leave of them, exhorting them to union, harmony, and mutual condescension and concluded by recommending himself to prayers. Thus ended the great Council of Nicaea. The council concluded its session on the twenty-fifth day of August, 325 CE, a month after the commencement of the twentieth year of the reign of Constantine, who ascended the throne on the twenty-fifth of July 306 CE.

Arius's disagreement with Alexander centered on his mixing of God with his creation removing Jesus from human society, from the universe of moral turmoil, placing him in the unchangeable heavens implying that if Jesus is God himself, he cannot intervene on behalf of mankind.

Alexander did not accept Arius's point of view because it leads to the conclusion that Christ was a man, which is the Jewish position. If Jesus owed his son-ship to adoption and his immortality to promotion by God, he would only be a Prophet and still a human.

To this argument, Eusebius, bishop of Caesarea, responded saying that God cannot have offspring because he is unimaginable, indescribable, and omnipotent. On that point, Constantine totally agreed !

326 CE

Constantine sent a letter to bishop Alexander insisting that Arius's view that Jesus was earthly man promote by God was acceptable demanding that the church of Alexandria reinstate Arius and his followers and restore their rank.

328 CE

Alexander passed away with his assistant Athanasius, who was both a brilliant theologian and chief defender of Trinitarianism, becoming bishop of Alexandria with his most famous works *Against the Heathen* and *The Incarnation of the Word of God* used to develop orthodox theology. Athanasius believed that Jesus, as Christ, entered the world in human form to lead men back into the harmony with the Father from which they had fallen away.

335 CE

Synod of Tyre discussed the failure of Athanasius to abide by Constantine the Great's order to reinstatement Arius and his followers into the Alexandrian church and restored to their rank with the Bishop being excommunicated.

337 CE

Constantine I became the first Arian Christian emperor when he was baptized by Eusebius on his death bed in Nicomedia. He believed that Jesus was an extra-ordinary man who entered the world to lead humanity back into harmony with the Father.

338 through 376 CE:

Beginning with Constantine the Great, the emperor began to involved himself in church affairs due to the battle raging between bishops over the *being* of Jesus and his relationship to God the Father with the prevailing question being – Was Jesus an extra-ordinary human being or was he God in the flesh?

Constantine I (306 – 337 CE): ***Arian***: Believe Jesus to be God's subordinate.

Constantine II (337 – 340 CE): Arian

Constantius II (337 – 361 CE): Arian

Constans I (337 – 350 CE): ***Anti-Arian***: Believe Jesus to be God.

Julian (361 – 363 CE): Pagan

Jovian (363 – 364 CE): Anti-Arian

Valentinian (364 – 375 CE): Anti-Arian

Valens (364 – 378 CE): Arian

Theodosius (379 -395 CE): ***Anti-Arian***

376 CE

The decisive moment for the formation of the Christian Bible came with the writing of Athanasius *39th Festal Letter* which instructed Christians of North Africa to read only approved text which stated that Jesus was consubstantial with the Father and nothing less. He ordered all scripture not approved by

Council of Nicaea to be destroyed. Upon receiving this news, monks at St. Pachomius monastery gathered their sacred books and buried them in a hillside near Nag Hammadi, Egypt while monks at Qumran buried their holy scripture in the cliffs above the Dead Sea with the followers of the Jerusalem church burying their sacred books near Joppa.

379 CE

Theodosius, a practical minded and decisive Spanish general, became emperor of the Eastern Empire (379 – 395 CE) with his first campaign being to defeat the Goth army in the Balkans. With the Balkans pacified, he returned to the imperial city of Milan and asked Anti-Arian bishop Ambrose (339 – 397 CE) to instruct him in the Catholic faith. The following month, he issued *Edict of Thessalonica* mandating anti-Arian orthodoxy being the only legitimate Christian religion. He offered Arian bishop of Constantinople, Demophilus, the choice of accepting the *Nicene Creed* or going into exile. He ordered the governor of Egypt to expel Lucius from Alexandria and install anti-Arian Peter. The affairs of Antioch were settled with equal dispatch with Arians and other heretics forbidden to occupy any church or meet together for worship within the walls of any town.

381 CE

Council of Constantinople added wording to the Nicene Creed which concluded that Jesus was fully human. Words added were: "He was crucified for us under Pontius Pilate, and suffered, and was buried, and on the third day he rose again, according to the scriptures, and ascended into heaven, and sitteth on the right hand of the Father."

386 CE

After sixty-years of raging debate within the church over the meaning of Trinity, three theologian brothers, the Cappadocian's, explained that Father, Son, and Spirit should not be identified with God because the divine nature of God is unnamable and unspeakable. Trinity should not be seen as a literal fact but as a paradigm that corresponds to the real facts in the hidden life of God meaning that God has the ability to express himself wholly to the world in each of these three manifestations if he so chooses.

390 CE

Apostles Creed first appeared in a letter written by Ambrose, bishop of Milan, to Pope Siricus in Rome with nothing in it said about the divinity of Jesus. The creed in its present form was not introduced to the public until the 8th century.

392 CE

Augustine, bishop of Hippo, is considered one of the greatest Christian thinkers of all time. He believed that the grace of God was indispensable to human freedom. He framed the concepts of 'original sin' and 'just war'. He wrote in *To Simplicianus* that Adam's sin had enormous consequences for the world, as man's power to do right was gone because he was dead spiritually as sin made it impossible for the sinner to think clearly and especially to understand higher spiritual truths and ideas. He developed the concept that the Catholic church is the spiritual 'City of God,' distinct from the earthly city.

In *On Free Choice of the Will*, he addresses why God gives humans 'free will' that can be used for good or evil. He believed that Adam's guilt did not destroy his ancestors freedom of will.

In *On Care to Be Had for the Dead*, he was the first to view human beings as a unity of two substances: soul and body.

In *The Literal Interpretation of Genesis*, he took the view that everything in the universe was created simultaneously by God, not in seven calendar days as Genesis would require. He argued that the six-day structure presents a logical framework but was not a literal passage of time in a physical way.

In *City of God*, he rejected the immortality of the human race as proposed by the pagans.

In *Just War*, he was the first theologian to assert that Christians should defend ones-self and others when necessary.

In *Literal Interpretation of Genesis* he believed that the Bible should not be interpreted as literal, but as metaphorical. While each passage of scripture has a literal sense it does not always mean that scripture is history, at times it is extended metaphor.

In *Confessions*, his early life of being a carousing drunkard who fathered a child out of wedlock, painted for him a negative view of priests being allowed to marry when historically, until that time, the apostles were married and with children.

In *Decretum Gratiani* the idea that women cannot be ordained priests, lead, teach or be witness can be found.

393 CE

New Testament was canonized at Council of Hippo with all gospels confirming Mary Magdalene's spiritual leadership and unique relationship to Jesus excluded and deemed "heretical." Scripture such as *Gospel of Mary Magdalene, Gospel of Philip, Gospel of Thomas* were excluded. Scriptures that confirmed and validated woman's leadership in the earliest forms of Christianity, such as *The Acts of Paul and Thecla, The Sophia of Jesus Christ* and *Pistis Sophia* were excluded.

400 CE

Theophilus, patriarch of Alexandria and leader of the Egyptian Christian church between 385 CE and 412 CE, wrote *The Vision of Theophilus*, which is the story of the holy family's travels in Egypt, China, India, and Tibet saying that after the crucifixion, family travel continuing on until the end of the first century, suggesting to scholars that Jesus and Mary Magdalene passed from the scene toward the end of the first century.

425 CE

Apostolic Constitutions give a complete list of New Testament books minus Revelation of Jesus Christ with 1 Clement, 2 Clement, and eight books of the Constitutions added.

431 CE

Emperor Theodosius II (408 – 450 CE) insisted that the Council of Ephesus affirmed that Jesus was made of the same substance as God the Father.

While Jesus had two natures before his baptism, the two natures merged to form a single nature after baptism. The council also declared the divine motherhood of Mother Mary.

Jesus became God on earth!

For scholars, the cost of stripping Jesus of his humanity, eliminated the reality that he was a human being; the cost of eliminating Mary Magdalene as Christ's consort, his spiritual equal, strips modern Christianity of a female model on how the process of love can unite mankind from within which is both flesh and spirit, both human and divine.

451 CE

Pope Leo I (440-461 CE), established the primacy of Rome on the basis of the inherited authority of Apostle Peter and the concept of the pope being the mystical embodiment of Peter. He called himself the heir to the throne and deputy of Peter having received his apostolic authority using terms derived from Roman law.

Council of Chalcedon stated that: "Jesus is perfect both in deity and in humanness; this selfsame one is also actually God and actually man." This affirmation was caused by a major conflict that existed between the schools of theology in Alexandria and in Antioch. The Alexandrian school taught that Jesus was divine, a God figure, while the Antioch school stressed that Jesus was fully human because of the saving virtue. As a compromise, the Council concluded that Jesus was "complete in Godhead and complete in manhood, truly God and truly man, in two natures, without confusion, without change, without division or without separation, coming together to form one person."

485 CE

The beginning of the end for the Western Empire can be dated to 383 CE when Magnus Maximus, commander of the Roman legions in Britain, crossed over into mainland Europe, capturing France and Spain before trying to expand his territory into Italy which led to his defeat at the hands of Roman Emperor Theodosius.

Upon the death of Theodosius in 395 CE, the western empire was divided between his two sons with the western region consisting of Italy, Spain, Britain, and North Africa ruled by his ten-year-old son Honorius and the eastern region consisting of the Balkans, Turkey, Middle East and Egypt being ruled by his eighteen-year-old son Arcadius.

Due to its immense size, the Roman Empire began coming under severe military pressure from all sides and from political unrest within. As such, the eastern and western empires slowly drifted apart, accelerated by military and economic cost dealing with the Goths in the west and the Huns in the east. In the case of the Hun tribes led by Attila, it was a loose confederation of highly mobile, well-armed clans which could easily reach 700,000 persons in number.

In 439 CE, Roman envoys were sent to Attila to arrange a peace agreement whereby Rome agreed to pay Attila 700 lbs. in gold per year (USD $ 19 million in 2024) as tribute to avoid conflict in the East. While this agreement was being concluded in the East, Goths led by Geiseric, seized Carthage in North Africa with the loss being a financial blow to the western empire as now some of its wealthiest provinces in the Mediterranean no longer belonged to Rome. The fall of Carthage also meant the Vandals could easily blockade the commercial harbor of Alexandria disrupting shipments of grain to Constantinople which was critical. From *History of Attila*, Roman historian Priscus, describes the Goth leader:

> Geiseric was of medium height and limped as a result of a fall while out riding. He thought deeply, said little, and despised luxury. He had a violent temper and was single-mindedly acquisitive and remarkably far-sighted. He was prepared to sow seeds of discord and incite hatred in order to stir up others to his advantage.

As soon as Attila received word that the eastern Roman fleet had set sail for Sicily to confront the Goths, he opened his Danube offensive ending imperial control in that area by 442 CE. In 449 CE , as sole head of the Hun nation, he sent his trusted bodyguard Edeco and his secretary Orestes to the imperial court in Constantinople, asking why the signed treaty with Rome had been violated demanding back payment of six thousand pounds of gold owed, but not paid (USD $ 163 million in 2024 dollars), based on the agreement made ten years prior. In *History of Attila*, Priscus of Panium, a Greek historian, gives a picture of Attila based upon their personal relationship:

> While he did not look Roman, he was not ugly in any way as reported nor did he exhibit any depravity or irrational behavior as in reality he showed great intelligence and common sense. He showed no madness nor exhibited immorality as he was loyal to his clan members who revered him as he always acted with moderation, with frugality and restraint. He wore no jewels and during dinner was served simple food using a wooden plate and mug. He was especially fond of coarse bread, whitebait, handmade soft cheese and green figs.

Historians have chosen 485 CE for the Fall of the Roman Empire because this is when the western faction of the Roman Empire was destroyed, thus ending its reign over the world. Romulus Augustulus (485 - 511 CE), who was last Roman emperor, was over-thrown by Germanic leader Odoacer (433 - 493 CE), who had control over the tribes to the north of Germany notably the Vandals, Franks, Angles, Saxons, Goths, Lombards, and Burgundians. Odoacer, who was viewed as being a soldier and statesman, was the first non-Italian (Barbarian) to rule over the Empire. He introduced few important changes to the administrative system of the empire thereby maintaining the support of the Roman Senate. He was an Arian Christian who rarely intervened in the affairs of the Trinitarian state church of the Roman Empire. As an Arian, he believed that Jesus Christ did not always exist but was made by God before time and that Son of God was only a title, that Jesus was distinct from the Father and therefore subordinate to him with the title Son actually meaning of the "same in essence" as God.

553 CE

Fifth Ecumenical Council of Constantinople declared the doctrine of Perpetual Virginity of Mother Mary followed by the doctrine of Immaculate Conception of Mother Mary in 1854 and doctrine that Mother Mary was consumed both body and soul into heavenly glory in 1950.

567 CE

Based upon Astro-archaeology, the study of astronomy as it was practiced in ancient times, it is believed by scholars that the "Star of Bethlehem" appeared on March 2 with the early church choosing December 25 as the first Nativity Feast (Christmas) because that date that was easy to remember because it fell on the first day of the Winter Solstice on which the lengthening of days could be found. Gospel of Luke reports the visit of the 'Shepherds' to venerate the newborn Christ child, whereas Gospel of Matthew records the visit of the 'Wise Men'. For scholars, Luke's intended Gentile audience needed to know that the Christ child had been born under humble circumstances whereas Matthew's Jewish audience wanted to know of Jesus's divine royalty as a descendent of the house of David.

610 CE

An Arab merchant from Meca, of the tribe of Quraysh, named Muhammed ibn Adballah (576-632 CE), while on a retreat on Mount Hira, was torn from his sleep by a divine visitation from the angel Gabriel. During this visitation, not only did Gabriel instruct Muhammad to write the Koran, he informed Muhammad that Allah, the high God of the Arabian pantheon, was identical to the God worshipped by Jews and Christians alike.
From a Muslim perspective, Islam did not start with Prophet Muhammad's revelation but is the original faith given to Adam, the first human and prophet. From Adam onwards, all prophets were sent by Allah to guide the people to the same core belief: submission to Allah, the One true God.

Christianity and Islam parted ways over their different understandings of the nature of God. In Christianity, God is understood as a Trinity – one God in three persons (Father, Son, Holy Ghost), a concept rejected by Islam where God is viewed as a single entity, without any partners or associates. Where Christianity views Jesus as being Son of God, Muslims view Jesus as being a prophet of God; same view held by the Jewish faith.

CONCLUSION

*A*s strange as it may seem, ancient religions didn't require the individual to believe one thing or another since religion was all about proper practices – how you treat your fellow man. There were many gods and many ways to worship them with no single path to the divine as ancient religions were not overly interested in the afterlife but more concerned about the quality of life in the "here and now." Among the many things that made Christianity different from other religions is the fact that Christian leaders insisted that it mattered what one believed. The Church insisted that it held the truth and that every other belief was in error with this truth, involving claims about God, about Jesus, about salvation, and about eternal life. As a result, followers were forced to appeal to church authorities as to what they should believe with these leaders, claiming that they were appointed by the apostles that Jesus choose to instruct them so they could pass along his sacred teachings.

Orthodoxy and the relationship between the early Church and early heretical groups is a matter of academic debate. Walter Bauer, in *Orthodoxy and Heresy in Earliest Christianity* proposed that in the earliest Christianity, heresy was an original manifestation. It was only after the legalization of Christianity, which began under Constantine I in 313 CE, that the Church, with his support, began to formulated canons of Christian truth in the face of major Christological disputes over the *being* of Jesus and relationship with the Father.

Sacred writings, inspired by God, but not approved by Church Fathers in the 3rd century, were ordered destroyed with the earthly life of Jesus disappearing from the record books; a literary victory for the followers of Apostle Paul's theology and great loss for mankind.

During the process of passing down God's word, a problem arose in the Christian Church, the truths being taught in one congregation were different from the truths being taught in another. By the fourth century CE, through way of coercion, there was only one denomination of Christian thinking – today, there are over 200 in North America alone and over 45,000 world-wide.

Biblical scholars agree that Jesus was a first-century Jew living under Roman occupation and that this occupation had split its captive people into feuding sects and warring factions. They also agree that Jesus was a prophet who taught the imminent coming of the Kingdom of God and that he attained a following in Galilee as a teacher of wisdom but that he aroused the ire of the temple priests, conservative Jews, and Roman authorities who thought his aim was rebellion. Scholars agree that the Virgin Birth story is a metaphor used by evangelists to highlight the purity of Jesus's life while on earth. They also agree that it was the soul of Jesus that was resurrected to meet the Father upon death as it was released from its sinful flech, which was its prison while on earth.

BIBLIOGRAPHY

*H*illel the Elder, who was a Jewish religious leader, sage, and scholar, was active in Jerusalem at the time of Jesus. He was recognized as being the highest authority among the Pharisees. When a prospective convert asked him to explain the Torah while he stood on one foot, Hillel gently chided the man: "What is hateful to you, do not do to your fellow man: this is the whole Torah; the rest is explanation; go and learn." So it is with this book, sources given - Go and learn.

Against Heresies by Irenaeus

A Marginal Jew: Rethinking the Historical Jesus by John Meier

A New New Testament by Hal Taussig

An Easter Reflection by Bart Ehrman

Ante-Nicene Fathers Library by Alexander Roberts, James Donaldson, Arthur Coxe

Ante-Nicene Fathers Library by Rev. A. Cleveland Cox

Antiquities of the Jews by Josephus

Apologies by Justin Martyr

Archko Volume by McIntosh and Twyman

Authentic Gospel of Jesus by Geza Vermes

Authentic Gospel of Jesus by Hyam Macoby

Battles of the Bible by Chaim Herzog and Mordechai Gichon

Belief of the Blessed Judas, the brother of our Lord, who was surnamed Thaddaeus by Eusebius.

Bible as History by Ian Wilson

Bible Unearthed by Israel Finkelstein and Neil Silberman

Biblical Archaeology Society (BAS)

Birth of Christianity by Paul Barnett

Born of Woman by John Shelby Spong

Brothers of Jesus by Jeffrey J. Butz

Bruder Jesus by Schalom Ben-Chorin

Christian Theology by Alister E. McGrath

Christianity and History by Herbert Butterfield

Christianizing the Roman Empire: 100-400 by Ramsay MacMullen

Christians and the Roman Empire by Marta Sordi

Church History by Bruce L. Shelby

Church History Second Edition by Bruce L. Shelby

Confessions by Augustine

Criticism of the Gospel of John by Bruno Bauer

Dead Sea Scrolls by Andre Dupont-Sommer

Dead Sea Scrolls by Michael Wise, Martin Abegg Jr and Edward Cook

Dead Sea Scrolls and the First Christians by Robert Eisenman

Dead Sea Scrolls Deception by Michael Baigent and Richard Leigh

Dead Sea Scroll Uncovered by Eisenman and Wise

De Virus Illustribus by Jerome

Did our Lord visit Britain as they say in Cornwall and Someret by Cyril Dobson

Drama of the Lost Disciples by George F. Fowler

Early Christian Doctrines by J.N.D. Kelly

Early Christology Club by Jeremy Bouma

Early High Christology Club by Martin Hengel

Early Israelites: Two Peoples, One History by Igor P. Lipovsky

Ecclesiastical History of the Church by Eusebius

Embassy to Gaius by Philo

Epic of Atrahasis

Epic of Gilgamesh

Essene Children of the Light by Stuart Wilson and Joanna Prentis

Evangelical Dictionary of Biblical Theology by Walter Elwell

First Apology by Justin Martyr

Flavius Josephus by William Winston

Flavius Josephus: Translation and Commentary by Steve Mason

Four Witnesses by Robin Griffen Jones

From Jesus to Christ by Paula Fredriksen

From Jesus to Christianity by I. Michael White

Gnostic Gospels by Elaine Pagles

Gnostics by Tobias Churton

Gnostics: First Christian Heretics by Sean Martin

Golden Legend by Jacobus de Voragine

Gospel According to Paul by Robin Griffith-Jones

Gospel Birth of Mary by Marylyn Meyer

Gospel of Jesus by James M. Robinson

Gospel of Mary by Marylyn Meyer

Gospel of Mary Magdalene by Karen King

Gospel of Philip by Jean-Yves Leloup

Gospel of Truth by Valentinus

Hegesippus the Nazarene: Fragments from His Five Books of Memoirs by James Trimm

Hillel, If not Now, When by Joseph Telushki

Historical Jesus: The Life of a Mediterranean Jewish Peasant by John Dominic Crossen

Historic Figure of Jesus by E.P. Sanders

Histories by Cornelius Tactius

History of the Church from Christ to Constantine by Eusebius

History of the Christian Church by Philip Schaff

History of the Renaissance by Jacob Burckhardt

Holy Blood Holy Grail by Michael Baigent, Richard Leigh & Henry Lincoln

Holy War by Karen Armstrong

Homilies and Recognitions by Clementine

How We Got the Bible by Neil R. Lightfoot

James the brother of Jesus by Robert Eisenman

James the Just in the Habakkuk Pesher by Robert Eisenman

Jerome Biblical Commentary

Jesus by Marcus J. Borg

Jesus A Life by A.N. Wilson

Jesus After 2000 Years by Gerd Ludeman

Jesus and the Essene by Dolores Cannon

Jesus and the Word by Rudolf Bultmann

Jesus Dynasty by James Tabor

Jesus Family Tomb by Jacobovici and Pellegrino

Jesus I never knew by Phillip Yancy

Jesus in the Nag Hammadi Writings by Majela Franzmann

Jesus lived in India by Holger Kersten

Jesus the Man by Barbara Thiering

Jesus the Pharisee by Han Maccoby

Jesus the Pharisee: A New Look at the Jewishness of Jesus by Rabbi Harvey Falk

Jesus through the Centuries by Jaroslav Pelikan

Jesus, Uncovering the Life, Teaching and Relevance of a Religious Revolutionary by Marcus J. Borg

Jews in the Time of Jesus by Stephen Wylen

Jewish Apostle Paul by Dr. Eli Lizorkin-Eyzenberg

Jewish Gospel of John by Dr. Eli Lizorkin-Eyzenberg

Jewish War by Josephus

Joseph d' Arimathia by Robert de Brown

Judas: Betrayer of Friend Jesus by William Klassen

Judas Iscariot and the Myth of the Jewish Evil by Hyam Macoby

Kosher Jesus by Rabbi Shmuley Boteach

Legends of the Jews by Louis Ginzberg

Life of Anthony by Plutarch

Life of Christ by Fray Yepes

Life of Constantine by Eusebius

Life of Flavius Josephus by Josephus

Life of Jesus by David Strauss

Life of Mary Magdalene by Rabanus Maurus

Lives and Deaths of the Holy Apostles by Dorman Newman

Lost Bible by J.R. Porter

Lost Books of the Bible by William Hone

Lost Gospel by Bart Ehrman

Lost Gospel by Simcha Jacobovice and Barrie Wilson

Lost Gospel Q by Thomas Moore

Lost Histories by Joel Levy

Lost Religion by Bart Ehrman

Lost Ten Tribes of Israel by Steven M. Collins

Maccabees, Zadokites, Christians, and Qumran by Robert Eiseman

Mary Magdalen by Lesa Bellevie

Mary Magdalene: Bride in Exile by Margaret Starbird

Mary Magdalene: Christianity's Hidden Goddess by Lynn Picket

Mary Magdalene Revealed by Meggan Watterson

Mary Magdalene: The First Apostle by Ann Graham Brock

Memoranda by Hegesippus

More than a Carpenter by Josh McDowell

Nag Hammadi Library

On Creation of the World by Philo

On the Aims of Jesus and His Disciples by Hermann Samuel Reimaws

On the Life and Times of Jesus the Messiah by Alfed Edersheim

On the Virtues by Philo

Physics by Aristotle

Picture of a Prophet by Leonard Ravenhill

Quest For the Historical Jesus by Albert Schweitzer

Rabbi Jesus by Bruce Chilton

Radical Jew by Daniel Boyarin

Real Jesus: Then and Now by Geza Vermes

Real Kosher Jesus by Michael L. Brown

Rediscovering the Teaching of Jesus by Norman Perrin

Reluctant Parting: How the New Testament's Jewish Writers Created a Christian Book by Julie Galambush

Resurrection by Geza Vermes

Resurrection by Hank Hanegraaff

Resurrection by Porter, Hays and Tombs

Resurrection of Mary Magdalene by Jane Schaberg

Revelation by Elaine Pagels

Revelation: Four views, Revised and Updated by Steve Gregg

Revolution in Judaea by Hyam Maccoby

Roman History by Cassio Dio

Samaritan Woman Reconsidered by Eli Lizorkin-Eyzenberg

Search for the Twelve Apostles by William Steuart McBirnie, PH.D.

Secret Archives of the Vatican by Maria Luisa Ambrosini

Secret Teachings of Jesus by Marvin W. Meyer

Secrets from the Lost Bible by Kenneth Hanson Ph.D

Self-consciousness of Jesus in Light of the Messianic Hope of the Times by W. Baldnsperger.

1001 Surprising Things You Should Know about the Bible by Jerry MacGregor

Ten Lost Tribes by Steven M. Collins

The Authentic Gospel of Jesus by Hyan Macoby

The Dead Sea Scrolls Deception by Michael Baigent and Richard Leigh

The Historical Figure of Jesus by E.P. Sanders

The Historical Jesus: The Life of a Mediterranean Jewish Peasant by John Dominic Crossen

The Jewish Gospel of John by Eli Lizorkin-Eyzenberg

The Jewish Apostle Paul by Eli Lizorkin-Eyzenberg

The Life of Jesus by Ernest Renan

The Magdalene Legacy by Laurence Gardner

The Origin of Satan by Elaine Pagels

The Quest of the Historical Jesus by Albert Schweitzer

The Reluctant Parting by Dr. Julie Galambush

The Woman with the Alabaster Jar by Margaret Starbird

Theory of Forms by Plato

They Walked with Jesus by Dolores Cannon

Traditions of St. Thomas by A.M. Mundadan

Twelve Caesars by Suetonius Gaius Tranquillus

Twelve Chosen by Ian Fleck

Twelve Christ Chose by Asbury Smith

Unknown Life of Jesus Christ by Nicholas Notovitch *(The Life of Saint Issa: Best of the Sons of Men)*

Urantia Revelation

What Did Jesus Really Look Like by Jack Anderson

When Jesus became God by Richard E. Rubenstein

Who Was Jesus by N.T. Wright

Who Wrote the Bible by Richard Friedman

Who Wrote the New Testament by Burton L. Mack

Why the Jews Rejected Jesus by David Klinghoffer

Woman with the Alabaster Jar by Margaret Starbird

Zealot by Reza Aslan